CATHOLIC ANGLICANS TODAY

CATHOLIC ANGLICANS TODAY

Edited by

JOHN WILKINSON

DARTON, LONGMAN & TODD

London

First published in 1968 by
Darton, Longman & Todd Ltd
64 Chiswick High Road, London W4
© 1968 Darton, Longman & Todd Ltd
Printed in Great Britain by
Balding & Mansell, London and Wisbech

232 50994 8

'There is to be remarked, embarrassing Laud and his followers in this early stage of the Great Quarrel, just the same difficulty which embarrasses High Churchmen or so-called 'Anglo-Catholics' today. It is impossible for them to give a clear definition of their position, because they, while abhorring the word Protestant, are essentially Protestant in refusing unity and in preferring a national religion, which can include any degree of heresy, to an international religion which excludes all heresy.'

Hilaire Belloc, *Characters of the Reformation*

Contents

IN A CHANGING WORLD

The Authors

Since all the authors are clergy, no attempt has been made to provide all the details which can be found in Crockford. In each case the date of ordination as deacon coincides with the beginning of the first curacy.

LESLIE HOULDEN: Cuddesdon and St Mary, Hunslet, Leeds, 1955. Tutor for a year at Chichester Theological College, and from 1960 Chaplain Fellow of Trinity College, Oxford, Consultant to Lambeth Conference 1968.

IEUAN ELLIS: Cuddesdon and St Alban, Hull, 1965. After reading theology at Cambridge and gaining a B. Litt. at Oxford is now teaching in the Department of Theology at Hull University.

ALAN WILKINSON: Mirfield and St Augustine's Kilburn, 1959. Ph.D of Cambridge, where he served as chaplain of his college, St Catherine's, for six years. Now incumbent near Bristol and lecturer at St Matthias' College of Education, Fishponds. Hulsean preacher at Cambridge last year.

FRANK HAWKINS: Chichester and Tavistock with Gulsworthy, diocese of Exeter, 1961. From 1964 a lecturer and tutor at Chichester Theological College.

NEVILLE TIDWELL: St Stephen's House and St Columba, Southwick, diocese of Durham, 1958. From 1960 to 1968 successively Tutor, Chaplain, and Vice-Principal of St Stephen's House, Oxford, and now on the staff of St Bede's Theological College, Umtata, South Africa.

THEODORE SIMPSON, c.r.: Chichester and Ellesmere
Port, Cheshire, 1960. Went to Community of the Resur-
rection in 1963. Author of *Today's Ministry and Tomorrow's
Church*, 1966. Now on the staff of the Federal Theological
Seminary, Alice, South Africa.

CHRISTOPHER BRYANT s.s.j.e.: St Augustine's
Canterbury and St Paul, Clapham 1929. Member of the
Society of St John the Evangelist from 1935, and from 1955
to 1968 Superior of St Edward's House, Westminster.

JOHN WILKINSON: Cuddesdon and St Dunstan and All
Saints, Stepney, 1956. Tutor, St George's College,
Jerusalem and author of *No Apology* 1962, *Interpretation and
Community* 1963, and *The Supper and the Eucharist* 1965. From
1963 Editorial Secretary to SPG and USPG.

JOHN GUNSTONE: Mirfield and St James the Greater,
Walthamstow, 1952. Since 1958 at St Augustine's, Rush
Green, Romford, and now Ecumenical Officer for diocese
of Chelmsford. Author of *The Liturgy of Penance* 1966, *The
Feast of Pentecost* 1966, and *Christmas and Epiphany* 1967.

MARK GIBBARD s.s.j.e.: Cuddesdon and All Saints,
Wellingborough, 1933. After teaching at Warminster and
Cheshunt Theological colleges became member of SSJE in
1943. Author of *Tomorrow's Church* 1950, and *Unity is Not
Enough* 1965. Ecumenical traveller since 1950.

COLIN HICKLING: Chichester and St Luke, Pallion,
Bishop Wearmouth, 1957. After four years on the staff of
Chichester Theological College has since 1965 taught in
Department of Theology, King's College, London.

Preface

'We must make a row in the world.' The words were Hurrell Froude's, the place Oriel College, Oxford, and the date 1833, the year of the Assize Sermon. Through the determination of Froude and his colleagues in the Oxford Movement a Catholic pattern of thought took shape among Anglicans, and the row went on for a century. So too did the quest for new forms of holiness and devotion.

Throughout the nineteenth century the movement remained a militant minority, feared, vilified, and even persecuted. In return it was loud, resilient, and above all cohesive. The definition of its ideas carried it forward until in the 1930s it had become an accepted feature in the Anglican Communion. Today, however, 'Catholic Anglicans' have lost their definition as a party, and though they are 'of the Church' they have paid for their acceptance by being to some extent engulfed by the Church. It is true that the Church as a whole has absorbed many of the lessons which Hurrell Froude had set out to teach, but it cannot yet be relied upon to give them expression in its official decisions and pronouncements.

To devote a book to the narrow issues of Anglican party-churchmanship would be untimely. The writers of these chapters wish neither to make a row in the world nor to form a new Catholic party. But all of us are convinced that the Catholic tradition in Anglicanism provides us with an authentic way of being Christians. We wish to say why. And we believe our reasons will be welcome both to those who, like ourselves, have their roots in this tradition, but are dissatisfied with the older patterns of Catholicism, and also to the growing number of conservative evangelicals who ask serious questions of us, and deserve serious answers.

To claim the title 'Catholic' is to adopt an attitude to the past. But, as the Vatican Council has demonstrated, there are two sharply-divided interpretations of the Christian past. One group of Catholics, rightly standing for the continuity of the faith down the centuries, seem to want Christian truth to be an addition of all the truths which the saints have uttered. For them the Communion of Saints is a kind of university which never retires its professors. Here the difficulty is to co-ordinate the vast accumulation of prayer-material, law, and doctrine which is crowding the attic. There is so much available that the work of co-ordination is never complete: and this group is hesitant to lose anything which has ever been valuable.

The other group sees the Communion of Saints as a succession of faithful witnesses to Christ, faithful because each in his generation took the risk of re-interpreting the Christian gospel to his contemporaries. Their difficulty is to be sure that the gospel which they themselves reinterpret is in fact the Christian gospel by the time it has been expressed in new terms, for there is a danger that a new medium will make a new message, and that the faith itself will be cut down to fit some temporary need.

What is the relation between an eternal gospel and a rapidly-changing world in which it must be preached? If the two are to be brought into relation with each other it is essential that Christians should discover how their faith meets newly-emerging needs. Christians must seek to meet the deeply-felt needs of their non-Christian contemporaries, and to meet them in intelligible terms. To do this they may have to change the language in which their gospel is to be couched, and the emphasis which was made in past circumstances. But unless they bring the gospel, and nothing less than the saving gospel of Christ, to the world of their day, their mission is fruitless. Here their grasp of history is of special importance, for only by a study of the many ways in which their predecessors have dealt with the needs which emerged in their own days can they hope to see the range of the truth within which they stand, and have the confidence to work out new answers instead of repeating the old ones.

One of the most impressive, though least-publicised advances which has been made in the last decade, was that of a meeting between the Eastern Churches who did and those who did not accept the Christological doctrine of the Council of Chalcedon. The meeting was held on the island of Rhodes after fifteen centuries when the 'orthodox' had described the others as 'monophysites'. To the Churches involved it had seemed – as indeed from many Anglican textbooks it had seemed – that they were divided by a question of truth or heresy. So, at least, it had appeared to the Fathers of Chalcedon. Yet when the two sides sat down together and explained their positions they formally agreed that there was nothing in their Christologies which need divide them. What for so long had seemed a question of clear white and black turned out to be – not grey, some convenient compromise – but not a question.

We believe not that the Church possesses the truth, *but that it should be possessed by the truth*. If the Holy Spirit is leading us, as we believe, into all truth, we expect to be shown more of it as we go on. And the most we can hope for this book is that it is within the area of truth, and speaks in a language which will make sense to some of our contemporaries.

THE CHRISTIAN GOSPEL

ONE

The Bible and the Faith

LESLIE HOULDEN

There has never been a time when the Bible has been more attractively, conveniently and painlessly presented for the Christian's use than the present. Translations into brave attempts at contemporary English appear constantly. Editions with helpful notes by distinguished experts and series of commentaries designed for every shade of competence abound. Yet despite all, the dish often fails to satisfy, and gives rise to unease. Of course sometimes (and for many Christians nearly always) it does nothing of the sort; it is still simply the pure milk of the Word. But this is because they impose limitations which for others have proved impossible and even undesirable. They use the Bible largely or exclusively as the basis for prayer and the means of edification; and often in practice they attend chiefly to those parts of it which lend themselves most naturally to this purpose. The disquiet arises when the Bible is used in other ways, when questions of other kinds are raised, and when the Bible as a whole is opened for frank examination. Then, modern translations and useful notes, far from finally answering questions, merely pose them more acutely and lead on to others more far-reaching. The strangeness of the cultures lying behind the biblical documents, problems of historicity and the sheer unwieldy bulk of the books all force themselves upon the attention. In other words, all the questions which arise when modern skills are applied to these books, and modern interests (e.g. historical or anthropological investigation) are brought to bear upon them impose themselves all the more stridently.

Catholic Christians have sometimes felt a certain detachment from these questions. Their emphasis on the tradition of the Church as authenticating doctrine and their strong dependence upon the sacraments in practical devotion have relieved the anxiety which a more exclusive reliance upon scripture might have generated. Such relief has perhaps been dearly bought and may be psychologically helpful more than it is rationally respectable, for in the structure of the faith, changing attitudes to, and any new questions about the Bible are equally important for Christians of all traditions. Nevertheless in some ways, a Christian of a Catholic outlook ought to find himself predisposed to understand the perspectives opened up by fresh approaches to the Bible. In particular, in the light of his strong Church-awareness, he will not find it hard to see that the biblical documents themselves, from first to last, are the product of a society or community sharing a certain outlook of faith, and do not exist in their own independent right. Nor will he find it hard to see that this community is a changing thing, sharing in a constant succession of cultures, and that the biblical books have their roots in these varied settings and are formed by them. He will no doubt be daunted by the sheer weight and complexity of modern biblical scholarship, but its basic modes of operation should cause little searching of heart.

It is not our purpose to attempt a survey of the many questions raised for the believer by modern attitudes to the Bible. The literature on that subject is enormous in volume and ample in quality.[1] We confine ourselves to an area often neglected but of great importance for the Christian who sees that faith depends not only upon the Bible but upon the work of the Spirit in the Church as an articulate society. It is the delicate and complex matter of the relationship of the Bible with the Church's faith.

[1]On the central question of historicity in the gospels, see especially H. E. W. Turner, *Historicity and the Gospels*, Mowbray 1963, and Dennis Nineham, *History & the Gospel*, S.P.C.K. 1967

The New Testament documents spring from the believing and worshipping Church. They fix the faith and adoration of the Church in words, according to certain specific literary forms (like epistle, gospel and apocalypse), and, at the time of their writing, according to the needs and conceptions of certain specific circumstances (those of Paul and his audience, or Matthew and the Church for which he wrote). But once they have come into existence, they begin to acquire authority, at first only locally and in small degree. From that moment, these fixed forms of words not only express faith but also mould it. Faith itself continues: held in environments increasingly removed from those out of which these books came. The books travel and are brought to bear upon that faith in senses remote from their original purpose. The church in Alexandria reads the Epistles to the Corinthians in the light of its own faith, its own thought-forms and its own problems; and while certainly allowing its own way of thinking of the faith to be affected by them cannot attempt to simulate the problems and ideas of Corinth years before. So an interchange is inaugurated which continues from that day to this, between the documents, increasingly authoritative, first formed *by* the Church, then data *for* the Church, and the faith as held by those receiving the documents. This relationship is one of infinite complexity and shifts continually; for though the documents remain the same, they are read by ever-changing eyes.

Our task is to examine some aspects of this interchange and to try and see how it works. How does Christian doctrine emerge from scripture? Or, if this is not the right question (in that the New Testament itself expresses already existing faith), how is doctrine related to scripture? What exactly is happening when appeal is made to scripture, either in general or to particular texts, in support of a doctrine? Does the producing of a biblical text in any way clinch a doctrinal argument, and if so, why? To what extent should a Christian seeking authority for a belief or a practice, look first for a biblical text and regard his search as likely to end in settling the matter, one way or the other? And if this procedure seems crude and unsatisfactory, what alternative is there? To appeal to biblical themes? But they too are not easy to disentangle, for the Bible does not seem to speak with a single voice.

In practice, such questions as these are most likely to be answered with the New Testament in mind. But there was a time, a considerable period of about two centuries, when the Church did not possess a 'New Testament' as an authoritative collection of books, but simply a series of writings and groups of writings (like the letters of Paul) which were gradually acquiring the status of a fixed and authoritative collection. We shall begin by going back to that period, when 'scripture' meant simply the Old Testament, taken over by the Church from Judaism, and we shall see whether the situation of the Church at that time casts any light upon our questions. From the literature of that period, in fact from the time when the later books of the New Testament were being written, there is a passage in a letter of Ignatius, bishop of Antioch, dated about AD 112, which will give us a useful start.

He writes to the Church in Philadelphia, where dissident groups are appealing to the Old Testament in support of positions which they have adopted.

'I urge you, do not do things in cliques, but act as Christ's disciples. When I heard some people saying, "If I don't find it in the original documents, I don't believe it in the gospel," I answered them, "But it *is* written there." They retorted, "That's just the question." To my mind it is Jesus Christ who is the original documents. The inviolable archives are his cross and death and resurrection and the faith that came by him.'[1]

However much or little Ignatius, writing on the eve of his

[1]Ignatius to the Philadelphians, as translated by Cyril C. Richardson in *Early Christian Fathers*, Library of Christian Classics, Vol. I, S.C.M. Press 1953, p. 110.

martyrdom, saw in these words, both the distinction which he draws and the principle which he erects have vast implications for Christian faith. The 'original documents' are the books of the Old Testament, and with them he contrasts 'Christ', and he goes on to 'unpack' that name to mean 'his cross and death and resurrection and the faith which came by him.' It is a question of which is to be the measure of the other: the old or the new.

We are fortunate to have this brief glimpse of Christian minds at work on this question at a most interesting moment in Christian development. It is enough to enable us to use it as a specimen, presenting in a relatively simple form several problems with which Christian doctrine perennially faces us.

In the first place, what, more precisely, is in question? In a rough way, no doubt Ignatius and those to whom he writes were at one in affirming the scriptural status of the Old Testament: they accepted it as authoritative for Christians. They differed in the way they saw this authority working. Any reasonable man will readily admit that the Old Testament presents formidable difficulties if it is to be used as a basis for belief. As a way of entering into an understanding of Judaism or of Israel's history and institutions over a very long period, it is indispensable. As a way of getting the feel of a response to God which is (considering the great length of the period involved) amazingly consistent, it is incomparable. But as a document of authoritative doctrine it looks both inefficient and risky. How should one set about using this vast collection of writings for such a purpose? Even to a reader like Ignatius and his contemporaries, much less sensitive than we are to their shifting historical background, product of more than a millennium, they all too clearly lack the handiness of a creed, the considered clarity of a set of conciliar decrees. It is no wonder that even by the time of Ignatius, when the Church was not yet a century old, there was room for disagreement and uncertainty. There was no universally agreed or obvious way for Christians to handle the Old Testament.

The truth is that the Church had already (it is clear from the New Testament writings, mostly in existence by this time) produced a set of quite disparate answers to the crucial question of its relation to its Jewish heritage, and to the Old Testament in particular, not all of them equally satisfactory from a doctrinal point of view. These answers were not fully worked out, not wholly conscious, and certainly the disparity between them was not clearly perceived. They jostled side by side in writings of various kinds, in Christian prayer and discourse. All of them served as principles of selection for Christian writers as they sought to give an account of the Old Testament basis for Christian faith. We shall distinguish three of these answers and estimate their value for understanding and formulating Christian doctrine.

1. Many Christians in the second century still saw the division between the Church and Judaism as far from absolute. The Church was the new Israel, in unbroken development from the old. She was the true inheritor of the promises, the life and the institutions of Israel. At the end of the second century, Christians in North Africa were buying their meat from the kosher butchers, and in the fourth century at Antioch there was intense devotion in the Church to the martyrs of the Maccabean revolt of the second century BC. To this day, an Ethiopian Christian observes the Jewish food laws, keeps Sabbath as well as Sunday and circumcises his male offspring. This view regards persisting Jews as either apostates or, more gently, erring brothers. It is of course entirely comprehensible: the Church began, in an age of many Jewish sects, as one such sect among others. It is not unfair to define the Church of the first years as the group of Jews who believed that Jesus of Nazareth was the promised Messiah of God. Even the incorporation of Gentiles on generous terms did not go beyond some Old Testament prophecies and the hopes of many Jews, particularly those living outside Palestine in the cities of the Mediterranean world.

In this view, the stress is on two features which have an undoubted place in a final picture but, as we shall see, do not merit such a dominating one. The first feature is continuity; the second, Israel as the people of God. The new Israel succeeds to the old, and essentially the two are one. If the logic of this view is pursued, it is clear that the role of Jesus is minimal. He is simply the one who stands at the parting of the ways, where the Church continues the main line of development and Judaism disappears down a false trail. His life is an incident, however important an incident, in the history of Israel, which is the continuing entity. It is of course true that this view is rarely held in isolation, but it constitutes one identifiable strand in Christian thinking and devotion which is not always set in relation to other more satisfactory ways of expression. In a diagram, it looks like this:

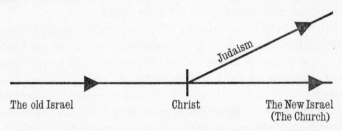

The old Israel   Christ   The New Israel
(The Church)

2. A second view places less value on continuity, much more on the parallelism between old and new. But while showing that each element in the life and institutions of the Church has a counterpart in the old Israel which foreshadowed it, this view is clear about the superiority of the new and about the distinction between it and the old. Nevertheless, taken by itself, it provides no clear way of deciding what in the Old Testament is of Christian value, apart from the mere fact that a plausible parallel is discernible in the arrangements of the Church. Thus, it so happens that Sunday is the parallel in the life of the Church to Sabbath in the life of Israel, in the sense that each is the specially observed day of the week in the society in question:

but it is hard to see any intrinsic doctrinal reason why there should be in old Israel such an equivalent to the Christian institution, if that should be taken as the datum, or why the reverse should be true, if one looks at it the other way round.

Moreover, the role of Jesus is even more incidental in this second scheme than in the first. It is true that he stands between old and new, and alone gives rise to the new, but he plays no really vital part in the logic of the scheme itself, for it is chiefly concerned with the parallelism between two sets of religious institutions and ideas and with the items of equipment which each set possesses. It is almost as if there were an inventory of kit which 'a religion' ought to have; and clearly in theory one could make a similar comparison between the Old Testament religion and any other religion that one cared to select. There is nothing in the logic of the pattern to demand that the Church be seen as *the* place where the true counterparts are to be found.

At the very least, this view has an undoubted place in Christian edification. It is devotionally helpful to see Jesus as a new Moses or a new David, to see Easter as a new Passover, baptism as the Red Sea crossing for each of us. The question is whether it can be trusted to roam unchecked in areas where Christian *doctrine* is being formulated. In the New Testament and in the early Church generally, nobody was much disposed to distinguish sharply between the writing of devotional literature and theology, and in many ways this was salutary. But when it comes to stating doctrine clearly, the effect can easily be unfortunate. The helpful analogy is elevated to the status of theological statement, and is unable to sustain the role.

It is not difficult to find more examples of this model. Baptism is the counterpart not only of the crossing of the Red Sea at the Exodus but also of the rite of circumcision; the eucharist parallels the Jewish sacrifices, the Christian priesthood the Aaronic, a Christian emperor one of the pious kings of Judah. In each case, so far as this view is concerned, though the Christian is in no doubt that the new supersedes the old, in fact the stress is on what the two parallel institutions share. This obscures the newness of the Christian institution and the differentiating features of both. Thus, when baptism and circumcision are set side by side, what really makes the parallelism work is the fact that they both fall into the category: 'rite of initiation into the people of God'. This, however, by no means exhausts the meaning of either rite, and, as far as baptism is concerned, it fails to draw attention to its chief significance as the rite of entry into relationship with Christ, or to its organic connection with the central facts of the gospel. Seeing its biblical basis in relation to the Jewish rite has in fact served to obscure the most important things which Christian doctrine has to say about it. Exactly the same situation arises with regard to sacrifice and priesthood, which, while they may bring out certain important ideas about the eucharist and the Christian ministry, all too easily obscure more important ones which relate them directly to the core of the gospel.

Before we leave the example of baptism in relation to this scheme of thought, we ought to examine the other Old Testament counterpart to which we referred, the crossing of the Red Sea by Israel at the Exodus. Here, the common element which leads to the choice of this event as significant is not, as in the case of circumcision, baptism's function as the rite of initiation, but rather the idea of deliverance from the old life of sin and death (= Egypt and the life of slavery to which Israel was subjected there) into the new life of freedom in Christ (= the Promised Land which lay, in due course, on the far side of the Red Sea). But even more important for the imaginative and devotional usefulness of this parallel from the Old Testament has been the fact that both in it and in baptism water figured prominently. For the proper understanding of Christian baptism in relation to the central insights of the gospel, even for its proper understanding in relation to a whole long sequence of God's saving acts in which the Exodus is seen to have an important place, this fact is totally fortuitous. Yet it is easy for it to draw attention away from central considerations to ideas which, though devotionally rich, are doctrinally peripheral. It makes for a neat and elegant pattern, and is soon regarded as a providential gift for theology.

Put in a diagram, the second view appears thus:

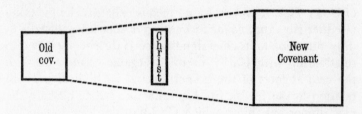

Here, the new is certainly more than *merely* parallel to the old: it supersedes and transcends it. But essentially it does no more than reproduce it. Because the old comes first, in effect it calls the tune, determining what is seen as really significant in the new, and exerting pressure in the direction of Judaising the new. Moreover, though Christ certainly stands between the two, the lines connecting them just fail to go through him.

3. When it is a matter of framing Christian doctrine, no scheme will be fully satisfactory that does not have Christ at its centre; and not just formally so, as in the two diagrams above, but structurally, integrally so. He must be the lynch-pin of the whole pattern, indispensable to its existence and coherence, and vitally affecting each part of it. The following diagram expresses this conviction, as far as the relation of the Old Testament to the Christian dispensation is concerned:

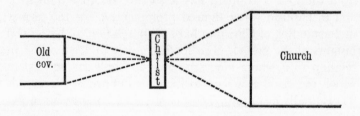

In this diagram, all the lines which join the Church to the Old Testament pass through Christ, and he alone makes the contact possible. The positive values of the other two schemes (in the first case, continuity, in the second, parallelism) are preserved, but in a new setting. What the diagram does not make clear is the exact nature of Christ's mediating position. In fact, it is a double role: he is both selector and transformer.

First, he selects. Not everything in the Old Testament is grist to the mill of Christian doctrine. It is no doubt true that we must study the Old Testament as a whole if we want to get a balanced and complete picture of the formation of Judaism; true also that Jesus sprang from that process. But that is not our present concern. What interests us here is neither what Judaism in the time of Jesus was like nor what the historical Jesus was like, but the doctrinal significance of Christ for the Church and her gospel and the way the expression of that significance is related to the Old Testament background, when the Old Testament is regarded as authoritative scripture. We repeat: Christ selects from the Old Testament certain images and insights at the expense of others. For example, the idea of 'Christ' (Messiah) itself receives, when attached to Jesus, a significance much greater than its rather meagre occurrence in the Old Testament would suggest; while the crudely nationalistic strain which is prominent in many parts of the Old Testament is abandoned or treated in a purely figurative way.

The process of selection also has the effect of bringing together themes and images which were not connected at all in the Old Testament: e.g. Jesus appears as both Messiah and Suffering Servant (cf. Isa. 53), as Second Adam (1 Cor. 15:22) and as New Moses (2 Cor. 3:7-15). It is true that, in their background in ancient Israelite thought and imagery, some of these figures were probably connected with each other, but these links are not at all explicit in the Old Testament itself. The images come together only because they throw light on the significance of Jesus.

Jesus not only selects; he also transforms. In other words, he is not controlled by the images and insights which he derives from the Old Testament, but himself controls them. This control is exercised not only over the actual using of an image or idea but also over its meaning. To take an example, the sense in which messiahship is attributed to Jesus is different from its use in popular Judaism. In the straightforward sense he does not correspond to what ordinary Jews expected of the promised great king who would deliver Israel from its oppressors. In the gospel of St John, the suffering and death of Jesus are portrayed in regal terms, to make clear the conviction that Jesus was never so truly king as when, to the ordinary observer, he looked least like it. We might be inclined to describe this change as a 'spiritualising' of the concept of Messiah: Jesus is not a king like Augustus or David or Herod, but a 'sort-of-king' to those who accept his teaching. But this is not quite adequate, because there issues from him a society, the Church, which is identifiable, with membership and organisation, and in which his rule is accepted in all areas of life. And the cross remains the sharpest expression of his rule. The result is that we are led to re-define the whole notion of *rule* (implicit in messiahship) in terms of generous self-giving and service. Because his authority is exercised in this way and has these characteristics, the community which stems from him came to see such authority as the ideal for its own life and conduct. The concept has not only been selected from the Old Testament but also transformed by its application to Jesus.

Putting this in another way, we can say that the idea of Messiah in the Old Testament is useful and important for Christian doctrine only because it has been selected by Christ and only as it has been transformed by him, above all by his death. It has, that is, no intrinsic right to a place in the pattern. Its place is given and determined by Christ. The same is true of all other Old Testament concepts and institutions which find an echo or a replica in the Christian dispensation. Thus, it may well be the case, as many Christians have held from the first century, that the sacrifices of the Old Testament provide a doctrinal background to the Christian eucharist and the Old Testament priesthood to the Christian clergy. But if this is to be so, one essential condition has to be fulfilled, that is, that the argument has to work according to our third diagram and not according to our second. In other words, any usefulness which this background has is wholly subordinate to the central data concerning Christ. If the imagery of sacrifice helpfully illuminates the meaning of the eucharist, as expressing liturgically the Christians' relationship to God through Christ, then it has a valid place in doctrinal statement. Otherwise, though it may have a place in the more freely imaginative language of devotion, its presence in doctrinal patterns will merely mislead. The first kind of statement will, after all, always be optional, for the use of those who find it religiously helpful; the second ought to aim at more careful expression which will command wide acceptance.

The model illustrated in our third diagram applies not only to biblical images like messiahship or institutions like sacrifice, but also to great all-embracing biblical themes such as *covenant* or *righteousness* and to far-reaching characteristics of biblical thought like eschatology. In cases like these, it is easy to stress the continuity between the Old Testament and Christian doctrine. In both (if we take the example of eschatology), God is seen as acting in history towards determined ends. In both it is right to describe his purpose as ultimately redemptive. But here too, Christ transforms. For the New Testament writers, the object of God's redemptive purpose is not precisely what it was in the Old Testament. Its defining lines are set by the life, death and resurrection of Jesus, and he himself appears as embodying that purpose, initiating its realisation among men. The Old Testament provides analogies and directions for thought, but could not of itself lead us to guess the place to which they would lead.

When Ignatius found it necessary to correct the Philadelphians' use of the Old Testament, we do not know what sort of argument they had been putting forward. It may have been something corresponding to either of our first two models; it may have been a quite simple appeal to Old Testament law as still binding upon Christians (presupposing diagram 1), or what was in effect a Judaising of some Christian idea or institution (diagram 2). In any case, in repudiating their views, Ignatius appeals to our third model. It is Christ alone who is the selector and controller of Old Testament images and ideas as they pass into the Christian Church for doctrinal use. The Church is to use them in the light of the basic data concerning him as the agent of God's purpose.

It will be clear that there is nothing simple about a claim to derive one's doctrine from the Bible. Up to now, because we took as a specimen a passage from Ignatius, from a time before the New Testament had been assembled or recognised, we have been seeing what happens when the Old Testament is used as source or backing for Christian doctrine. We need to go on to see how the New Testament affects the picture; but before that, there are one or two elaborations to be made to the argument we have already presented.

We look again briefly at the three thought-models illustrated in the diagrams. There is no difficulty in seeing that the first of them was bound to be prominent in the Church's early days before she became clearly aware of herself as an independent institution. Elements of it survive, especially in liturgy; for example, the *Exultet*, the deacon's proclamation at the Easter Vigil in the Western rite, movingly affirms the continuity of the Church with the old Israel and of Easter with the first Passover night (while also owing much to the second model. But we should be wrong to fear that such surviving elements constituted any threat to our proper holding of the faith; the wider context in which they appear always acts as an adequate corrective, in this case the Easter message of Our Lord's resurrection itself.

But it would be a mistake to suppose that its distorting

influence upon doctrine was confined to the Church's first years. When Stuart kings of England identified themselves with the godly kings of Judah like Hezekiah and Josiah and modelled Christian polity on Old Testament precedents, there was a highly significant use of the first model for doctrinal purposes. Its failure to be a permanently valid analysis of the gospel's implications for political life is an indication of the inadequacy of the first model.

Despite examples such as this, no Christian body has ever ordered itself exclusively according to this model, seeing itself as simply 'Judaism with Jesus as the Messiah'. Always in practice, the more important ways of using the Old Testament background have been the second and third models, with the tensions and confusions between them largely unresolved. The main harmful effect of the confusions has been, as we have suggested, to obscure the direct connection of all Christian doctrine with the central facts of the proclamation about Christ and the relationship with God which he opens up for man.

Alongside this source of muddle and partly related to it is another. It concerns not, as in the former case, the criteria for making selection from an unwieldy mass of material, but rather the manner of regarding the matter that is selected. By what analogy are Christians to understand the role of the doctrinally significant parts of the Old Testament? Many Christians have taken them as having the same sort of authority as a legal text: timeless words about which the chief question is that of establishing the right interpretation, there being no question of going behind them to anything else (such as their cultural provenance or the beliefs of the people who produced them). They are simply oracles given to the human race as saving truth: the task of man is to understand them as sheer words, at most to develop their implications.

Sometimes and for some purposes, when this approach has been taken, it has not seemed necessary or desirable even to make selections from the authoritative scripture. When it

is a question of supporting or establishing doctrinal tenets it
is scarcely avoidable; but when the purpose is shifted or
widened to that of using the scripture as from end to end a
book of life-giving spiritual truth, then, whatever extravagant
interpretations (e.g. reading uncongenial stories as allegories
of acceptable truths) may become necessary to render it
intelligible, it is possible to see it as 'the interminable mono-
logue of God'[1] – to accept it as sheer words, which are to be
savoured and cherished. Between this use of Scripture (of
which Origen and Augustine were the brilliant exponents,
influencing the whole Christian tradition), and its use for
strictly doctrinal purposes, the line is often hard to draw,
still harder to adhere to firmly.

We referred to the extravagant interpretations to which
the Christian interpreter has often resorted in order to make
scripture (seen as sheer words) Christianly intelligible. This
means, in effect, that he sets up a criterion above scripture in
terms of which he judges it: he knows, in approaching
scripture, what it must turn out to mean. That criterion is the
faith, the doctrine. Often he will not see it in these terms:
he will not go through the process of finding that scripture
must be interpreted in this elaborate and improbable way in
order to make it doctrinally satisfactory. Rather he will say
that, whatever the appearances, this is what scripture must
be intended to mean, for it must speak with a single voice.
Only when historical criticism makes us see what the original
writers are likely to have had in mind, and when we see their
meaning as *the* meaning, do we find the old exegesis strained
or forced and realise that 'the faith', Christian doctrine, has
really been in control. Until this happens, it can scarcely
be perceived that there are two distinct ways of using
scripture as a ground for doctrine: first as oracles, sheer
words; second, as a witness, in a wide variety of ways, to

[1]Peter Brown, *Augustine of Hippo*, London 1967, p. 253. His chapters
22 and 23 give a most vivid and illuminating account of Augustine's
attitude to and use of the Bible.

what lies behind it, the basic data of the faith, the 'cross and death and resurrection' of Christ.

The two ways lead to quite different conceptions of Christian doctrine as a whole. The first almost always leads in the direction of the itemised, propositional view of doctrine. It is more likely to put forward tenets of faith (e.g. the virgin birth of Our Lord or the descent into Hell) because they are evidenced in scriptural texts and in the form in which they are scripturally supported rather than because of any necessary coherence with the central Christian data.

According to the second way, doctrine is what the central data lead us to infer about God and his purposes, and it is no more than this. It is, in other words, a homogeneous, consistent articulation of what God has done in Christ, not a series of mysteries or a set of detached articles of belief.

Sometimes there may be a clash between the two ways. The texts may seem to point to a tenet in such a form that it cannot be brought into connection with the central data. It seems not to meet them in any vital way and becomes a doctrinally useless pious curiosity. In such cases, the tenet loses its status as 'doctrine' and must enter some other category: perhaps mere fact of history, perhaps legend. Most often, it will be an edifying story which, in the idiom of some early Christian writer, served as comment on the central data: it is not doctrine but poetic variation upon a doctrinal theme.

Perhaps the simplest way of illustrating the unsatisfactory nature of the first way is to show how it operates in the closely related matter of seeking ethical guidance from the Bible. Faced with a new moral question, Christians turn to the scriptures. The procedure often used could not unfairly be described as ransacking the Bible to discover some incident or statement which could conceivably bear upon the problem. An obvious example is the scriptural sanctioning of the policy of apartheid by the Dutch Reformed Church in South Africa on the basis of ancient stories in Genesis about the relations between peoples formerly inhabiting the Tigris-

Euphrates valleys and surrounding areas. It is easy to see how this method can yield results totally out of harmony with the moral implications of the central data of the gospel. The New Testament itself repeatedly shows these to be chiefly love of God and love of the neighbour, duties taking precedence over all others, and guiding the working out of all others.

By a second route we arrive again at Ignatius' formula; not the documents but Christ, 'his cross and death and resurrection', are the primary authority for doctrine.

In some of our examples, we have already had in mind the whole Bible, but what is the effect of the development which took place after Ignatius' time, the formation of the New Testament canon of scripture?

In our third diagram (p. 12), we left the Old Testament box open on the side pointing away from Christ, in order to suggest that not everything in the Old Testament directly leads to him: he selects and transforms. Though the way of relationship with God which the Old Testament portrays can be said to lead to Christ, so that we say that he 'fulfils' the Old Testament, yet there remains to the end in the Old Testament a certain imprecision and ambiguity which only he resolves. He completes the pattern – but only if it is looked at in a certain way. Only he makes us see it in that certain way. Only Christ himself determines that we give greater significance to this feature rather than that; and to some elements he gives a prominence and clarity which is not found in the Old Testament at all.

In the same diagram, we also left open the 'Church' box on the side which looks to the future; but the sense this time is different. The point here is to enable us to distinguish between Christ and the New Testament scriptures which bear witness to him. Those writings themselves lead us to distinguish two levels in the witness they bear. In the first place, they give evidence of a central proclamation of the redemptive acts of God in Christ, a proclamation formulated in a variety of ways but always agreeing on the death and resurrection. This proclamation, the basic Christian data,

was from the start the Church's *raison d'être*. This she celebrated in her life of charity and in her eucharistic assemblies;
this she communicated to all whom she reached; on this
basis she planted herself in city after city of the Roman world.
We see it in its simplest form in 1 Corinthians 15:3ff, more
elaborately in the apostolic speeches in Acts (e.g. 2:14–36,
13:16–41), in poetic liturgical form in Philippians 2:6–11.
This proclamation has moulded every writer in the New
Testament. Amply witnessed to in those books, it goes on to
have a life of its own in the Church, even after the New
Testament books have been written. It is substantially
identical with what the Church came to call its 'rule of faith';
it finds concrete expression in forms of words like baptismal
creeds, liturgies, material for the instruction of converts, and
eventually the formal statements issued by councils of Church
leaders. Frequently, as would be expected, the *words* used to
express it are those of scripture, but the *content* goes behind
scripture and is in essence older than even the earliest books
of the New Testament.

In the second place, around the central data the New
Testament writers have used a wide variety of literary
forms with a wide variety of aims. The evangelists, each with
the needs of a particular audience in mind, each with his
own theological outlook, gave the traditions about Jesus' life
and death – not disinterestedly and objectively, but on the
basis of the central data, the life, death and resurrection
seen as revealing God's purposes and making them effective
for man. Paul wrote to Corinth to answer questions and to
correct abuses: but he makes his judgments in the light of the
basic proclamation. The writer to the Hebrews expounds the
central data in his own rich idiom, but still he is addressing a
community which faces specific problems and runs certain
risks, and these shape his exposition. The Revelation of John
sets the central data against a backcloth of the whole cosmic
plan of God, but still he writes in order to meet the needs of
the seven churches addressed in the second and third chapters.

At both levels there is a meeting of God's acts in Christ

with a response from specific elements in the Christian community. The two interact from the first moment of each encounter: the acts cannot be spoken of at all without acquiring the colour of the mind which speaks. Even the simplest statement of all (1 Cor. 15:3ff), which Paul says he inherits from the Church before him, is not free from his own typical emphases. Nevertheless, the two sides of the inter-action can be distinguished; and clearly they carry different degrees of authority. God's acts are the saving initiative to which faith responds. The response of the primitive Church, seen in the New Testament books, is, however edifying, in principle simply a response, like our own. In as much as both are responses to the action of God, we can range ours alongside theirs. The special value of their response as against ours lies in its directness, its immediacy, and its free-dom from the accumulations which time loads upon the Church's theological tradition. The New Testament gives the inestimable benefit of what we may regard as a set of *worked examples* of faithful and authentic response to the acts, from the earliest years. The examples are extensive enough to give us the idea of 'how the game works', how, that is, the central data give rise to doctrinal and ethical thinking in the context of human life. The New Testament books fulfil, in other words, for Christian doctrine a function not unlike that of the examples which the writer of a mathematical textbook uses to illustrate a theorem. That is, they enable us to go on and work out our own problems for ourselves by the right methods. If we are wise, we shall constantly refer back to the examples in order to check that we are on the right lines. But there are two things we shall take care not to do: we shall not mistake the examples for the theorem itself; and we shall not suppose that the examples limit the range of the theorem's application. That application will widen indefinitely as we find new practical problems which our principle helps us to solve.

If this analogy holds, it leads us to a view of the authority of scripture which is both strong and creative. The basis of

Christian doctrine is twofold: the redeeming acts of God in Christ, and the continuing relationship with God which those acts establish for man. The Old Testament provides the basic religious formation and the stock of ideas and images which Christ and the early Church used (by selection and transformation) to render his acts intelligible. The New Testament shows the new relationship at work.

Because of their authenticity and their immediacy, both historically and religiously, to the acts, these writings always continue to be directly useful to Christians for edification and for growth in true personal and collective response to God. But for this to happen rightly, it needs to be balanced by their use in a different and more indirect way as a ground for doctrine. Here, we have suggested, they function as specific examples of how the theorem works – examples from a particular period and a particular set of circumstances. New circumstances, new patterns of thought and discourse, produce the need for a continuous stream of new examples, which indeed look back to the first (and subsequent) ones for the guidance they are qualified to give, but do not see them as limiting the area in which the theorem (i.e. the central Christian data) is applicable. In particular, there is no special need for the new doctrinal formulations to use the words and phrases of the old. Indeed we should be on our guard if we find ourselves using them, for they are unlikely to retain their old sense in a changed world.

Christian doctrine is, in sum, the intellectually articulate response of the Christian community to the central data in continually shifting circumstances of culture and thought. The novel feature of our own and recent days has been simply the heightened awareness of these things, bringing with it a new possibility of clarity in our relationship with the formulations of the past, including the New Testament itself. This clarity confers freedom which ought to be received as a blessing.

Catholic teaching, with its emphasis on the role of tradition, has always possessed the seeds of this freedom. It has often used tradition as in effect a burden on the back of scripture, and seen both as vehicles of fixed, oracular authority. By comparison with this, the Reformation plea, continually reiterated, for a return to scripture alone, could only be a liberation. It was intended to be a liberation which would give the Word of God free course in the hearts of his people. But, as we are now able to see, there was a need to penetrate further and to make further distinctions, if scripture is not in some ways to obscure him to whom it witnesses.

'Tradition' is a way of referring to what we more generally call the work of the Holy Spirit. The more general term is to be preferred because there is built into it that flexibility and openness to present and future, to the thought and circumstances of the secular world, which we have been commending. Christian doctrine is not a changeless body of truths, formulated and listed for ever, nor is its transmission like the careful handing on of a priceless heirloom which is preserved untouched. Of course in some senses, Christians have long admitted this; they have known that doctrine develops. But that development has been seen as simply the making explicit of what was implicit from the start: in other words, as a self-contained process, taking place in the midst of the world's ordinary history, but detached from it, working by its own inner momentum of grace. Such a view is hardly borne out by the facts. Each growth does not in reality just add enrichment to the already existing stock, as if all took place in the isolation of a cultural incubator and as if there were a settled validity about the fruit of each generation's work. Rather, it is a matter of a series of responses to the divine acts in Christ, responses which always have an experimental nature. They are always attempts to solve a specific problem: how, in the light of *these* circumstances, thinking as we do in the world we live in, do the data appear, and what response do they demand of us? This means that the test of good Christian doctrine lies in its appropriateness as response. It also means that no response is the last word: the terms of the experiment change.

FURTHER READING

J. BARR, *Old and New in Interpretation*, S.C.M. Press 1966

J. L. HOULDEN, *'We offer this bread and this cup'* in *Theology*, October 1966

M. WILES, *The Making of Christian Doctrine*, C.U.P. 1967

J. KNOX, *The Humanity and Divinity of Christ*, C.U.P. 1967

R. A. NORRIS, *God and World in Early Christian Theology* Black 1966

O. CHADWICK, *From Bossuet to Newman*, C.U.P. 1957

W. M. ABBOTT (Ed), *The Documents of Vatican II – Revelation*, Chapman 1966, p. 107ff.

G. W. H. LAMPE and K. J. WOOLLCOMBE, *Essays on Typology*, S.C.M. Press 1957

L. HODGSON and others, *On the Authority of the Bible*, S.P.C.K. 1960

R. P. C. HANSON, *Tradition in the Early Church*, S.C.M. Press 1962

TWO

The Gospel of the living God

IEUAN ELLIS

One can see why the ancient Jews stopped pronouncing the name of God. It becomes debased in human speech. Leslie Dewart, in his interesting book, *The Future of Belief*, proposes that the name 'God' be discontinued, and instead of devising new titles it would be better to speak about God without naming him at all.[1] Certainly, we must take the Second Commandment seriously and reserve a special place for silence about God. But complete silence at the present time might be taken to mean that there is no God at all.

The most urgent concern in theology in this secular age is a restatement of the doctrine of God. This ought to be an ecumenical enterprise since no single school of theology has all the necessary insights. Some reviewers opposed traditional metaphysics to *Honest to God* and claimed that if Bishop Robinson had been more versed in them he would not have made so many mistakes. But Professor Dewart's book questions whether these same metaphysics can any longer express the reality of God. Dewart actually says that because of its conceptual inadequacy – in particular, a dichotomy between God's essence and existence – 'scholasticism provided the condition of the possibility of modern atheism'.[2] We need thinkers who are familiar with the past but who can share in the fundamental rethinking attempted by the 'secular theologies'.

Honest to God was not the earliest attempt of its kind. Two

[1]L. Dewart, *The Future of Belief*, Burns & Oates, p. 214.
[2]Dewart, op. cit., p. 163.

years earlier, in 1961, appeared the first publication of the so-called 'Death of God' School, William Hamilton's *The New Essence of Christianity*. Hamilton held that the experience of the 'holy' was possible only within a traditional pattern of society but that this pattern has now broken down. The second member of the trio, Paul van Buren, published *The Secular Meaning of the Gospel* in 1963. He argued that the 'holy' experienced by men in the old society was nothing more than the expression of human attitudes and desires: 'Christianity is about man and not God.' This is shown by its language, which he rigorously examines, since he finds that the word 'God' is not about a fact that we can 'prove'. Thirdly, Thomas J. J. Altizer, in *The Gospel of Christian Atheism* (1966), holds that 'God' had become immanent in Jesus and finally died in his crucifixion. But this death or end of God is a necessity if we really are to experience the value of the gospel.

No longer is this St John of the Cross speaking of the absence of God, of faith discovering at the summit of the ascent that there is 'nothing', but rejoicing in union. Nor is this a doctrine of *Deus absconditus*, the God who hides himself but who is present in his hiddenness. The theism of Christians is not absolute; it is relative and conditioned because of the nature of God. It is possible to say that God 'exists' or God 'is' but only if you recognise that God is not bound by these terms. But, however much he is beyond our grasp, Christians believe that God is *real*; he is not simply a concept in our minds. Yet according to these thinkers we do not need the objective fact of God, and it is sufficient to hold only to the man Jesus.

The case is best argued by van Buren, and it hinges on two matters: Jesus was a man, not God incarnate; and the fact that men talk about God does not necessarily mean that there is a God. Van Buren holds that language about God is not the sort of language which deals with scientific facts; it cannot convey something real and objective which can be verified. So it had better be understood as language describing human attitudes and viewpoints. In that case, the expression 'God' is unnecessary and we can talk, instead, about man committing himself to some perspective that gives meaning and wholeness to life. Van Buren does not despise language about God – for the gospel is about the sanctification of life – but we ought to be quite clear that the subject of it is man himself.[1]

This argument assumes that statements about man and statements about God have a quite separate history and use. What about Christ, in whom statements about man and God have a common reference? Van Buren claims that Christ's 'divinity' is a description of a perfectly human existence of great worth and unique significance. As such, he believes, Christ is to be confessed as 'Lord' by us but not as the 'God' of traditional belief.

How valid is this argument? Two questions need to be considered. First, if one views language about God in this way, why is it necessary to ascribe absolute significance to Jesus? Why is Jesus absolute rather than the Lord Buddha or Socrates, unless one believes that he has some significance beyond his merely human life? Traditional Christian doctrine has said this and, quite logically, follows it up with assertions about Jesus as the one who reveals God, revealing not simply that there is a God but also what God is 'like'. We shall return to this point when we discuss the gospel portrait of Jesus.

Secondly, is van Buren justified in his clear demarcation of language? Can we agree that there is one definite type of language which we use to convey facts and another distinct kind which is merely expressing how we feel? Surely, if both kinds of language are used by persons they cannot be so far apart. Even if I do not convey facts, I may still be referring to some reality 'beyond' or 'outside' myself in the language of poetry and symbol. And I could be referring to such a reality when I use language about God.

[1]P. van Buren, *The Secular Meaning of the Gospel*, S.C.M. Press, p. 85f.

Further, language about God and language about man
cannot be separated so rigidly, otherwise the objectivity
of God is seen only in terms of him as the 'Wholly Other',
and if we cease to believe in the 'Wholly Other' then man
(*pace* van Buren) simply becomes the subject of the language.
But this confuses the variety and many-sided character of
Christian talk about God.

We also need a wider understanding of what language
does. It is not simply a copy or picture of something else;
somehow it is important in itself. Words stand for the reality
which they describe, and certainly words about God are not
bare expressions. There is an objectivity about such language:
it may not be the objectivity of physical objects and scientific
facts but it is the objectivity of something which challenges
us in the way that other persons do.

Van Buren's work is important and deserves far more
than this summary treatment. But he does not prove his
case either about Jesus's non-transcendental meaning or
about religious language only referring to some human
wish-fulfilment.

However, the 'Death of God' theologians see themselves
as evangelists, and their 'gospel' should be sympathetically
understood. They are Americans dissenting from their own
society in which church-going is the habit of 95 per cent of
the population. But this religious obsession of the most
advanced technological society in the world may be mere
escapism. More than ever before man needs to find meaning
and a sense of purpose in his existence. Yet he cannot
simply summon 'God' to his aid, for God is at a discount in
much modern thought and, in any case, it is idolatry to
make him only the answer to man's problems. The 'Death
of God' writers take the nihilism of Nietzsche seriously:
man must find the answer to his search for meaning in
himself.

This is fundamentally a question about history and man's
existence in history. No man is alone: part of his search for
meaning about himself is because he is bound up with other

people, with society, and with a whole world of activity. What is the meaning of this existence which presses in upon him? Is he faced by an apparently mechanistic universe with no possibility of free decision on his part? Or is there hope in the fact that his existence is historical? Man's life is not static but moving: there is the past as well as the present, and we look to the future. So long as there is a future, the question of man's meaning and value is not foreclosed.

This is, surely, a secular concern; it is the theme of popular songs and of a general philosophy of life which reflects either hopelessness or a yearning for identification. But it is also a religious concern. Man's religions have traditionally been the expression of these different attitudes to history, since religion has been the field in which man has concentrated his quest for meaning. There is the way of negation; in Buddhism and the monistic religions the human personality seeks to rid itself of the limitations imposed by historical existence. There is also the way of positive encounter, which has taken the form of theories of history and man's place in it, particularly in the highly-developed theistic religions. Amongst the latter, Christianity occupies a vital place with its preoccupation with history and the centrality of an utterly human figure, Jesus himself, who gives history direction and significance.

Yet the 'Death of God' school reject religion and any association of Christianity with religion. Why? The reason lies in their attitude towards history. They are strongly individualistic in their thinking and they emphasise Christ because he stands for the individual against the depersonalising forces of history. History can have no promise: they see it largely as a cyclic process and they reject religion because it is so involved in history, particularly in its cultic and sacral aspects, and because it is strongly societal in its expression. Behind some of these ideas lies Bonhoeffer's plea for a religionless Christianity. But there is also Karl Barth's influence, in his repudiation of man's religion. These writers look at religion differently from their nineteenth-century

Liberal Protestant and radical predecessors who found comfort in the fact that religion was universal and, therefore, Christianity could not be exclusive. But Altizer, who examines this specifically, rejects religion and holds to the uniqueness of Jesus as a new phenomenon in history.[1] This echoes Barth who interprets religion purely as an invention or product of man, and revelation, which comes from God alone, is the annulment of it. One can see how this could lead to a Christian atheism. In Barth's case the judgment on religion comes from his fundamental distinction between the divine and the human; human reality has no relation to the truth. But this may be all too easily inverted; if the human is given no meaning, it may react and exclude the divine. Altizer shows how a rigid view of revelation culminates in the 'Death of God' theology. The judgment on human history, passed by Barth and his followers, is taken to its ultimate conclusion.

This view of history nullifies the aim of secular theology to provide a gospel for modern man. Instead, we must affirm a more positive understanding both of history and religion which takes the following form. Christ can be encountered in human history, and he does not nullify that history; however, he is not the secular Jesus but he bears the claim of God. Christ fulfils the promise in history and allows the man of faith to see the future operating in the present. The Church is the agency in which this takes place, and this is not the 'ideal Church' but the human institution involved in history and therefore 'like' one of the religions. All this is prepared for in history itself and bids man consider God's purpose which begins with Creation and stretches to the final age.

Christianity is about man's search to discover meaning about himself. The Incarnation means that man is met as man by God himself, and history takes on a new dimension. To understand how this takes place we must emphasise that historical existence is not a bare series of events, but some-

[1]Thomas J. J. Altizer, *The Gospel of Christian Atheism*, Collins, ch. 1 passim.

thing in which human beings are involved. A true historical existence is one in which I encounter other human beings. When I meet someone I am already on the road to discovering something about myself. But I can do this only if I do not withhold myself from this other person, only if I am 'open' to him, as he must be open to me. The highest expression of this is love, which is a giving of the self; and no one will deny that love and care for others gives meaning to oneself and to life.

Historical existence understood like this means that I can also encounter men of the past. I do not set out simply to discover *facts* about them; modern historiography is an attempt to lay hold of their self-hood, what they were like in themselves and what they understood existence to mean, because this is vitally important for me also. The necessary factor is that the historical record about them shall preserve this understanding of theirs.

In the record about Jesus, the material is more than adequate. We are presented with a person whose openness invites my own openness and aids my discovery of myself. Here we make full use of the current movement in theology known as 'the new quest of the historical Jesus',[1] The synoptic gospels give us the 'kerygma' about Jesus, i.e. the gospel-preaching selection and interpretation of his words and works. Until very recently some scholars would have said that that was the only way to reach Jesus, via the faith of the early Church. But we see that there is a second way of approaching him, by means of the understanding of history that we have described. It is possible to discover the selfhood of Jesus. The gospel accounts enable us to do this because – despite their mythological material – they preserve unaltered precisely those sayings and scenes in which Jesus made his intention and understanding of existence most apparent.[2]

This is a fundamental point. It means that we are dealing

[1] See J. M. Robinson, *A New Quest of the Historical Jesus*, S.C.M. Press.
[2] Robinson, op. cit., p. 69f.

C

with a totally human Jesus who can be encountered in history. He can be met like other great men, like the Buddha or Muhammad, for instance. A fully self-conscious faith is not necessary at this stage. This Jesus has great relevance for modern man's search for meaning because, on any count, his is a human life of great significance and worth. Jesus has always fascinated men who would never countenance orthodox Christianity.

But what does a real encounter with Jesus involve? It means considering his claims about himself and God. The Buddha appears to teach little about God, and Muhammad's strict monotheism does not allow him to say more than that he is *the* prophet. But Jesus's remarkable selfhood is bound up with his consciousness not only that there is a God but that he is in some quite unique relation to him. One cannot single out Jesus as a great, or perhaps the greatest, human personality and ignore the key to his self-understanding which makes the achievement possible – his belief in the kingdom of God (God's sovereign presence and immediate rule in the world of men) and his own mission to proclaim and live out the claims of that kingdom. Nor can one remain in a state of 'objectivity' or plain hesitancy about the Jesus of history; he makes the same demand as the Christ of the kerygma, that one shall be as existentially involved in the question of God as he is. Meeting Jesus in history does not abrogate the claims of faith, as older theologians thought it did. The secular theologians fail to see this logic of the 'new quest', and they present the human life of Jesus without showing how it challenges us.

This quality of the life of Jesus means two things: it tells us about the character of God; and it also has something profound to say about our historical existence.

Jesus calls us to believe in the living God who is utterly concerned with this world and its history. The very fact of Creation is a personal involvement for God. The Incarnation fulfils the logic of a theism as personal and meaningful as this. God is compassionate, merciful and loving, and that is why Christ's life displays such attributes.

Christ who reveals God in this way must, therefore, have more than ordinary human significance. Theology attempts to express this: Christ is confessed as Lord, and as Son of God. His pre-existence, work in Creation, and eternal intercession for men, each points up the perspective in which the life in Galilee 1900 years ago is to be seen.

But the perspective begins with the human life, and that is the material point. The transcendental Christ did not deify human life, so that what went before had no meaning or significance. It is in a genuine human existence that the compassion, mercy and love of God are lived out; and because of this man has hope.

Thus, any tendencies in theology which play down the historical and human elements must be avoided. This includes some overstatements of traditional Christology and also the de-historicising tendencies of some Protestant orthodoxies. Traditional Christology has sometimes treated the human nature of Christ as having no real function except as a sleeve or organ for the operation of the divine Word. But we must look back to the question of St Irenaeus: What does it mean to have an historical man, a real figure of flesh and blood, in whom God acted? Such a Christology will not begin with the divine life in heaven, about which we know nothing. It goes on the datum of the historical life of Christ. And, secondly, the actual events of this life and not the mere fact of it are essential. The human figure, what he does, how he acts and expresses himself, is someone on whom faith can dwell. Faith cannot, of course, rest only on historical probabilities, but neither can it rest on the assumption that 'the question of Jesus Christ is not a matter for historical enquiry'[1]. Present-day historiography allows us to make no such easy judgment. If it were true then Jesus Christ would be abstracted out of human history, and he might become so idealised (the 'only real man' etc.) that we could have no

[1]See, for instance, E. Brunner, *The Mediator*, Theosoph Publ., p. 170f.

part in him, no part, at least, for which we could find a meaning. As it is, however, human faith is invited by *human* faith, in the man in the gospel, who had his own decisions to make, and worked out his belief in the situation in which he was placed. This is the really human Jesus and not the merely human Jesus of the secular theologies.

Man's search for meaning is matched by God's concern that it shall be met and answered in human life and history. That is why the Incarnation means the glory of man. That is why, as Rudolf Bultmann says, 'the question of God and the question of myself ultimately are identical'[1], if Bultmann means by that that we shall never find God if we avoid re-solving the inadequacies and contradictions of our lives and all that prevents that wholeness of life which Jesus himself manifested.

Hence Christ's words, 'I have come that you may have life, and have it more abundantly.' This is not something vague; it is about a new form of human existence. And it brings with it a change in our personal history. The full life which I live in Christ means that the promise of history is no longer about something purely in the future. It has moved into the present. There is a finality about this experience. Events are no longer formless or unconnected to anything (as the atheistic Existentialist would say), or just stretching away to some human Utopia in the future (as Marxists would say). *God* directs them. I am presented with the immediacy of God, to whose existence I must now be totally related. This event the biblical writers call the 'Eschaton'. The word means 'the *Last*'; it denotes the end of a merely human history, and it concerns something palpable, no less than the new lives of men and women who are reborn and know for themselves what Christianity means. The sign of this is the Church. This is the new society in the world which exists to preach Christ and to proclaim how our human life is now changed.

[1] R. Bultmann, *Jesus Christ and Mythology*, S.C.M. Press, p. 53.

'In the Church', says Luther, 'great wonders daily occur, such as the forgiveness of sins, triumph over death, the gifts of righteousness, and eternal life'.[1] That is the reality of the Church, for all these are eschatological happenings; they are all descriptions of the miracle of faith when it meets with the living God.

The 'Death of God' writers lack this eschatological reference to the Church. Partly, this is a reflection of the Barthian repudiation of religion and, therefore, of a religiously-involved Church. But it also derives from their understanding of man's existence which empties human history of any real meaning. They cannot see the value of the Church as an historical phenomenon spread abroad amongst human society. This point of view is also found in some writers who propose a 'religionless Christianity'. We must oppose this tendency as we rejected the abstract idealisation of Christ out of human history. Their solution to man's religious quest means separating him from a great deal in his existing experience; similarly, their attitude to the Church involves a contrast between the ideal and the actual body of believers.

But the Church is necessarily involved in human society. Its message claims to answer to all man's history and activity. A sign of this is that it reflects society in its organisation and even in the fact that it can use general religious experience to express its own distinctive understanding of the transcendent. A cry for religionless Christianity is right if it castigates the Church for retaining outdated structures long ago abandoned by society and unworthy forms of religious expression and worship. But it is wrong if it means a retreat to an invisible Church.

The secular theologians show the weakness of their position in their attitude towards worship. Any denigration of 'religion' will be suspicious of cult and ritual. Religionless Christianity can find no real place for corporate worship and the communal activity of praising God. The approach of

[1]Quoted in P. Lehmann, *Ethics in a Christian Context*, S.C.M. Press, p. 63n. 2.

these writers is primarily intellectual and moral. But so many elements are involved in man's experience of God, and worship is one of the most important because it unites various aspects of this experience. This point can be illustrated from the missionary activity of the Church. Where religious life has been found narrow and superficial, it is sometimes because missionaries have rejected indigenous worshipping forms, though these have been evolved in a long tradition in society and answer to various needs in it. A spiritual vacuum has thus been created which imported forms of worship, relating to a different situation, have not filled. Worship draws on many factors to express the reality of God in the richest possible way.

Certainly the Christian understanding of God cannot be understood apart from a consideration of worship.

Christian worship takes its character from the experience of the living God who meets man's quest in history. It consists of a proclamation about historical acts and about the living society which arises out of these. Every act of Christian worship is also an historical event itself. It directs the Christian to that final history in which every man shall own the living God. Christian worship is thus profoundly eschatological in character. Its central act, the eucharist, proclaims that the last age is experienced *now*.

Christian worship is *effective*, and it claims to convey something real. Cultic forms are very important to this end. Van Buren's restricted understanding of language vitiates his case at this point; but it is exactly the powerful communicative properties of symbol and metaphorical expression (as well as, of course, gesture and action) which give worship its openness and reference to objectivity. Some of this effective symbolism and language was not Christian in origin but was taken from existing experience which found it valuable.

This sanctification of existing life and experience, which worship expresses, brings us to the final matter. My encounter with God discloses the future. But it suggests how the past is also full with meaning. When I turn to the Bible I find there a consistent world view of God's purposes in history which begins with Creation itself. Behind the individual act of faith and behind the activity of the Church there is a preparation which constitutes all history.

The biblical writers do not speak about God in his timelessness; he is always in his 'time for man'. So man is placed in a dynamic process which stretches behind him as well as before him. Faith occurs in a context and has a background. It is not 'my faith' but the faith of the Church which professed it before me. Faith is evoked in answer to the preaching of the Church and in meeting other Christians and seeing how their belief works. But the man of faith is also a member of human society and the product of its evolution, just as the Church itself is bound up with society. He must believe that all these forces which influence him so deeply have their purpose in the mind of God. Faith must look back to Creation itself.

Significantly, this is where much secular theology has little to say. The 'Death of God' writers have no satisfactory doctrine of Creation because they cannot see how human history and activity can bear the divine. We miss here the cosmic vision of Teilhard de Chardin who saw how evolutionary theory could be integrated into theology and become a factor contributing to our self-understanding.

This is also a weakness in much Protestant theology. Paradoxically, biblical theologians can often be faulted on this subject. They stress faith and see its eschatological bearing, but they speak little about continuity. Despite the massive restatement of the doctrine of Creation by Karl Barth, Protestant scholars still make statements which imply that 'grace destroys nature'. But this makes grace completely arbitrary; it takes faith out of its dynamic relation to history and leaves so little reason for Creation that it might even be evil. Thus, the unity of divine and human in Christ is endangered, because no value or worth is really given to the human. But Jesus Christ the *man* is necessary to faith's decision. The traditional Catholic scheme may have too readily assumed that there is a natural progression from nature to grace, which does not do justice to the creative newness of faith. But a better way would be that suggested in St Irenaeus's doctrine of recapitulation. God is consistent in his purpose; Christ sums up in himself all that has gone on before.

We must certainly re-examine what theologians have meant by 'total depravity' and ask what possible use this view of human nature has today. To stress grace at the expense of Creation seems to imply that God has not all along been faithful. The question whether man retains even the formal semblance of the *imago Dei* is, surely, the question of the real continuity of redemptive history.

'Creation is grace', as Barth himself reminds us. The living God is Creator. Neglect of this understanding, and a narrow concentration on certain theories of redemption, has caused a reaction in the cry for a 'religionless Christianity'. Part of our answer to modern atheism must, therefore, be a recovery of a theological understanding of Creation. It is a necessary counterpart to eschatology. We must certainly be alive to the implications of evolutionary theory though without repeating the mistake of liberal theologians who saw history only in terms of a quite mechanical development.

* * *

None of this is meant to suggest that modern questions about the doctrine of God are easily settled. But the aim of secular theology to answer man's urgent quest for meaning can also be met by Catholic theology without complete compromise or talk of the 'Death of God'. The sincerity of the secular theologians is not denied; the only question is the adequacy of their attempt. It should be recognised that this theology is not simply a response to an apologetic situation but arises out of certain preoccupations in modern Protestant thought.

Many problems remain. We do need a restatement of what God is all about. Much of the difficulty concerns language. How can God be described? Professor Dewart's book is a valiant attempt to analyse the language used by a particular tradition of Christian thought. God is not a being, but is it satisfactory to describe him as 'Being Itself'? Dewart proposes, instead, that God is a 'reality beyond being'. But here we must object that a reality is something that is, and whatever is belongs to being. At the end of his book Dewart counsels silence as a necessary part of our thought about God.

The attempt of secular theology contains a warning about method: to disregard the experience of men who claim to deal with God is a handicap from the start. Tillich proposed that one should start with secular experience and he appealed to the universal sense of an 'Ultimate Reality'. But do all men sense it, and what is the content of this 'Ultimate Reality'? It could be something quite pantheistic and impersonal and of little relevance to a concrete belief such as Christians affirm about the Incarnation. Surely religious experience should be accepted as the datum for examining the reality of God. A purely intellectual approach to the being of God may lose sight of the fact that religion is a way of life, a system of worship, a form of personal mysticism, etc., in all of which the religious man claims to speak of God from working knowledge. Dewart himself betrays a too markedly philosophical approach in his deprecatory remarks about worship.[1]

In the task of reconstruction, a large place must be given to a new theology of religions. As a result of Barth's influence this has been neglected, with unfortunate results, as is shown in some of the secular theologians. They allow no positive evaluation of religion, yet here is a whole field of experience which cannot be empty and has great contemporary relevance. This can be said without any need to go back to a consensus of religions on the old liberal pattern which Barth rightly rejects.

[1]Dewart, op. cit., p. 204.

Lastly, justice must be done to the distinctive nature of the Christian experience of God. When Christians talk about God encountering men in history they believe that they have a record for it. This is the Bible which itself is historical and forms a vital part of the data for interpreting history. Christians cannot fail, when speaking of the God they know, to use biblical language. This does not remove any of the difficulties of language but it means that the Christian doctrine of God must have a completely biblical character and it suggests that there are certain limits to our thinking about God. If this involves a tension with the conceptual approach beloved of Catholic tradition, that cannot be helped. Only too often Catholic philosopher-theologians give the impression of being quite unbiblical in outlook – though biblical theologians for their part often seem to assume that to declare, 'the Bible says,' is to avoid conceptual difficulties, when manifestly this is not so. The tension must be creative, and it ought to concentrate on the following problems.

The biblical writers do not speak of some general religious dimension known as 'God', 'The Absolute', or 'The Holy', but quite specifically of Him who is the God and Father of Jesus Christ. Knowledge vouchsafed of him in Christ – faith-knowledge – is different from other knowledge. But does the Bible require us to say (like Karl Barth) that faith-knowledge is *wholly* different? If so, then Christians and modern atheists would start off on the same footing (as some neo-Orthodox theologians claim), for neither can have anything to do with 'God' until, in the case of the Christian, God in his grace encounters him and reveals that he 'is'. How would a new understanding of the eschatological nature of the Church clarify this ancient discussion?

Granted that conceptual language is necessary, can it not be brought closer to the biblical point of view about redemptive history? If we conceive of God as *actus purus* or the metaphysical 'Absolute', we treat him as unchanging essence, outside the flux of the time process and in total contrast to the contingent and transient existence of man. It is hard enough on this view to account for the actual event of personal relations between God and man. But it is still less adequate in dealing with the mystery of the divine and the human in Christ. The two-nature Chalcedonian theory is under attack for this reason. In some way, we must talk about the divine and the human in Christ as distinct but not separated, united but not confused. But doctrine should use something more satisfactory than out-of date theories of 'nature' and 'substance' if it is to have any relation to the personal life of Jesus, which the gospels present to us.

To recognise the biblical approach is necessarily to face the question of 'myth'. If one speaks of God acting in history, one must use mythical language; God has to be described somehow in symbolic utterances drawn out of changing human experience. The biblical writers used symbols and metaphors belonging to their experience. Many of these must now be changed. The so-called 'de-mythologising' programme must be accepted: if God is described in the physical and spatial symbols of a past age his immediacy may actually be hidden. But the necessity of myth remains. De-mythologising is wrong if it empties the myth of God's action and understands the imagery only to mean that my search for meaning and the question of the existence of God are ultimately identical. We need new symbols to refer to history which is the essential content of Christian myth. Far more work on myth is needed from Catholic writers, particularly since the de-mythologising school has a restricted understanding of image and symbol which could be enriched by thinkers from another tradition.

A fresh and positive understanding of history would help all this discussion. Certainly, a vision of history in the purpose of God could answer the concern of secular man – history with Christ as its centre and the Church as the paradigm of the divine and human interaction in history. There is every reason for censuring Christian theology if it is introverted and circumscribed. Pope John's address to Vatican II asked the Church to adopt an ecumenical and historical perspective: to 'look to the present, to new conditions and forms of life . . .' That is a recognition of theology's concern with what man is saying, man whose flesh Christ wore. Against Karl Barth we have got to make sense of human culture, but we must do more than take it at its face value. If we can see that the history which encompasses all our concerns is alive with transcendence, then we shall want to wrest a meaning from all that goes on within it. Both secular and religious man meet in their search to discover what life is about. But only faith can see the extent of the promise in history and its loving continuity from beginning to end.

FURTHER READING

D. E. JENKINS, *Guide to the Debate about God*, Lutterworth Press 1966. *The Glory of Man*, S.C.M. Press 1967

J. MACQUARRIE, *God-Talk*, S.C.M. Press 1967

J. MOLTMANN, *Theology of Hope*, S.C.M. Press 1967

T. W. OGLETREE, *Death of God Controversy*, S.C.M. Press 1966

THE CATHOLIC CHURCH

THREE

The Authority of the Church

ALAN WILKINSON

'Never accept authority: whether of a jealous god, priest, prime minister, president, dictator, school teacher, social worker, parent, or of anyone else whatsoever, unless, in your own seriously considered view, there are good reasons for it.'

Dr Ronald Fletcher, the sociologist who wrote these words five years ago in *New Society*, was expressing the new attitude to authority which is characteristic of the world of the 1960s. This new attitude affects the exercise of authority in every sphere of life. Thus in the helping professions, there are those who strongly advocate 'non-judgmental counselling'; it is said that the helper should not impose his solution but elicit it from the client himself. In schools until comparatively recently, the teacher stood in front of a class arranged in rows and instructed the pupils. Now classes are often arranged in small groups, and learning is regarded as a mutual and freely-ranging process in which the children use their own initiative under the guidance of the teacher. In new methods of religious education the starting point is, as far as possible, the experience of the children. Canon Eric James tells how he was asked to lecture to youth leaders on the problem of authority and the teenager. He was asked not to prepare the second lecture until he had listened to the results of the group work and questions resulting from the first; and this was the method he was asked to adopt throughout the series. The Church is also increasingly using small groups for teaching purposes; the priest steps down from the pulpit and puts himself 'at risk' by inviting discussion and critical questioning.

In social life there has been a strong reaction against formality and ceremony. Before the war a pile of visiting cards would greet the new occupants of a house in the university district of Cambridge. Whereas thirty years ago a good deal of social life still had its appropriate dress and behaviour, this mode of living is now regarded not only as antiquated, but also as life-denying. Life, it is argued, should be allowed to create its own forms spontaneously; an external authoritarian structure gravely cramps and distorts. For many, the metaphysical scores have been torn up; 'playing it by ear' is a significant modern phrase.

The astonishing developments in science and technology create a tendency to deny that anything from the past can be authoritative. We are trained to venerate the latest in any series. This may be a reasonable assumption when buying a new car. But Plato or Shakespeare do not grow out of date in the same way as an early computer becomes obsolete. 'Pre-Freudian' has the same ring as 'prehistoric'. Psychologists, sociologists and anthropologists are commonly credited with not only having provided explanations for experiences and phenomena formerly treated as beyond criticism and self-authenticating; they are regarded as having explained them away. The use of the word 'merely' is a pointer: 'religion is merely a night-light for the neurotic'; 'God is merely a symbol for society'. For those Christians who believe in infallibility, it was much easier to grant this to Councils before modern communications revealed to the general public the dissensions and manoeuvrings behind and within the Second Vatican Council. If it has become difficult or impossible to believe in an occasional transubstantiation of the words of the Church into the words of Christ, a reading of (say) one of the new Pelican commentaries on the gospels makes it difficult or impossible to hold a naively romantic view of revelation as having been conveyed to man untouched by human hand.

It is often remarked upon, to the discredit of the Church's

authority, that while it on the whole keeps to generalised pronouncements on war and race, when it comes to the minutiae of sexual ethics the Church is often eager to speak categorically. By contrast, humanists are often ready to be specific, dogmatic and categorical about issues of war and race, while insisting that questions of sexual ethics are either a purely private affair, or can only be approached very tentatively. The teenager complains that the Church is much more eager to condemn fornication than Vietnam.

The so-called 'scientific' way of thinking is often considered to be the only sure way to truth. Therefore, it is worth spending some time discussing the popular contrast between authority in religion and authority in science, between 'a closed dogmatic system' and 'an open-minded adventurousness open only to the facts'. One reason why science sometimes is able to give us clear answers is that the scope of its questions is limited to the mechanisms of life rather than to its purpose. 'Can't you give me a clear answer to the problem of evil?' 'No, but I can give you a clear answer to those questions you ask about the behaviour of rats under that hormone compound which we are testing.' I don't believe that man can be for long content with the *how* of life alone. Indeed concentration upon techniques alone can be a drug, like overwork, taken to prevent us from facing disturbing questions.

It has a very different effect if one begins a statement with 'He' rather than 'I' – contrast for example, 'He's dancing' with 'I'm dancing' (to adapt an illustration used by Bishop Ian Ramsey.) 'He's dancing to keep warm under the capitalist system,' says the Marxist. 'He's reverting to tribal behaviour,' says the anthropologist. 'He's typical of 10 per cent of the population,' says the sociologist. 'He's dancing so well that he will win the prize,' says the ballroom manager. The nearer the man dancing approaches the status of an object, a specimen, an example, the more easy it is to deal with him with scientific precision. But much of religion, philosophy, literature and art deals with experiences like 'I'm dancing' a much more personal, inward and complex texture of experience to try to present.

I want now to recall the common antitheses between science and religion, and then to suggest under four headings that in fact these antitheses are often false. Religion is subjective, people say, but science is objective; religion is dogmatic, science empirical; religion is authoritarian, backward-looking, introverted; science is authoritative, ever marching onwards with excitement and expectation, pushing backwards the frontiers of ignorance; religion deals with hopes and intangibles, science with hard practical facts; religion asks for personal commitment, science for personal detachment; religion is part of man's infancy, and it operates through an oppressive and restrictive community, 'explaining' an ever-narrowing area of mystery; science is part of man's maturity, exciting, individualistic, and explains mysteries as ignorance. Religion is concerned with poetry, science with prose.

The first heading concerns the relation of the individual to the authority of the scientific and religious communities. W. G. Pollard, a leading American physicist, is also an Episcopalian priest, and in *Physicist and Christian* (1962) he compared his own experiences of knowledge through his two communities. 'Only physicists can really know the truth of physics; everyone else has to take it on faith . . . The Church, too, is a community whose distinctive life and unique power of understanding can only be shared by those who have subjected themselves to the full process of incorporation into that community.' A report of the American Association for the Advancement of Science showed that high school students had no idea of the important part played by excitement, imagination and delight in scientific discovery, nor had they any conception of the essential place of the community in scientific knowledge.

Both becoming a Christian and becoming a scientist involve incorporation into a community, sharing its accumulated knowledge and wisdom, growing into its outlook, and

venerating its saints. Only when one has *received* a tremendous amount can one begin to make an original contribution.
Forsyth wrote, 'None should depart from tradition but those
to whom it is dear. None should be entrusted with the destruction of the past but those who love it'. Like the Hebrew
prophets or St Francis of Assisi one can only stand over
against the community through the resources which the
community provides. Pollard quotes Robert Oppenheimer's
Reith Lectures:

> 'Each of us knows from his own life how much even a
> casual and limited association of men goes beyond him in
> knowledge, in understanding, in humanity, and in power.
> . . . Each of us knows how much he has been transcended
> by the group of which he has been or is a part; each of
> us has felt the solace of other men's knowledge to stay his
> own ignorance, of other men's wisdom to stay his folly,
> of other men's courage to answer his doubts or his weak-
> ness'.

This is very far from the popular picture of the scientist
as an inspired individualist, advancing only in so far as
he despises the authority of community knowlege.

The second heading concerns the common antithesis
between religion as subjective and personal, and science as
objective and impersonal. In fact, in recent years, there has
been a considerable convergence. In science there has been
a growing recognition of the importance of personal commitment and the place of non-cerebral factors in discovery.
Michael Polanyi said in *Personal Knowledge* (1958):

> 'I have shown that into every act of knowing there enters a
> passionate contribution of the person . . . Personal know-
> ledge in science . . . commits us, passionately and far
> beyond our comprehension, to a vision of reality . . . Like
> love to which it is akin, this commitment is a "shirt of
> flame" blazing with passion and, also like love, consumed
> by devotion to a universal demand.'

The phrase 'scientific method' implies a standardisation of practice which is far from the actual truth; the finished paper makes neat and cerebral, what was often arrived at initially through the authority of aesthetic attraction, intuition, or what can only be called a sense of constraint against the obvious facts.

Two scientists wrote on this theme in the *Times Literary Supplement* for 25 October, 1963. H. C. Longuet-Higgins declared:

'To repeat, the scientist is by nature an artist. His ways of thought are primarily intuitive and imaginative. He does not use the Scientific Method, this is a convenient fiction'.

P. B. Medawar made the same point more elaborately.

'(1) There is no such thing as a Scientific Mind . . . (2) There is no such thing as The Scientific Method . . . (3) The idea of naïve or innocent observation is philosophers' make-believe . . . (4) Induction is a myth . . . (5) The formulation of a natural law begins as an imaginative exploit'.

Discovery comes then, not through the elimination of personality, but through personality, through *all* the ways we have of knowing anything to be true. (It is interesting that in social work and in psychiatry, there is a move towards the recognition that the personality and love of the social worker and psychiatrist are the most important healing factors.) Discoveries happen when people are willing to leap beyond the obvious facts, are willing to turn back on the laboratory stair and see whether this incredible hunch could possibly work, whether this odd constraint can be validated.

The nature of religious authority and its validation is not as dissimilar as is often supposed. There is at least one major difference, however. Even in the most costly personal involvement in science, one is never on the bench in the experiment in quite the same way as in religious faith. As in love, one cannot surrender and conduct a controlled experiment at the same time; the 'I' that observes and calculates must be drawn in with the 'me'. But faith arises *out* of experience – *all* my ways of knowing something, or more importantly someone, to be true and trustworthy; it goes beyond experience as one's marriage vows do, but they are also based upon a corpus of accumulated experience, in which acts of faith or curiosity, at first tentative and half-hearted perhaps, have been validated by reason, emotion and experience, and tested by communal consensus, and so have been made the foundation for other more venturesome acts of faith and hope.

The ways by which a person moves from not knowing God to faith in God and commitment in baptism, are not unlike the ways in which a person moves from not having met a particular woman to the moment when he is taking her unconditionally for better and for worse. For revelation is of God himself, not of propositions about God; propositions exist to articulate experience. Theology is mere information, mere knowing about, until it is vivified and verified by prayer. Theology is concerned with being consecrated by the truth, with the doing of truth. Fr Benson wrote:

'The use of the intellect is, that by knowing the things of God we may attain to the experimental knowledge of God's love. Otherwise our learning is only like a staircase leading to the top of a ruined tower'.

For Anglicans, authority is many-stranded, a series of cross-checking and cross-illuminating authorities. 'Authority ... is single in that it is derived from a single Divine source ... It is distributed among Scripture, Tradition, Creeds, the Ministry of the Word and Sacraments, the witness of saints, and the *consensus fidelium* ... It is thus a dispersed rather than a centralised authority, having many elements which combine, interact with, and check each other ... Liturgy, in the sense of the offering and ordering of the public worship of God, is the crucible in which these elements of authority are fused and unified in the fellowship and power of the Holy Spirit' (Lambeth Conference 1948). The God who creates is the same God who redeems. The world to which Christ came was the world which the Father had created through the Son. We should therefore expect to discover that experience confirms the authority of the Christian faith, though this may not be immediately apparent. The struggle and suffering of the Cross make sense in a world which so obviously 'groans in all its parts as if in the pangs of childbirth' (Rom. 8:22). If one compares the contemporary analysis of human nature by psychiatry with that by traditional spiritual writers, one notes striking similarities, for example between the ideas of *accidie* and 'depression'. Modern psychiatry discovers how many of our problems are rooted in anxiety, fear and envy. The central message of the New Testament is 'Fear not'. One understands more of the difficulties of being God from one's own experience of being a parent.[1] As children grow older the loving parent gives them greater freedom, without which there can be no maturity, though the wrong exercise of this freedom may lead to disaster.

The third heading I might call 'Models and Mystery' adopting the title from the illuminating book by Bishop Ian Ramsey. It is said that science sticks to the facts and concerns itself with prose statements. But 'facts' is an odd word. Place a stick in a glass of water; I say that it is not bent because I adopt the normal convention of giving authority to touch and ignoring sight. Facts only make sense in some conceptual scheme, and we accept a very large number of facts upon authority. Any statement at all implies an act of faith – for example, in the reality of the world to which we communicate, as every scientist relies upon the intelligibility and stability of the world he is investigating.

[1]*Editorial Note:* For an extremely interesting account of man's awareness of God, see the chapter called 'Ten day Voyage' in R. D. Laing's *The Bird of Paradise.*

Now it used to be thought that the physical world was really like a system of billiard balls; the language of late nineteenth-century physics presented itself as prose reality, simple description. But we realise now that many scientific descriptions are in fact models enabling us to be articulate about reality. Both in science and in religion the deeper we penetrate into reality the more language eludes us, especially if we are personally committed, as in relationship with a human being or God, where we encounter the difficulty of making clear statements which begin with 'I'.

> *Words strain,*
> *Crack and sometimes break, under the burden,*
> *Under the tension, slip, slide, perish,*
> *Decay with imprecision, will not stay in place,*
> *Will not stay still.*
>
> T. S. ELIOT, FOUR QUARTETS

It is characteristic of the spiritual insensitivity of our society that many people today seem to think that poetry, metaphors and symbols are long-winded ways of obscuring the obvious. Technological society finds metaphoric and symbolic thinking unfamiliar, and worse still disturbing, because of its capacity for awakening sides of our nature which we seek to put to sleep, the why and the mystery of life, the oddness and the strangeness of it all. The writings of educationalists like David Holbrook make it clear that aspects of our present educational system maim or destroy the imaginative and poetic faculties of many children. The language of devils is not strange to anyone who has suffered mental illness, it perhaps is the only language for a present reality, and the de-mythologisers seem at times like the psychiatrist who would shut off sections of the sick mind with tranquilisers rather than face and exorcise its terror. 'The symbol awakens intuition where the language of abstraction can only offer rational explanation. The symbol addresses every side of the human spirit, whereas the language of abstraction is bound to confine itself to a single thought. The symbol strikes a chord in the very depths of the soul, whereas the language of abstraction touches only the surface of the mind like a passing breeze' (J. J. Bachofen). A prose conceptualised version of the biblical faith is as worthless as a prose conceptualised version of *King Lear*. It is one of the major defects of Western religion that it is so often preoccupied with the workings of the conscious mind of the educated adult. But unless Christ redeems the sub-conscious as well, the whole man cannot be redeemed, and the subconscious is largely reached through primordial images. We who wish for a more naturalistic and more rational style of worship should take heed.

God is not God of the gaps, for Christianity is about the Incarnation, the sacraments, a man, a bath and a meal. It is not about the occult. Spiritual writers are always very matter-of-fact when it comes to stigmata and visions; of course they happen, but they are very peripheral. The Christian is like the novelist or the poet or the painter in that he is concerned about the oddness of the ordinary, the transfiguration of the natural. Ronald Hepburn wrote in a recent humanist symposium *Objections to Humanism* about the programme to strip religion of its various encumbrances:

'There may survive, however, moral concepts of a rich-ness that shows up the meagreness of the humanist's own. And there may survive ways of seeing humanity, trans-figurations of the supposedly familiar world, which – even when we are quite unable to assimilate or domesticate them – can haunt and trouble and goad the imagination.'

Bishop Ramsey sees theology as 'the guardian and spokes-man of insight and mystery'. Here again, there has been a recent shift of emphasis in Christianity as in the arts; when we speak of mystery, it is not an escapist world of fabricated mystery, but the awareness of the oddness of the normal, the strangeness of birth and death, of love and bread, wine and water.

The fourth heading concerns the popular contrast between

the dogmatism of religion and the openness of science. Certain preliminary points must be made.

' "Authorities" are trustworthy not only according to their expertness but also in proportion as they are free and determined to reckon honestly with new discoveries' (A. R. Vidler).

The authoritarian has no real authority, in this sense. The Church has got to accept willingly, generously and courageously the pluralist society in which she has no automatic status or authority of office. In a sacral society Church and politics became so intertwined, that heresy was inevitably politically orientated, and often dangerous socially. But the Church has learnt in the last hundred years that the Holy Spirit guides us into truth dialectically. There has also been a shift of attitudes in science. A good deal of late nineteenth- and early twentieth-century science was characterised by a self-assured dogmatism that sounds strange today; we solve one problem only to find three new problems have grown in the same place. A little knowledge of the history of science modifies the popular estimate of the scientific community as always open to new discoveries. Darwin was fiercely criticised by various biologists and supported by some Churchmen. In 1864 the President of the Royal Society in giving its highest award to Darwin expressly omitted the theory of evolution from the grounds of its award. Twenty-three years after the publication of the *Origin of Species* Darwin was buried near Isaac Newton in Westminster Abbey.

In any case we must be sympathetic to the problems created by a wholesale re-orientation of attitudes. The more deeply a belief affects one's life, the harder it is to change. Changing the layout of *The Times* is rather less difficult than changing one's wife. Many people today find it hard to realise that the centre of the world has shifted from Europe to Africa and Asia. Because Christian faith is the 'Yes' of the whole person not to a theory but to the experimental knowledge of the personal God, it is no more healthful to be constantly digging up the foundations in the cause of intellectual stimulus than to be always taking the temperature of one's marriage. Belief in a relationship is different from belief in a scientific theorem. A wife who finds that her husband is a thief cries 'I know, but I still believe in him.' This is as creditable and understandable as the cry of Job, 'Though he slay me, yet will I wait for him.' The Church is not a religious debating society, but a worshipping community. Nevertheless it is also an apostolic community, and to be truly apostolic it must be as ready to listen and learn, as to teach and speak. It was a healthy sign of a new openness, of a new readiness to hear what God is saying through the agnostic, when the Anglican Church of Canada commissioned a leading Canadian agnostic to write a critique of the Church now published as *The Comfortable Pew* by Pierre Berton. Like the scientific community the Church is international; charges of 'a conspiracy to conceal the facts', for example about the Dead Sea Scrolls or the authorship of the epistles are as absurd today in one community as they would be in another, although the Roman Church is only just emerging from a system of censorship.

Christianity is a revelation through history, therefore it is peculiarly vulnerable to new discoveries, textual, archeological and historical. Because Christianity claims that in Christ we find revealed the fullness of Truth, the modern Church is always bound to take account sooner or later of new discoveries in every field, hence the number of studies with titles like 'Christ and Freud', 'Christianity and Evolution', 'Christ and Politics', 'Christianity and other religions'.

In a pluralist and empirically minded society, mass communications expose at least some of the more ill-founded claims to unquestioned and transcendent authority. So the Church is ceasing to have the authority of office and increasingly is having to earn its authority on the open market. Contrast the authority of Christ with the authority of a policeman. The policeman is obeyed in his own realm whether he is a wise and good man or not. Those who encountered Christ usually felt that he was a person of authority in his own right; this authority was not derived from his holding a publicly recognised office like that of a lawyer or scribe. 'The people were astounded at his teaching, for, unlike the doctors of the law, he taught with a note of authority' (Mark 1:22). When the people tried to make him fill the office of Kingship that they had chosen, he slipped away (John 6:15), Christ's authority derived from his person – from his insight, command, compassion and otherness. He realistically accepted the titles of 'Master' and 'Lord' but redefined them in terms of the servant (John 13:13). Moreover, what he said with his lips, he embodied in action; he not only spoke the truth, he did the truth. The bread broken and the wine poured out were not just picturesque parables; what he said on Maundy Thursday night he did on the cross the following day. This complete identification of word and action is one reason why his authority was and is convincing. 'The doctors of the law and the Pharisees sit in the chair of Moses; therefore do what they tell you; pay attention to their words. But do not follow their practice; for they say one thing and do another' (Matt. 23:2–3).

The authority of the Church is authoritative when it follows Christ's method. The authority of Christianity derives from the authority of Christ, and the authority of a person as a person ('I was enormously impressed by him when he walked into the room') is very different from the authority of a person as meteorologist ('he can tell you anything you want to know about the weather'). Both the person as person, and the person as meteorologist are authoritative, but in very different senses of the word. Christ always refused to be authoritarian; again and again when asked one question he would reply with another; he would not save the questioners from the necessary spiritual and moral effort. He did not come to purvey information, but to be and to do the truth.

Franz Jägerstätter was an Austrian Roman Catholic, the devout sexton of his village. He was executed at the age of 36 in 1943 because he refused on Christian grounds to join Hitler's army. He is one of the most authoritatively Christian men of our time, because out of the resources of faith which he derived from the liturgy and sacraments of the Church, he was able to defy the apparently authoritative blandishments of the Church to conform. His Bishop said of him after the war, in words which might have been used about Christ by the High Priest after the crucifixion, 'Jägerstätter represents a completely exceptional case, one more to be marvelled at than copied'.

Newman ended Tract 1 addressed to the clergy in September 1833: 'Exalt our Holy Fathers, the Bishops . . . and magnify your office, as being ordained by them to take part in their Ministry.' Though the Tractarians and their successors devoted much theological writing to show that episcopacy is of the *esse* of the Church, the office that was really magnified by Anglo-Catholics was that of the parish priest. The judgments of the Privy Council in the later nineteenth century brought ecclesiastical authority into contempt, by on the one hand allowing greater latitude to the liberal churchmen, and by trying on the other hand to enforce a narrow interpretation of ceremonial and liturgical directions when it came to Anglo-Catholics. For the most part protected by the parson's freehold, and encouraged by the gradual breakdown in discipline and the failure to produce an acceptable revision of the Prayer Book, many Anglo-Catholics developed a congregationalist type of Catholicism, looking for its authority largely to Rome, though there was dispute as to how much of that authority should be accepted. Two good results of this appeal to Rome were that Anglican spiritual and liturgical life became less insular, and that Anglican worship became more splendid as it began to use more of the created world.

There were two main reasons for this appeal to Roman

authority. Firstly, they believed that Rome with its full churches had the means for converting England; therefore on pastoral grounds they adopted Rome's discipline, spiritual methods and liturgical manners. Secondly, the Anglo-Catholics had an inferiority feeling about Anglicanism dating from Newman's secession. Many did not believe that the Anglican tradition had either authority, spiritual depth, romance or integrity. They mistrusted an appeal to a Catholic tradition in the West which was independent of the Latin tradition, as being fatally compromised by Protestant elements, as well as being State-imposed. Ten years ago the vicar of a parish in a northern town where a crematorium had just been built, told his parishioners that he would refuse to conduct any cremations, as cremation was contrary to 'the teaching of the Church'. A sizeable number of Anglicans were until recently brought up on a strict eucharistic fast as being 'the teaching of the Church'. Up until a few years ago in one Anglo-Catholic parish, there were deliberately no organisations like the Mothers' Union, which would have brought the parishioners into contact with other traditions of churchmanship in the diocese. But we have now reached a new stage. The crumbling of the monolithic façade of Roman Catholicism since Vatican II has implicitly given a new validity to many of the special features of the Anglican tradition which had previously been despised by many Anglo-Catholics. The Prayer Book emphasis upon the communion of the people as an integral part of every eucharist, is now respected in almost all Anglo-Catholic churches, largely because this is now also Roman teaching. The new phenomenon of a variety of liturgical usage in Roman Catholicism, has led to a considerable Anglo-Catholic willingness to adopt the revised Anglican services prepared by the Church of England Liturgical Commission in place of various approximations to the (old) Western rite. The former ideal of some Anglo-Catholics that every Western Catholic should be a Latin is disappearing. At the Vatican Council many people realised for the first time that there was within the Roman Church a body of Christians who were Catholic, though not Latin, namely those usually called the Uniates. The Melchite (Uniate) patriarch of Antioch, Maximos IV, said bluntly: 'We must therefore begin to convert the Latin West to catholicism, to the universality of the message of Christ . . . a levelling conformity is not reconcilable with catholic universality.'

The failure of Anglo-Catholics to magnify the personal role of the English vicar into the office of the continental priest is evident, though the Catholic movement has given a much greater spiritual depth to the English priesthood, and for this, one of its greatest gifts, we ought to be grateful. The title 'Father' has a very different tone from 'Vicar' or 'Sir'. 'Father' implies an affectionate respect for a priestly authority. (Illustrative of the lengths to which the copying of the Roman manner can go is the practice of a few extremists of advertising a visiting preacher as 'The Parish Priest of X' rather than as the 'Vicar of X'). For most English people, the terms 'parson', 'vicar', or 'clergyman' come more naturally to the lips than 'priest' when used of the incumbent. Two different ideas of authority are implied in the two sentences: 'We must get *the* vicar at once'; 'We must get *a* priest at once'. The Englishman is unlikely to say 'any priest will do', for he puts personal relationship before sacramental function. Upon what traditionally has the authority of the English vicar been based? More upon his superior educational and social status than upon being the dispenser of sacraments essential to salvation; he has been judged more by the frequency with which he visited the people than by the frequency with which he celebrated the eucharist. The new mobility of populations, the ecumenical movement within and beyond the Church of England, the disappearance of the old kind of slum parish (with heroic priests like Father Wainright) where so many were materially dependent upon the Church: all these and other factors have contributed to the gradual disappearance of the congregationalist Anglo-Catholic priest who wished to be closely linked only to like-minded parishes at home and like-minded dioceses overseas.

Thirty years ago Anglo-Catholics were ashamed to belong to a Church which included a Bishop Barnes. Now Anglicans find themselves complimented by Roman Catholics for belonging to such a wisely tolerant church. In *Doctrinal Development and Christian Unity*[1] a Dutch Jesuit writes that we can learn much from the attitudes to episcopacy taken up by those very Reformation divines, whose importance Norman Sykes devoted so much labour to publicise ten years ago, and Anglo-Catholics so much labour to minimise. Anglicans used to become Roman Catholics largely because Roman authority seemed to be certain and clear. But when a leading English Roman Catholic theologian left that Church he said of the Pope 'one who claims to be the moral leader of mankind should not tell lies'. It can no longer be argued that at least the authorities of the Church of Rome command obedience among its members because they speak with a note of simple authority. Until very recently a sizeable number of middle-class Roman Catholics in America and some European countries, limited the size of their families by contraceptive methods forbidden by their Church. Since the latest encyclical the extent of their refusal to accept 'simple authority' has become even more obvious.

There is then no simple, easy way to truth. God has designed the world in such a way that we have to exert considerable effort in order to understand it. The Lambeth Conference of 1948 was right to see doctrinal authority as many-stranded and cross-checking. In the future the authority which the Church will command in the world will depend very much upon the manner of the exercise of authority within the Church. Whatever the faults of the proposals for synodical government in the Church of England, at least they do try to resolve the tension between the clericalist notion of the Church as represented by the Con-

[1]Edited by Nicholas Lash, 1967.

vocations, and the democratic notion of the Church as represented by the climate of opinion which produced the Enabling Act and the Church Assembly. The proposed structures imply that those exercising authority in the Church should be representative and accountable; and that this authority should be as widely shared as is practicable, however much the bishop in his diocese, and the priest in his parish, rightly have to accept a final responsibility. The authority which the Church commands, will also be related to its readiness to move away from relying upon the authority of the pronouncement, buttressed by legislation, social convention and political pressure. The truth must be done in full view of the public, with the type of painstaking and expert sifting of evidence in relation to principle which we saw in *Putting Asunder* (1966). It will also be enhanced by a genuine dialectic within the Church, which the increasing number of lay theologians will do much to foster. This is not the place to discuss *Honest to God*. But it is clear that it exposed several major problems which had been neglected, and in doing so, caught the ear of many who had despaired of theology ever saying anything to their condition, or who had previously never read any theology at all. The Church will gain a more ready hearing as it becomes more grateful for the voice of God speaking through those who reject God, or say that they do not know him. Isaiah spoke of Cyrus king of Persia as God's anointed. 'I call you by your name, I surname you, though you do not know me' (Isa. 45:1, 4). But if the Church is to grow into a mutually fruitful relationship with the world, then this means that the Church must use her authority to free men as far as possible from the fears, superstitions and social pressures which can make both genuine belief and genuine unbelief impossible. The superstitious fears which in part create the demand for indiscriminate baptism, are an obvious example.

Has the Church then no teaching authority? Is it no longer to be thought of as sent by God? Is it to be regarded no more as (at least) the chief sacrament of Christ's presence in the world? That the Church is a divinely created and divinely commissioned body with authority is not in question. What is in question is the nature of that authority and the manner of its exercise. The apostolic mission of the Church can only be properly carried out if the Church is prepared to seek for no other kind of authority than that of Christ, if like Christ the Church is prepared to be stripped and unprotected. The true scandal of the Church will then become more apparent. It is for example, scandalous and ridiculous to those trained to think that only the latest can be valid. Indeed a theologian like John Hick (in *Evil and the God of Love* 1966) urges us to modify Augustinianism in favour of the thinking of an even more ancient theologian, namely St Irenaeus. 'Every age is equidistant from eternity'; the Christian past has the right to be heard, for in the Communion of Saints it is a present reality. The Christian Faith (says Dr Mascall)

'contains partly developed, partly undeveloped, a whole treasure of riches exceeding anything which we at any particular time are capable of grasping or utilising'.

Equally we must not get into the habit of assuming that there will come a day when the world will really listen to the Church because it will have been perfectly reformed, without 'spot or wrinkle'. (Christ spoke with authority and clarity, and still men crucified him.) The history of the Church from Abraham onwards, and the nature of the Bible itself, are both clear evidence that God works and speaks through imperfect media. When Christ appeared to St Francis of Assisi to convert him, it was in a partly-ruined church, while he knelt before the broken-down altar. God displays his greatness in the lowliness of the instruments he employs. When Jesus is truly set forth in embodied word, then the Holy Spirit takes the things of Christ and makes them contemporary and authoritative. The Church will always (to quote Dr Mascall again) be 'black with the sins of its members but comely with the beauty and holiness of its Head'. However, our age does not easily think in terms of an inner

D

eternal reality which is different from the surface and temporal appearance. To the world this kind of language sounds all too easily like a complacent justification of hypocrisy. It is clear then that the unworthiness of the minister (or the liturgy or the community) can hinder the effect of the sacrament. The seed is sown, but it falls upon stony soil. This truth needs to be stressed, for Christians have a tendency to retreat before uncomfortable facts into a comforting world of 'eternal reality'. However much faith goes beyond experience (it isn't very obvious that God has 'put down the mighty from their seat and exalted the humble and meek'), nevertheless it must grow out of, and be tempered by, experience, otherwise it may be largely escapist fantasy.

Professor MacKinnon said in a broadcast on 'Authority and Freedom in the Church':

'humility is a fundamental attribute of the divine as disclosed in Christ . . . But humility is more often than not presented as a kind of submissive obedience to the Church's traditions, to her institutional and organisational development, irrespective of the historical and social factors which may have shaped it, and the built-in consequences of the past decisions of her leaders. Much less is said of the extent to which those who exercise such authority must display humility in their turn; much less too of the extent to which the styles of triumphalism in, say, the Roman Catholic Church, or (again I speak as an Anglican) the elaborate ceremonial masquerade of Establishment distort not only the manner but the substance of an apostolic presence to the world . . . Whether our ecclesiastical leaders recognise it or not, we confront the unlimited opportunities, as well as perils, of a post-Constantian age'[1].

---

[1] *Listener*, 23 March 1967.

FURTHER READING

A. M. ALLCHIN, *The Spirit and the Word*, Faith Press 1963

CHARLES DAVIS, *A Question of Conscience*, Hodder and Stoughton 1967

W. G. POLLARD, *Physicist and Christian*, S.P.C.K. 1962

A. E. J. RAWLINSON and W. L. KNOX, 'Authority' in *Essays Catholic and Critical*, S.P.C.K. 1926

L. S. THORNTON C.R., *Revelation and the Modern World*, Dacre 1950

JOHN M. TODD (ed), *Problems of Authority*, Darton, Longman & Todd 1962

BERNARD WALL (trans), *Priest and Worker, the autobiography of Henri Perrin*, Macmillan 1965

R. R. WILLIAMS (ed), *Authority and the Church*, S.P.C.K. 1965

GORDON C. ZAHN, *In Solitary Witness, The Life and Death of Franz Jägerstätter*, Geoffrey Chapman 1966

One section of this essay first appeared in the London Quarterly and Holborn Review for January 1967 and is reproduced with permission.

FOUR

Ministry in the Church

FRANK HAWKINS

Who is 'the traditional clergyman'? Is it the comic: the innocent, bumbling, ineffective figure of caricature? Is it the reassuring: the bishop in the House of Lords, the parson in rectory or vicarage, secure in the stability of yesterday's social order? Is it the well-meaning amateur? Such pictures concern and confuse us when we consider the ordained ministry. We do not lack suggestions and proposals for practical improvements – nor, on the whole, the zeal to implement them. But there is a failure to distinguish between the essential 'tradition' of ministry, and what is 'traditional' but accidental. Unless we know what the ordained ministry is for, and why it is necessary, we cannot begin to see what must be discarded or changed.

Historically, our Church has accepted the Catholic tradition of a threefold order of ministry, but this tradition is now challenged, and if we are to respond, we must discriminate between historical and sociological accidents and permanent theological truths. To accept that there are such truths is in effect to accept a tradition of ministry, but it is not simply to approve the system which happens to exist today. Where the present system obscures or suppresses the very truths it should reveal, it must be changed.

To discover these permanent truths about the ordained ministry we must return to historical and theological origins. But it is theology, not archeology, from which we must derive our evidence. The particular patterns of ministry which served the early Church cannot serve us today. If we are to adhere to the threefold order of bishops, priests, and deacons, it must be because we are sure that this order will enable us to preserve from yesterday what we must apply for today and tomorrow.

The people of God are called into an elect, holy, and priestly body in Christ. It is their privilege to be established in Christ; it is their responsibility to share in Christ's mission to the world. The apostolic ministry is called to share a comparable privilege and to exercise a comparable responsibility. It is therefore Christ who determines the establishment of the Church and its missionary activity. And God determines Christ's mission since it is from God that Christ is sent, and to God that Christ returns in glory.

It is important to remember both the sending and the return, for to share the mission of Christ is also to share his return to the Father. The early Christian communities accepted this truth more readily than we do. For them, identification with Christ's mission meant more than seeing and accepting Christ: it meant that Christ (himself the 'apostle' of God) had sent apostles 'to the ends of the earth' so that all the world could be brought back and united with the Father in him. By being identified with Jesus Christ, Christians were committed to take their part in the whole of God's plan or 'economy'.

No one disputes the fact that Christ called the apostles to share in his mission and its fulfilment. But can it also be assumed that the apostles appointed others to continue their work, or is this merely a mistaken notion of the second-century writers? When we see how the New Testament speaks of Christ and his twelve chosen apostles, we cannot help noticing in the historical accounts of their relationship something more than a historical occurrence in the past. Christ and the apostles provide an example which suggests how the Christian communities are to understand the permanent relation between God and his people. The gospel traditions set out to clarify what was involved in 'apostolic' ministry, and the part it played in the larger economy of God.

The earliest description of the ministry brings out its essential connection with Christ's mission and the whole of God's plan. 'And God has set some in the assembly, first apostles, secondly prophets, thirdly teachers, then powers, then gifts of healings, helps, governments, different kinds of tongues' (1 Cor. 12:28). St Paul distinguishes three callings from the rest by a definite order or sequence: *first* apostles, *secondly* prophets, *thirdly* teachers. These three callings may be taken to represent the three accepted categories of revelation in the Old Testament. Just as under the Old Covenant the Word of God was revealed in the Law, the Prophets, and the Writings, so under the New Covenant Jesus Christ is revealed as the word of God through the distinctive personal witness and activity of Christian apostles, prophets, and teachers.[1] This personal call to reveal Christ distinguishes these three callings from others in the Christian assembly.

The three callings, essential to a Christian assembly, suggested fidelity to the Old Testament revelation and an essential continuity of the Old and New Covenants. But under the New Covenant the call to reveal Jesus Christ, besides the proclamation of the gospel, involved liturgical responsibilities. Word and liturgy together created and sustained the uniquely Christian character of the assembly. Since in the eucharist they proclaimed Christ both in the spoken Word and in the action of thanksgiving, prophets and teachers, as well as apostles, had the right to take a distinctive part in the liturgy. The apostle naturally presided as the community founder but in his absence his place was filled by a prophet or teacher.

What we have seen in the earlier pattern of ministry is confirmed by inference from evidence slightly later, when Christian communities look back to apostles and prophets as the foundation of the church (Eph. 2:20, 3:5; Rev. 18:20), or to the association of prophets with the apostolic mission (Acts 11:27, 13:1-3). Teachers are sometimes linked with the

---

[1] J. P. Audet, *La Didaché*, Paris 1958, pp. 439ff.

prophets (Acts 13:1–3; Eph. 4:11). Outside the New Testament the pattern is confirmed by the *Didache* (perhaps written between 70 and 100 AD). It gives instruction for a situation in which apostles (11:3ff.), prophets (11:3ff., 15:1, 2), and teachers (11:1, 13:1, 15:1, 2) are the recognised 'ministers' of the Christian community, with clear liturgical prerogatives (10:7, 11:9, 15:1, 2; *cf.* Acts 13:1–3).

The later New Testament references do not suggest a contemporary experience of apostles, prophets, and teachers: the order does not seem to have survived the apostolic age proper. The apostles themselves were martyred or settled in communities; there were no more apostles as such. Prophets and teachers also settled in communities. 'Every true prophet desiring to settle among you is worthy of his food. In like manner a true teacher is also worthy, like the workman, of his food' (*Did.* 13:1). Unlike apostles, there were still prophets and teachers in the second century, but without their former status. These three callings thus had a necessary, but not a permanent, function in the church. They were necessary in the apostolic age itself, when they were held to be the divinely-called witnesses to Jesus Christ, but they were not self-perpetuating. The problem is evaded by recourse to a 'tunnel period', a mysterious period in which it is assumed that the different ministers mentioned in the New Testament were transformed into the threefold ministry as we know it. What is involved here is the nature and the authority of the apostolic 'tradition'. From St Paul onwards, the importance of tradition is recognised in the first century. *Kerygma* and *Didache* had fixed forms, and their apostolic authority was all-important.

The authority of the New Testament revelation itself rests on the basis of a handing-on of apostolic tradition, for it is a collection of written material recording what was originally spoken or written by apostles, prophets, and teachers. The New Testament itself has inherited their once-for-all historical character and assumed their function in revealing Jesus Christ. But from this fact alone we cannot draw conclusions about the ministry of the apostolic successors. The historical background to the formation of the New Testament makes it unlikely that the whole apostolic tradition is necessarily included. But there is, in fact, evidence that apostolic successors had a place in the apostolic tradition. The author of *Ephesians*, reflecting on the foundation ministry of the church, found it necessary to include evangelists and pastors after apostles and before prophets and teachers (4:11). The evidence of the *Didache* confirms that such successors were envisaged. 'Appoint for yourselves therefore bishops and deacons worthy of the Lord, men who are meek and not lovers of money, and true and approved; for to you they also perform the liturgy of the prophets and teachers' (15:1, 2; *cf.* 10:7). In the second century Hermas of Rome sees in a vision that past and present ministries together make a single whole, a tower: 'The stones that are squared and white, and that fit together in their joints, these are the apostles and bishops and teachers and deacons, . . . some of them already fallen on sleep, and others still living' (*Vis.* 3.v:1).

The New Testament singles out the apostle himself as the key to the nature and function of the apostolic successors. For the early Christian communities the apostle was more than a great foundation-figure of the faith. The Twelve had been commissioned by the risen Christ (and the New Testament assumes all 'apostles' were, or perhaps they were also commissioned by the Twelve) to take part in his own mission from the Father. The mission did not end with him, nor with his apostles. Until the second coming, the Parousia, communities had to be founded, and men called to share what Christ and the Twelve had begun.

This conception of apostolic ministry is illuminated in the New Testament by the parallels drawn between Moses and Christ and his apostles. Christ is the Law-giver of the New Covenant, (Matt. 5:17, *cf.* 5:21–27), but St Paul makes it clear that the apostle too is to be regarded as a 'Moses' of the New Covenant (2 Cor. 3:4–11). The apostle acts as the divinely-appointed law-giver for his own communities just as Christ does for them all. St Luke suggests this when he associates Christ's delivery of the Beatitudes with the choosing of the Twelve (Luke. 6:12ff.). Later Christian writers make the same connection with Pentecost, and Justin Martyr sees the text, 'For out of Sion shall go forth the law, and the word of the Lord out of Jerusalem' (Isa. 2:3 *LXX*) fulfilled in the apostolic mission.

> 'From Jerusalem twelve men went forth into the world, illiterate and without speaking ability; but in God's power they proclaimed to every race that they were sent by Christ to teach to all the word of God' (1 *Apol.* 39; *cf. Dial.* 24).

These comparisons confirm the character of Christ's commission to his apostles. They also suggest that the apostle's standing as a 'Moses' of the New Covenant has a bearing on the way the apostolic ministry was to develop.

Such an understanding of the Christian ministry is part of a coherent theological interpretation. The character of the newly-established Christian community itself, its gospel tradition, its liturgy, as well as its apostolic ministry, were all decisively of the New Covenant; yet they were interpreted and defined in the light of the Old. The apostolic preaching itself had shown what the events of the Exodus, the wanderings of the people of Israel in the desert and the entry to the Promised Land meant to the early Christians. The significance of people, ministry, and liturgy in the life of the community was expressed in terms of the wilderness journey; the redemption of the Exodus behind and the Promised Land as the goal ahead. If Christ was the Moses of the new Exodus, he was also the Joshua of the entry to the Promised Land. This was the background used to explain the mission apostles were called to share with Christ, and the leadership they exercised over the communities they founded. It is from this basis in the New Testament that the implications for the apostolic ministry are developed. Because the Old Testament had a necessary part to play in the revelation of the divine economy, and because there was some real parallel between Moses and Christ, Moses and the apostles, the concepts of authority and service, leadership and priesthood, worship and sacrifice, and succession and ordination could all be rightly applied to the Christian ministry. Some of these concepts are seen developing in the New Testament, others outside; but they have a common basis in the Old Testament.

The Old Testament provided a broad authority. But unregulated development of the pattern of ministry based on the Old Testament was prevented by the Christian belief that God had acted and spoken decisively in Christ. The Old Testament was to be applied not in a vacuum, but specifically to interpret the action of God in Christ. We have the authority of the New Testament for what may be applied from the Old; the early Christians found a given theological interpretation based on the Old Testament in their earliest traditions (1 Cor. 15:3, 4; 11:25). They believed that Christ himself had encouraged the use of the whole Old Testament for the interpretation of the gospel (Luke 24:25–27). The tradition of ministry, the process by which God's authority committed to Christ had also been committed to the apostles and the successors they had appointed, is consistently interpreted in Old Testament terms; this is not a late or secondary rationalisation of supposedly primitive forms. The Old Testament is the key to the earliest pattern of ministry: the apostle, law-giver of the New Covenant, is associated with prophets and teachers just as the Law of Moses is associated with the Prophets and the Wisdom writing. And the basis for this teaching is the parallel between the apostle and Moses, already drawn by St Paul himself.

The particular threefold pattern of ministry which emerged in the second century was both an expression of the distinctive Christian ministry of the New Covenant, and also a witness to the continuity of the divine economy in Old and New Covenant alike. It is seen already fully developed in the ordination prayers for bishop, presbyter, and deacon in the *Apostolic Tradition* of Hippolytus (*c.* 215). We must consider what theological and historical grounds justified both the development and universal adoption of this pattern.

The New Testament emphasises both the God-given freedom and dignity of the Christian people, and also the corresponding truth that God's people are subordinate only to God, and owe honour and allegiance to Christ alone as Lord. But the New Testament provides no evidence of a Christian community existing without recognised leaders of some kind. These truths cannot be isolated from their common origin: the specific pattern of God's activity in Christ. It is in Christ that God reveals himself to his people, and in Christ that he establishes them as his own. It is also in Christ that God establishes a ministry commissioned to represent his rule over his own people. In the New Testament these are not opposed but complementary aspects of God's presence with his people.

The apostle is the prototype of Christian leadership and super vision. He is to lead where Christ has gone before; he is to be with Christ a 'Moses' to his people and with Christ a 'Joshua' leading the way into the Promised Land. But there is more to the relationship than this. St Paul certainly saw his apostolate, and the communities he supervised, as belonging to Christ. Yet he still claims a particular and privileged relation and responsibility towards them (1 Cor. 4:15). He believes the apostle must reflect the Christ who is both Son of God and suffering Son of Man. The apostle shares the authority of Christ but like the incarnate Christ, he must exercise it in conditions of humility.

Leadership of Christian communities continued on these principles after the apostles, as all the evidence shows. Problems concerning the identity of the apostles' successors have tended to obscure the theological truth that in the New Testament the apostles possess a divine authority as Christian leaders not only for their own but also for subsequent generations. This is not only a conclusion from form-criticism; it is clear from the fact that attributes of God and Christ are applied to the apostles and their successors indifferently. Shepherding is the most important example.

In the Old Testament, shepherding the flock of God is properly God's responsibility. He can entrust this responsibility to men, and he can also revoke it. In the New Testament, Christ makes an absolute claim to this responsibility, and shows what is involved in being the good shepherd (John 10). The good shepherd has a special parallel in the Old Testament in the person of David, and the early Church made much of this. [1]After his resurrection Christ commissioned the apostles with this own authority (John 20: 21–23), an authority subsequently explained to St Peter in terms of shepherding (John 21). This pastoral responsibility was not confined to the apostles; it was shared with the community leaders who succeeded them (Acts 20:28; 1 Peter 5:1ff). The inference is that the pastor, the shepherd to whom is entrusted the care of God's flock, exercises a distinctive ministry which gives him the right to be a Christian leader, and shares the divine responsibility of pastoral oversight with Christ and the apostles.

In time this Christian shepherding came to be identified with the title of bishop. Originally the word 'bishop' simply meant 'overseer'; it was one of many designations employed to describe Christian leaders. The New Testament shows how this title, under the influence of the Old Testament and the gospel tradition, came to express the full meaning of Christian shepherding and oversight (Ezek. 34:11, 12; Jer. 23:2–4 cf. Acts 20:17, 28; 1 Peter 2:25, 5:1ff.). For a long time the word 'bishop' represented a specifically Christian leadership infused into an existing community structure with its own pattern of leadership. Only in the second century is there evidence of its general recognition as a particular office. It is possible that it is so recognised in the New Testament (1 Tim. 3:1ff.), and the word 'bishop' was used in the West to interpret the office of elder or presbyter as a

[1]The use of this theme in connection with the eucharistic liturgy, baptism, and early Christian art is explained by Audet, op. cit., pp. 415–433.

Christian ministry well into the second century. But because of its connection with Christ's shepherding, and the particular Christian appointment to this responsibility, it became the universally recognised title for the office of pastoral oversight of a Christian community.

Shepherding expresses God's care as well as his rule and authority. Christ, the good shepherd, cares completely for the people of God, and his oversight contemplates the ultimate return of all his flock to the Father (John 10:16). He shares the full scope of this oversight with the apostles and their successors. God's people are to be ruled and served not only 'to the ends of the earth' by the apostolic mission, but also to the end of time, and the Parousia.

St Luke, like St Paul, identifies the pastoral care and service of Christ with the figure of the apostle. He begins his gospel with the 'mighty wonder' of the majesty of God incarnate in the infant Jesus, and the Acts of the apostles with the 'mighty wonder' of God's power at work in the apostolic mission of the infant church. The gospel is pervaded by the theme of the Suffering Servant described in Isaiah; in Acts the mission of the apostles and their successors begins and ends with martyrdom.

In both Gospel and Acts God rules by sacrificial service, to which Christ and the Old Testament provide the key. The apostles' ministry, like Christ's is thus to rule 'like a servant' (Luke 22:26, 27).

The whole of Christ's ministry is shared by the apostles, but with the apostolic successors, pastoral oversight and apostolic service are distinguished. Paul and Barnabas 'appointed elders' in the gentile Christian church at Ephesus (Acts 14:23). These elders the Holy Spirit has made 'bishops', to shepherd the flock (Acts 20:17, 28). It is clear that St Luke is describing the same event and the same ministers. There are also others, appointed in a similar way, to assist the apostles (Acts 6:3-6) in service to the Christian community. These are 'deacons'. Like 'bishop', the word 'deacon' was first used to give a Christian interpretation to an existing office; in this case elders, or possibly prophets or teachers. As a title, 'deacon' emerges closely associated with 'bishop', as the New Testament shows (Phil. 1:1; 1 Tim.3:3ff., 8ff.). Apostolic oversight and service are represented to the apostolic communities by the ministry of the 'bishop' and 'deacons' who succeed to the ministry of the apostles.

The bishop represents the oversight of God to his flock, just as Christ revealed the authority of God to the apostles. Deacons assisted the bishop as the apostles had assisted Christ. Through Christ's commission, the apostles shared the sacrificial *diakonia* which Christ offered to the Father. The theology of the apostolic ministry not only reflects but shares the theology of the Incarnation: Christ's mission from the Father, and his sacrificial creation of the return of humanity to the Father in himself.

These are not the only apostolic successors recognised by St Luke. There are other elders, besides those appointed by Paul and Barnabas, who are associated with the apostles at Jerusalem. These apostles and elders together form the apostolic council or government of the church (Acts 15). For practical purposes this council is like the Jewish Sanhedrin, but it also has theological implications for the ministry. Once again the apostle is the key to the Christian interpretation. While every apostle reflects the divine oversight and service of Christ's ministry, not every apostle belongs to the Twelve. The Twelve form a special group related to Christ; they are associated with him as the foundation of the New Covenant, and its instrument of government. After the Ascension, the apostolic council under the presidency of James, the Lord's brother, was not simply the practical centre for government of the church. It was the instrument of divine jurisdiction for the New Covenant. St Paul's jurisdiction over the gentile churches, undoubted though it was, still had to be confirmed by the apostolic council. After the apostles, the principle was maintained at the local church level in the relationship of the presiding bishop and his college of presbyters.

Much that is implicit in the New Testament's picture of the development of the apostolic ministry becomes explicit in the earliest Christian writings outside it.

In about A.D. 95, there was a schism in the Corinthian church which involved its ministry. Writing to the Corinthians St Clement of Rome speaks at length of the majesty of God, and man's need to submit to his will.

'We should be obedient to God, rather than follow those who in arrogance and disorder are leaders in abominable jealousy' (14:1).

'For Christ belongs to those who are humble-minded; not to those who exalt themselves over his flock. The sceptre of the majesty of God, even our Lord Jesus Christ, came not in arrogant pomp or pride, though he might have done, but humble-minded, as the Holy Spirit spoke concerning him. For he says, "Lord, who hath believed our report? . . ." (16:1ff).

The schism is contrary to the will of God; it has upset the divine economy reflected in the Christian ministry.

'Is it right then that we should be deserters from his will? Let us offend foolish and senseless men, who exalt themselves and boast in arrogant words, rather than God. Let us fear the Lord Jesus Christ, whose blood was given for us. Let us reverence our leaders; let us honour our presbyters; let us instruct our young men in the lesson of the fear of God' (21:4–6; *cf.* 1:3).

Clement preserves deliberately the ambiguity of the term 'elder', which may mean a 'senior man' of the community or a recognised ministerial 'presbyter'.

Apparently the Corinthian schism had been caused by the jealousy of a small group of 'young men' (3:3–'the young against the elders'). The young men have rebelled against the authority of the ruling 'elders' who are in fact the appointed Christian leaders. Clement reminds the Corinthians that distinctions in the Christian community do not depend on age, but appointment. 'Let the flock of Christ be at peace with the duly appointed presbyters' (54:2; cf. 57:1, 2). He uses the analogy of an army, combining the ideal discipline of the Roman army with the inclusive military order of Israel advancing through the desert to the Promised Land (37). This leads him to the image of the body. 'So in our case, let the whole body be saved in Jesus Christ, and let each man be subject to his neighbour, according also as he was appointed with his special grace' (38:1).

Where leadership of the Christian community is concerned, Clement knows that Christian tradition distinguishes appointment to a pastoral 'oversight' of the flock, and Christian 'service'. The apostolic successors are appointed, and proved by the Spirit 'to be bishops and deacons to those who should believe' (42:4). The evidence of *1 Clement* does not suggest that there are bishops and deacons as such in Clement's own church, or in Corinth. These titles are not mentioned explicitly elsewhere in the epistle, and Clement refers only to 'leaders' or 'elders' (presbyters). This is confirmed by what we know of the Roman Church from *1 Peter* (5:1–7). Clement refers to bishops and deacons in terms of the Christian tradition of the division of responsibility between community leaders. Like the apostles, they have a necessary place in the economy of the New Covenant.

Other early writers associate bishops and deacons. Thus in the *Didache*, bishops and deacons are regarded as the proper successors to the liturgical functions of the apostolic prophets and teachers (15:1, 2). The theological background of this association is brought out again in the writings of St Ignatius of Antioch. In some passages he likens bishops and deacons to God the Father and Jesus Christ; they are a 'divine' ministry. 'Be zealous to do all things in Godly concord, the bishop presiding after the likeness of God and the presbyters after the likeness of the council of the apostles, with the deacons also who are most dear to me, having been entrusted with the diaconate of Jesus Christ, who was with the Father before the worlds, and appeared at the end of time' (*Magn.* 6, *etc.*).

Ignatius also witnesses to a fusion of the two patterns of the Christian ministry suggested by Acts. The presbyter or elder is not simply subject to Christian ministerial appointment as bishop or deacon; he has a Christian ministry in his own right as a member of the governing presbyterate of the Christian community, under the presidency of the bishop. The bishop and his presbytery establish and govern the local Christian community just as Christ and the Twelve established and ruled the New Israel. In pastoral oversight, the bishop reflects God the Father to his flock. In jurisdiction, he presides over his presbytery as Christ presided over the Twelve, as is shown by the following passage:

'When you are obedient to the bishop as to Jesus Christ, it is evident that you live not after men but after Jesus Christ, who died for us, that believing on his death you might escape death. It is therefore necessary, as your custom is, that you should do nothing without the bishop; but be obedient also to the presbytery, as to the apostles of Jesus Christ our hope' (*Trall.* 2).

In service, the deacons assist the bishop, just as the bishop himself assists the apostles and Christ in sharing their ministry. The fusion described by Ignatius hinges on the complex theological background to the bishop's ministry. But Ignatius clarifies the Christian significance of the presbyter in relation to the bishop, a significance obscured in those communities where elders were simply appointed to the ministry of a bishop or deacon.

Thus in the early second century, the three-fold order of bishops, presbyters, and deacons emerged as the recognised apostolic ministry, and by the time of Hippolytus, in the early third century, this order and its theological coherence was universally accepted.

The order is threefold because it reflects three characteristics of the apostles themselves: oversight, government, and service. These can never be accidental: they are essential to the fulfilment of the divine economy, and they enable ministers to participate in the whole divine action in Christ to complete God's purpose.

The people of God are ruled (as they are shepherded, established, and served) by God himself in Christ, and by those who have been chosen to share Christ's ministry. But the people of God also participate in Christ's mission and ministry, and they too reflect its characteristics. This is clear from the priestly character of the people of God (1 Peter 2:9–11; Rev. 1:6, 5:9). Thus the people of God as well as the Christian ministers share in Christ's priesthood. The ministerial priesthood is not separate from, or contrasted with, the priesthood of the whole body; it is complementary to it. Priesthood is not some extra function or qualification; those who shepherd, rule, establish and serve the people of God already exercise a priestly function. The apostles and the apostolic successors are priests not because they are so called, but because the ministry they share with Christ is priestly. The distinction between the priestly ministers and the priestly people is simply the distinction between shepherd and sheep.

The epistle to the Hebrews describes the high priesthood of Christ (like that of Melchizedek) as unique, personal, and exclusive. But this belief neither excludes the Christian people from sharing this priesthood; nor in the early Church was it understood to exclude the concept of ministerial priesthood. As the bishop represented God's rule in the life of the Christian community, so also he represents the high-priesthood of Christ when the community assembles for worship.

Clement of Rome, like *1 Peter*, sees the whole Christian body as priestly. In terms of oversight everybody has an appointed place, and must render obedience as if in an army, (37), and in terms of worship too everybody has his proper place.

'Now that we have peered into the depths of the divine knowledge, we should do all things in order, as many as the

Master (God) has commanded us to perform, at their appointed seasons. The offerings and liturgies he commanded to be performed with care, and not to be done rashly or in disorder, but at fixed times and seasons. And where and by whom he would have them performed, he himself fixed by his supreme will: that all things being done with piety according to his good pleasure might be acceptable to his will. They then who make their offerings at the appointed times are acceptable and blessed, for following the ordinances of the Master, they cannot err. For to the high-priest his proper liturgies have been assigned, and to the priests their proper place is appointed, and upon the Levites their proper services are laid. The layman is bound by the layman's ordinances. Let each of you, brethren, in his own order, give thanks to God, maintaining a good conscience, not exceeding the established regulation of his liturgy, and in reverence' (40; 41:1).

Clement compares the president at the eucharistic assembly with the Levitical high-priest of the Old Covenant. We might surmise that 'priests' and 'Levites' are presbyters and deacons: there are allusions in the descriptions to what is said of these orders elsewhere. This is less important than recognising that the laity are included as a proper priestly order, with their own 'liturgy' to perform in the eucharist.

Clement's analogy is deliberate, for he calls Christ 'the high-priest of our offerings' (36:1), and relates the Aaronic priesthood to Moses to emphasise the succession from Christ to the apostles (43; cf. 32:2, 4; 51; 53). This identification was general. Tradition spoke of James, the brother of the Lord, as bishop and high-priest of the church at Jerusalem. Prophets were given a high-priestly status in the communities where they settled (*Did.* 13). Justin Martyr associates the apostles with the high-priesthood of Christ (*Dial.* 42). The Old Testament parallels are developed in greater detail by later Christian writers, but their teaching ultimately depends on the identity of the apostolic ministry with the high-priestly work of Christ.

Early Christian writers saw their community manifested in its most representative form in the eucharistic assembly. The bishop together with presbyters, deacons, and people offered thanks to God through Christ the heavenly high-priest. It was not an accidental pattern, for it expressed the reality of the heavenly assembly around the throne of God. The liturgy of the assembly reflected the ancient and basic understanding of the Last Supper: the New Covenant established through the blood of Christ, and the anticipation of its heavenly fulfilment. Through the high-priesthood of the heavenly, exalted Christ, the slain Lamb standing in the midst of the throne of God, earthly and heavenly assembly and offering were united (Rev. 11:16, 14:1–3, 19:4, 6). It is this high-priesthood that the president of the earthly assembly represents, and this heavenly assembly which the eucharistic liturgy of the priestly body shares and fore-shadows.

For the New Testament and the early Christian writers alike, Christian ministers are never isolated from the Christian community itself. Any theology of the ministry must be incomplete if it neglects the reciprocal ministry of the whole body, for the body is orderly: each has his own place, and his particular ministry to fulfil to the benefit of all. But the community itself has a ministerial function: to co-operate with the apostolic ministry in order that the whole church may co-operate with God in Christ. This is the ultimate priestly function of the whole body, and why the ministerial priesthood properly represents it to God.

One cannot read *1 Clement* without being aware that the harmony and unity of the church depend on the human response to God's will, expressed in the structure and activity of the Christian assembly. One cannot read Ignatius' epistles without realising that the whole church must cling to the apostolic gospel and ministry in order to be united with the Father through Christ.

This mutual co-operation of ministry and people is seen not only in the eucharist but also in the method of appointing apostolic ministers. Because their ministry is essential, the candidates must be tested and approved by the whole church before they are appointed to exercise their ministry. The New Testament and the early Christian writers also witness to the importance of this testing in connection with its corollary truth: that apostolic ministers were to be regarded 'as the Lord' and honoured as such by the Lord's people.

This was in fact how the apostle stood in relation to his communities. It is reflected outside the New Testament in the ordinance of the *Didache* that itinerant apostles, prophets and teachers, when approved and found genuine, are to be received 'as the Lord' (11). Those to whom the *Didache* was originally addressed are urged to ordain bishops and deacons to succeed prophets and teachers, for 'they are your honourable men along with the prophets and teachers' (15:2). Clement urges the Corinthians to honour their presbyters (1:3, 21:6). In Ignatius the bishop is to be regarded as the Lord himself.

> 'Everyone the Master of the household sends to be steward over his own house, we ought to receive as him that sent him. Plainly therefore we ought to regard the bishop as the Lord himself' (*Eph. 6*).

Those to be appointed to the apostolic ministry were tested, approved and accepted by the whole Church, both because of their essential responsibility and their essential dignity within the Christian community.

The Acts of the Apostles and the pastoral epistles suggest that ministerial authority, and a special grace of the Holy Spirit was bestowed through the imposition of hands by a minister who had himself been apostolically commissioned. The tradition is confirmed by Clement, together with its theological background.

> 'The apostles received the gospel for us from the Lord

Jesus Christ; Jesus Christ was sent forth from God. So then Christ is from God and the apostles are from Christ. Both then come of the will of God in the appointed order. So preaching everywhere in country and town, they appointed their first-fruits, when they had proved them by the Spirit, to be bishops and deacons to those who should believe' (42:1, 2, 4).

Clement's difficulty (as the involved argument of chapters 43 and 44 shows,) is that although he knows it is theologically correct (and necessary to his purpose) to describe the apostles' successors as bishops and deacons, the words did not describe appointments but simply Christian ministries, in his own church. What is clear from chapters 42–44 is that the apostles did appoint successors.

Appointment to ministerial authority looks forward as well as back. Through Christ the power of the kingdom is already active in the present. God has deputed his power of judgment to the Son, and he promises the apostles that they are to sit on twelve thrones judging with him the twelve tribes of Israel (Matt. 19:28). In 'binding and loosing' sins the apostles bring the judgment and mercy of Christ at the Last Day into the present (Matt. 16:18, 19; 18:18; John 20:23: 1 Cor. 5:3). The apostles are assessors with Christ in judgment; they, like their successors in the church, exercise the powers of 'binding and loosing' sins with Christ, and on the day of judgment form a judicial presbyterate with the exalted Christ.

This is the permanent, because ultimate, character of the apostolic ministry; a character which is expressed in terms of worship as well as jurisdiction. The Revelation describes the throne of God and the Lamb as surrounded by the thrones of twenty-four 'elders': the 'patriarchs' of the Old and the New Covenants. The patriarchs of Israel and the Christian apostles, whose worship and jurisdiction centred on the earthly Jerusalem, form the presbyteral order of the assembly and worship of the heavenly Jerusalem. In face of the full reality of God's *episcope* and the high-priesthood of the Lamb, their representative exercise of these functions is concluded. But Christ's high-priesthood remains, and he is still accompanied by his heavenly 'presbyterate'; this is the place of the apostles and their successors in the heavenly establishment and liturgy.

The ministry of the early Church and New Testament seems remote from the practical concerns of ministry today. By historical development and against various social backgrounds, the pattern of the apostolic ministry has changed and changed again through the centuries and continues to do so. But our essential concerns must still be those of the apostolic period. We need not go back to find them, for we can discover and revive them in the tradition that we possess today. The tradition itself has of course undergone historical development. That priests preside jointly or singly at the eucharist, that they can preach and teach, baptise and absolve, are all developments of their inherent ministry within the limits of the bishop's jurisdiction. Besides his jurisdiction, the bishop has retained the prerogatives of ordination and confirmation. Through delegation by the bishop, the parish priest and the parish have become the basic pastoral unit of the Christian community. In this way, following the pattern of apostolic ministry, pastoral oversight is shared by the priest with his bishop. He is in effect the shepherd of the flock and the servant of God's people in his parish. These are changes which, apart from the fact that they can be theologically justified, are practically irreversible.

The parish priest of today cannot take first- or nineteenth-century systems for a model, but he must accept the fundamental theological implications of his care: sharing pastoral oversight with the bishop, co-operating with and serving his people in preaching and teaching, baptising and absolving, and presiding at the eucharist. These are the ways in which he is called and authorised to share in Christ's mission, and work towards its fulfilment.

These are the inescapable concerns of the Christian ministry. But they will be neglected, distorted, or obscured if the priest does not succeed in escaping from the variety of additional roles and functions he has inherited from his forebears. Modern society and the modern Church are encouragingly eager to do away with these, and rightly so if it means that ministers are to be freed for their essential work. The priest today needs a clear theological appreciation of what he is essentially called to do, and the confidence to attempt it, even if this means changing much that is familiar.

But he hardly gets it here!

FIVE

The Church's Teaching

NEVILLE TIDWELL

When is a retreat a strategic withdrawal and when is it a rout?
It is a question which troubles the mind of many a Catholic
today as he looks back on the past century. He feels he is
witnessing a series of retreats by the Christian Church from
its entrenched positions on questions of faith, morals and
discipline. First, holy Scripture, which had seemed so secure,
fell before the combined might of higher criticism and the
new sciences. This ancient stronghold was not readily given
up, nor when the withdrawal did take place was it at first
total. Initially only the Old Testament was surrendered,
and a stand was made at what was felt to be a position more
defensible (and more worthy of defence), the New Testament,
and especially the gospel records. Soon even these began to
yield before the critics' onslaught, but as the Christian front
fell back in one area it still seemed to renew itself in another.
For this was the age which saw the Catholic revival in the
Church of England and the First Vatican Council in Rome.
The 'Catholic' was – and perhaps he still is – distinguished by
his commitment to the Church and to her authority, to the
'tradition' and to the 'living voice'. The security and certainty, no longer guaranteed in the Bible, might perhaps be
found in the Church which had been promised indefectibility
by her Lord himself and whose teachings could be accepted
as those of the Lord himself.

But once historical criticism had been admitted, albeit
reluctantly, into any one of the areas formerly protected as
'sacred', in this case the Bible, then it was only a matter of

time before it spread into all the others. Doctrinal criticism – the historical study of the origins, formation, adequacy and truth of the statements of Christian belief – came close on the heels of biblical criticism, undaunted by the imperative, 'Highly Infallible. Keep out!'

The fact that Christian doctrine has a history, that it has 'developed' over the centuries, was not new to our Victorian forefathers, and they saw that it raised some very fundamental questions. For them, however, the two main questions were these: If doctrine has developed over the centuries (and it clearly has), then how can we distinguish true development from false, legitimate from illegitimate? And how can something be true and 'of the faith' today which was not known as such (at least implicitly) in an earlier age? To measure the distance we have travelled (or retreated) in the past hundred years we have only to examine our present-day questions about the same issues. We investigate the same facts of doctrinal development and biblical criticism but we ask today: How can something be *un*true today which was true yesterday? How can what was yesterday regarded as essential to a man's salvation be seen as any less essential today?

The last hundred years of critical study both of the Bible and of Christian doctrine have shown us the relativity of all doctrinal statements. We have come to see how much the formulation of a Christian doctrine belongs to a historical context, and how far the Church is culturally conditioned in everything she may say about faith or morals. We see how, on occasions, Christian dogmas have been built with sword in hand; how the strength and conviction with which Christians have maintained some doctrines may often have been due more to their polemical origins than to disinterested zeal for Christian truth. In short, we find that the Church, in defining its beliefs and in pronouncing on moral issues, has been and is subject to the same pressures, influences and motivation as any man or group of men reflecting upon and trying to reason out their experiences and convictions.

The Church has fought valiantly for the truth, but not

always with the best weapons or from the best motives. What we know about ourselves, the historical study of the formation of Christian doctrine shows to be true of the Church. The desire for truth is easily confused with the natural human desire to be victorious in argument; the firm refusal to be moved from or to reconsider an established opinion often reflects a human reluctance to admit error as much as a concern that the truth shall not be compromised; often too, and this is our own major temptation today, we desire a rigid system of belief more because we have fears about the breakdown of a familiar authority than because we are concerned for the truth. If it were possible to have questions of faith, morals and discipline firmly, finally and infallibly settled it would be so much easier to uphold established authority, to maintain the 'traditional' discipline and to cling to our customary distinctions between Catholic/not-Catholic, Christian/not-Christian, the true Church/not the true Church.

But when all this had been said, and when we have truly examined our motives for believing what we do, we must still acknowledge that a Christian may rightly be troubled by the Church's apparent failure to stand firm. Indeed he *must* be troubled when what seem to him to be essentials are at stake. And here the modern Christian, anxious about the Church, joins hands with the anxious Christian of the last century, threatened by biblical criticism in its infancy and the new sciences in the self-confident vigour of their youth. Samuel Wilberforce, for example, in 1861 wrote that, so far as he could see, if Darwin were right then 'the revelation of God to man as we Christians know it, is a delusion and a snare.' Not merely the truth or accuracy of certain details in the Bible were at stake, but, at least as Wilberforce was able to see it, the very fact of a divine revelation.

The Church today, and the individual Christian, are worried by reforms and renewal which involve retreat from positions once strongly held. But what is really felt to be at stake is not so much the truth of the assurance which comes

from a revelation infallibly guaranteed and out of reach of
analytical or historical criticism. This becomes clear when
we examine the usual form of any Christian arguments for
infallibility (or for any kind of absolute except God himself).
Generally it goes like this: the Christian revelation is God's
message of salvation, a message, therefore, vital to all men;
but on a matter so vital it is impossible that men could be
left in any doubt as to what properly belongs to it; therefore
God must have provided us with infallible guarantees and
sources of this saving knowledge. The argument is una-
shamedly *a priori*. That does not deny its validity, nor does it
establish it. But it does compel us to ask, 'If *we* need to believe
God must have done this, what, when we examine the
evidence has *God* actually done? If this is the only way we
can think God's revelation *must* work and *must* have been
given, then how does our theory look when we approach
the question in an *a posteriori* way and ask about the way in
which God, on the available evidence, appears *actually
to have given* his revelation?'

The upheaval in the Church today has had one especially
salutary effect, for it has driven Christians back to original
sources and opened up the (perhaps terrifying) possibility of
finding ourselves left no longer with a system of doctrine or
ecclesiastical institutions as the object of our faith and source
of our security, but with only God himself. We may well
find ourselves left only with those securities which God himself has provided and not those which we would prefer him
to have provided (or would ourselves provide if we were God).
We are made to face fundamental questions and forced to
distinguish between real and artificial problems. For we are
hedged in by pseudo-problems, some of which arise from
asking the wrong questions in the first place and others which
arise not from the basic data of theology itself but from the
logical implications of a developed theological position.
There is only one way of tackling these problems and only
one way of distinguishing real from artificial problems: to
press right through to the most basic questions about every

issue. In terms of the limited subject of this essay, the authority of the Church's teaching and the possibility of infallible guarantees of Christian truth, the most basic question concerns the nature of revelation itself. What is the nature of that vital saving knowledge given to the Christian? How is it communicated, preserved and transmitted? What kind of 'knowledge' is 'saving knowledge'? In what way is it tied up with words in doctrinal statements or in the Bible? These fundamental questions are the starting-point for any serious consideration of the authority and nature of the Church's teaching.

What kind of 'knowledge' is saving knowledge? Perhaps the simplest answer would be: 'Saving knowledge is *revealed* knowledge'. And such an answer would at least indicate that salvation is not the result of man's own efforts in research or discovery, but is something given, something which, but for the gracious act of the giver, we could never have. To say that knowledge, truth, or anything else, is *revealed*, is certainly to say that it is given to us, that we know it only because it was made known to us, and not because we searched it out; but it is not to say anything about the way in which it has been made known or given to us, about the method and means of revelation. Moreover, to speak of revealed *knowledge* raises the further question, 'What relation are we here asserting?', for all knowledge is a relation between knower and known. What we mean by 'knowledge' depends also on our understanding of the nature of the thing-known and on our understanding of what Aquinas called 'the mode of the nature of the knower'. What we understand to be the nature of the thing-known will determine or at least suggest for us the most effective ways in which it may initially come to be known and in which the knowledge of it may be communicated to others. To come to know that $2 \times 2 = 4$ and to introduce others to this mathematical formula is a process quite different from the way I came to know my own wife and may help others to come to know her by introducing them to her.

Few discussions of the nature of revelation in Christian thought today fail to quote William Temple's assertion that 'what is offered to man in any specific revelation is not truth concerning God, but the living God himself.' His point is not that it is possible for any man either to 'know' God as he is in himself, or without also knowing 'truth concerning' or 'facts about' God – Temple was not saying that Christianity has no intellectual content. The statement concerns only the nature of the *known*, the nature of only one pole of the relationship which all knowledge implies. And that nature is such that the relationship we have to the *known* in revelation is not so much one of 'knowledge about' – 'propositional knowledge' as it is often called – as it is 'acquaintance with'. The real content of the Christian revelation is not a system of ideas about God but God himself; what we claim to 'know' is something which has the nature of the personal 'revelation'' has to do with knowledge which I could not have except as a result of the *self*-activity of the revealer, an act of *self*-manifestation.

We all have some idea of what it means to 'know' another person as distinct from knowing things or facts and so, since our God is personal, we can understand why it is in the realm of personal values – the sphere of action, purpose and decision – that he may best be known, and why it is through a human person that he may be most adequately 'revealed'. This is why the person of Jesus Christ is at the centre of the Christian revelation and the revelation in him is called 'final'. Because God is personal it follows that, though he may perhaps be known in some way through philosophy and human reflection, yet he is most fully known in those ways in which the personal can be known. And secondly, because the content of the Christian revelation is the personal God, it follows that the 'knowledge' which a Christian has by revelation is not of the kind which, primarily at any rate, adds to the number of 'facts' he possesses or needs to assimilate, but rather it is that knowing-relationship which stirs up in men that inter-personal reaction which we call 'faith'. God's self-manifestation in Christ primarily invites men not to accept certain statements or ideas but to commit themselves to a person; it offers us not otherwise-unobtainable information but otherwise-unattainable integration and otherwise-undeserved reconciliation. Jesus Christ is at the very centre of our faith, not because he as God-made-man was able to speak through a human voice-box and a human brain the actual words of God, but because in Jesus Christ God and man are united in the most fully personal way. Revelation is reconciliation; it is not so much a communication as a communion. Does this kind of knowledge or truth need infallible scriptures or pronouncements to commend or communicate or guarantee it? Is it indeed the kind of truth that can ever be commended or communicated in such ways?

These questions lead us to consider the other pole of the knowing-relationship, the nature of man as the knower, as the one who receives revelation. What is the 'mode of the nature' of man as knower? And how does our answer to this question help us to see the real place of doctrinal formulae in our faith? God himself is what is revealed and he is the revealer, but for his own act of revelation to be effective – for it to be revelation at all – it has to get through to the recipient. But 'everything which is received, is received in the mode of the recipient', in a way and a form determined by the nature of the recipient. Since in our case the 'mode' of the recipient is the 'mode' of a man then the only knowledge of God we can have is a *human* knowledge. It is as if God were likened to the sun which no human being can look at directly without some form of protection for his eyes, just as no man can 'see God and live' – we cannot know God as he is in himself. But though we cannot gaze directly, at the sun, it is still known to us as a source of light by the shadows which it casts. So, similarly, God is known to us by the 'shadows' which he casts upon his creation, by the 'signs' of his activity in nature and history. Moreover, the shadow which the sun casts is given its shape and outline not only by the shape of the object the sun in shining on, and the angle of the

E

sun in the sky, but also by the kind of surface on which it falls—it might, for example, be corrugated. So, too, God's 'shadows' answer to the reality to a greater or lesser degree in proportion to the suitability of the media he uses (nature, history, or, best of all, the historical and personal life of Jesus of Nazareth) in proportion to the 'obliqueness' of the angle from which God approaches his creatures (in 'various ways ... of old ... by the prophets', but, 'in these last days ... by a Son' (Heb. 1:1–2), and also in relation to the 'contours' of the human mind which receives the revelation. The knowledge which we have of God or anything is *human* knowledge. All human knowledge starts as 'experience', our immediate and direct awareness of 'reality' and the original source of data for our knowledge. But so long as our experience remains 'wordless' it is not fully humanly intelligible, for only by words can the human knower interpret what is given in experience. With words he makes the experience both intelligible to himself and communicable to others. The 'mode of the nature of the human knower' is the mode of the rational, the way of one who by rational categories – at its simplest by the use of ordinary everyday words – comes to the fullest understanding of his experience and formulates what is given to him in that experience. Thus, although words and sentences are not themselves the *given*, the thing revealed, in the Christian revelation, yet, because we are human, we should not understand that revelation without the use of words; our knowledge of God, because it is human knowledge, must find expression in human words.

While we accept that our knowledge of God must be expressed in human words, we may yet believe that in the case of divine revelation the very words themselves are from God – are 'inspired' and infallible – and had to be planted in the minds of certain chosen recipients, almost without their knowledge. But this belief again would be based on *a priori* argument and must be tested against the actual evidence provided in the biblical records and the teaching of the Church. And that evidence points to the interesting fact that when a revelation is made, it is interpreted in words and ideas which are not simply given 'vertically' along with the experience but are derived 'horizontally' from the past. Thus Jesus reveals God to the apostles not 'out of the blue' but in a situation in which God was already known and understood in a particular way; Jesus is recognised as God's Messiah in a situation in which the idea of God's Messiah was already meaningful. The 'final' revelation in Jesus Christ was intelligible to the apostles only because the Old Testament before Jesus already witnessed to a revelation and provided the categories in which the person and work of Jesus could be interpreted. Moreover, the Old Testament itself contains an intelligible revelation only because there existed and exists a fundamental revelation of God in creation itself, a basic human ability to 'experience' the divine and a basic tendency to interpret this experience by means of a particular set of images and ideas. The words, images and ideas which are used to interpret what is given in revelation all belong to the human side of that divine-human encounter which is revelation. Because the words are human, whether they are used in the Bible or the teaching of the Church, they can only be understood as belonging to a very specific historical context and as the product of a specifically historical development of thought. The human interpretations of revelation, such as we find in the Bible and in the teaching of the Church, are properly not absolutes standing above the historical process, derived vertically from God, but belong to the horizontal and historical and are, in essence, the product of a dialogue between the present moment (and its problems and crises) and an inheritance from the past, a fruitful interaction of the present upon the past and the past upon the present. This is why the Church on the one hand cannot be enslaved by the doctrinal definitions of her own past history and yet, on the other hand, cannot abandon or cast off her inheritance, as though it counted for nothing.

The things so far discussed are already the commonplaces of modern biblical study. The biblical scholars have long taken for granted that God reveals himself in history, and have also recognised that these 'acts' of God without human words to proclaim and interpret them are devoid of meaning. In the Bible it is plain that the divine revelation given in events is a dialogue between an inherited past – a 'tradition' of faith – and the present life of the 'community of faith' (the Church, old or new). But what biblical studies teach us about the ways of God and the mechanics of revelation ought somehow or other to inform our thinking about every other aspect of theology, especially dogmatics. Certainly it has something to say about the Church's role as 'teacher' and about the nature and authority of the Church's teaching.

The major revolution in human thought in the West during the last two or three centuries, put simply, has been the exchange of a primarily *a priori* method of thought and investigation for one which is *a posteriori*. This revolution has taken place also in Christian thought about the Bible and the formulation of doctrines. We have moved out of an age in which the nature of the Bible and the authority of the Church's teaching are established on *a priori* grounds, and, today, any claims we may make on behalf of Bible or Church must be tested against, and shown to be compatible with, the actual facts, with what the Bible in fact is and what the Church is. The Christian today is faced with the suggestion that the Church and the Bible are not infallible, and with the question, 'Can the Church change her mind about a dogma or a moral law?' His fear, we have suggested, is that his whole notion of a divine revelation is in jeopardy. But this is really a fear for a particular *theory* of revelation, and a theory which we have seen reason to revise quite radically. However to revise our theory of revelation is necessarily to revise our thinking about the nature and function of the Church, especially in her role as teacher.

The nineteenth century was asking very different questions about 'developments' in the Church's teaching from those we are asking today. We have travelled far, and along new roads, in the past hundred years. It may be significant that this volume includes a chapter on the 'Authority of the Church' as well as one on the Church's teaching. The collected essays of Catholics in the Church of England of an earlier generation – e.g. *Lux Mundi* and *Essays Catholic and Critical* – understand by the authority of the Church simply and solely her right as a divinely commissioned teacher to make authoritative pronouncements on matters of faith and morals. Teaching in those earlier essays was the whole concern of the writer on 'Authority', and it was so because those essayists in common with all Catholics of their time firmly held to the idea that

> '*Still the Holy Church is here,*
> *Although her Lord is gone.*'

The Church's job was to act on behalf of an absent Lord. She had to guard and keep and hand on something that had been entrusted to her by her Lord before his departure. The gospel, Christian truth, 'revelation' was seen as a 'possession' of the Church. Revelation was something parcelled up before the Church came into being, and ready to be handed over when she was created to receive it. Revelation is seen, if not as 'propositional' or a system of ideas, at least as something finished, a piece of past history whose memory the Church is to keep alive. And the theology based on such a view of revelation betrays the fact that the fundamental question for the Church is always the question about revelation itself. It is really only in terms of that older view of things that such problems as 'Scripture and/or Tradition' are created and that Christians can ask such basically meaningless questions like, 'Is the Bible above the Church or the Church above the Bible?' Nor is it difficult to deduce what kind of attitude a Church seen in such terms will have towards the non-Christian world, or how its different denominations and parties will view one another. It will be clear from this volume of essays that to rethink one's theory of revelation is necessarily to rewrite one's theology from A to Z and to rebuild one's theological structures from the foundations upwards. Thus the older view of revelation saw doctrinal development in terms of an original 'deposit' of 'faith' – i.e. the teaching or intellectual content of Christianity – whose implications would be drawn out by the Church as the Holy Spirit brought 'all things to her remembrance' and led her 'into all truth'. This way of looking at the Church's role implies the older view of the Church's authority, the view of the Church as the old-style schoolmistress whose job is to get certain facts into the heads of her pupils, facts to be accepted on her authority, committed to memory and reproduced whenever they were needed – usually 'under examination conditions'. But it has been wisely said: 'the gospel is not so much that which the Church proclaims as the Church is that which proclaims the gospel.' The Church does not so much possess the truth as she is possessed by the Truth!

The Church, then, has not received a revelation as though revelation were a collection of facts or ideas that could be handed over, assented to and reflected upon. Rather she is herself an essential element of revelation. If the older view of the Church as possessing an infallible teaching authority seemed to set too high a value on the Church, it may well be that we must be prepared, in rethinking this question, to accord to the Church a yet higher value; we must be prepared to see the Church's function not simply as being the organ through which a revelation (given in the past) is handed on, but as the very place where that revelation occurs, the zone of revelation in the present and in every age. We must see in the Church not so much the institutional character – emphasised in the older view of her teaching role – but rather her 'sacramental' character. We must take very seriously her nature as 'The Body of Christ', as the meeting place of God and man today.

Much confusion surrounds Christian thinking about revelation simply because our English word 'revelation' is ambiguous. It may refer to the thing-revealed (the *revelatum*) or to the process, the manner, and the means by which the *revelatum* is made known (the *revelatio*). With Temple we may agree that the *revelatum* is God himself and that, as Temple continues, 'there is no such thing as revealed truth; there are truths of revelation, that is to say propositions which express the results of correct thinking about revelation, but they are not themselves directly revealed.' To say that they are 'not directly revealed' is to say that they are not the *revelatum* itself or any part of it but rather they belong to the *revelatio*. They are necessary conditions for communication between God and man but they are not themselves that which is communicated. Propositions and dogmatic definitions, human words and sentences, are the means by which the human recipient of revelation expresses what he has experienced. We must recall that all human knowledge starts from experience, but that it is properly *human* knowledge only when the experience has been given expression in rational categories. All Christian dogmas are therefore rationalisations and explications of the fundamentally Christian experience of God in Christ; they are what Temple calls the 'results of correct thinking about revelation'; they are the results of reflection upon an experience and an attempt to express the true significance of that experience.

There are various necessary distinctions to be made about that process of reflection-upon-experience by which Christian dogmas are produced. There is need especially to be clear that the Church is able to judge what is and what is not the 'result of correct thinking about revelation' not because she has been given, either as a whole or in the person of certain of her officers, a unique and supernatural logical equipment that other mortals do not possess, but simply because she is continually experiencing that which her dogmas try to express; she reflects upon a present experience as much as upon a past one. It is necessary also to distinguish between the kind of language a man may use to express his feelings when he is personally confronted by the living God and the language the Church may use when she tries to express her faith in such a way as to meet the challenge of wrong-thinking from within and intellectual attack from without; thus it has been said 'Jeremiah is as clearly revelational' – i.e. stands close to the living truth – 'as the Athanasian Creed is not.' Also we may distinguish not only stages in the Church's reflection upon her experience of God but also different kinds of reflection. We need in particular to be careful to differentiate between dogmas which are directly derivative from the Church's experience of God in Christ and other doctrines which are essentially logical deductions (that is to say, abstractions) from other doctrines. Thus, for example, most arguments for the immaculate conception depend on the idea of the sinlessness of Christ. This idea may or may not 'logically' necessitate the immaculate conception but it raises enough difficulties of its own. What in fact do we mean by the sinlessness of Christ? The problems surrounding this area of Christian belief illustrate well some of the points made in more general terms in the rest of this chapter. They show up very well just what tests a claim to infallibility must pass and just what kind of assertions can be regarded as in any sense 'necessary to salvation' or 'of the faith'. Do we mean by the sinlessness of Christ that he lived a morally blameless life? If we do then it seems we are making a historical assertion, and it should be historically investigated. Do the gospels show Jesus anywhere doing what may be considered morally wrong? The question is pointless because the gospels do not record every minute, every action and every thought of Christ's life. Even if they did, or if we could persuade all historians to accept the little that is recorded as sufficient evidence, to judge that Christ was sinless implies that we have in mind some absolute moral standard against which He can be measured. But who shall set that standard?

When we say Christ was sinless what we are really talking about is our 'experience' of his unique moral and spiritual integrity: we have seen him as one who knew the purpose of God as no other man does and who followed that purpose as no other man will. We should do better, then, to speak positively of the 'faithfulness' of Jesus, the fact that he alone of all men lived and died in unbroken fellowship with God. Since this is a matter of experience, the Church is able to speak of Christ's sinlessness with a certainty and conviction which she could not have about a matter of historical research. If our salvation is dependent on the 'faithfulness' of Jesus, it does not in the same way, if at all, depend upon historical research.

Similar reasoning might be applied to many other Christian doctrines – e.g. the virgin birth – whose true value lies rather in what they are saying about the nature of the Church's experience and understanding of Jesus than in any-they may appear to assert about matters of historical or biological fact. Thus one Christian who believes 'literally' in the virgin birth – I suppose, in any case, we really mean the virgin conception – and another who thinks of it as a 'symbolic' way of talking about the person of Jesus contradict one another, but only at the historical and biological level. If the virgin birth is a biological fact, it has in itself no saving significance. A Christian is free to believe that Jesus was born by a particular biological process, 'parthenogenesis,' but this belief is not something which the Church has the power, right, or need to make necessary to salvation. What matters is that the virgin birth – whether taken literally or as a symbol – expresses a particular insight into the Church's experience of Christ. On this both our Christians can agree.

The same would to some extent apply to the resurrection of Christ. It may well be the case that Jesus, after his death on the cross, was resuscitated and walked the earth once more 'with flesh, bones, and all things pertaining to the perfection of man's nature'. But, if so, it is a matter open to historical investigation, a matter of how well and in what way it is documented or proved by historical effects. But matters of history can never be certain; though the evidence may be plain and abundant, its interpretation is always a matter of presuppositions, of elements not present in the 'facts' as such. Thus there are as many possible interpretations as there are interpreters. The resurrection is closer than the virgin birth to the heart of the Christian gospel. It is the one thing without which our 'faith is vain, we are yet in our sins.' But if this fundamental article of faith were concerned with the manner in which Jesus survives through or returns from the dead, then its truth would depend merely upon the verdict of historians. Our faith is rather the Church's experience, beginning with the experience of the apostles and other chosen witnesses, that this Jesus who once lived and was crucified still lives, is alive again. This is the resurrection faith of the Church; it is the certain knowledge that her Lord still lives and is still present with her. It cannot be required of any Christian to believe, as a necessity of salvation, any particular way in which Christ lived through and beyond death. The empty tomb is not in itself an article of faith. It was not an article of faith not even, by itself alone, a proof of the resurrection, to the apostles themselves. Their faith was that Jesus after his death had appeared to them; they had experienced again the presence with them of the one they had followed from Galilee to Calvary. The *fact* that he now lives and reigns is the Church's doctrine and this is the fact which she can infallibly assert because the Church is the only place within creation where this knowledge is found and this experience shared. The *question how* Christ returned from the dead is a matter for the clever or the curious to solve.

With the resurrection we touch the heart of the question about the true nature and function of the Church, and thus of her role as teacher. It is above all else the resurrection faith of the Church which shows her to be not a community which possesses a revelation received and transmitted from the past, but a community which is the actual zone of revelation then and now. This same faith makes her not just a society which in her sacraments dispenses 'grace' deposited with her in the past for her to hand out to suitable candidates down the ages, but a society which is itself the primary sacrament from which all other sacraments derive and take their meaning. And the resurrection faith further marks the

Church out not simply as the community of believers who remember a Jesus who once lived and in whom God in the past made himself known to men, but as the community of those who, while they do remember God's act in Christ in the past, remember it as the act of one who is still alive and still actively present in his Body. In the process of revelation (*revelatio*) the most important, indeed the primary element, forming the 'bridge' between God and man is the 'chosen people', the community of faith. This, we have come to learn, is the vital clue to our understanding of the nature of the Bible; it is something which comes into being and becomes sacred only within the context of the history of the chosen people. Certainly this is true of the Old Testament in which one of the chief 'revealing events' to which the community looks back is its own formation. And for the Christian Church 'the historical event to which all distinctively Christian faith returns is not an event antedating the Church, or in any sense or degree prior to it, but it is the coming into existence of the Church itself' (Knox, *The Church and the Reality of Christ*). As Jesus in his earthly life, ministry and death was able to be the revelation of God because the things to do with Jesus took place within a community which was already the zone of revelation – the old Israel – so his resurrection, the fact that he still lives and reigns as Lord and Christ, is a revelation only within the new community of faith, the Christian Church. It is when the Church sees her true nature as the zone of God's revelation in Christ, that is as the Body of Christ, and lives this truth in every act and aspect of her existence that she cannot fail or has infallibility. To be infallible may mean either that one is 'incapable of error' or that one is 'not liable to fail in any action or operation'. It is in the latter sense that the Church can be infallible as she 'teaches' the truth by living it rather than by simply stating it. The Church, for example, has wisely never defined her doctrine of the Atonement; if she ever did she could not define it infallibly, but she could be, and is called to be, infallibly the atoning community, a community which, wherever and whenever she is at-one, cannot fail to bring at-onement to others and ultimately to all creation.

One of the reasons why the Church has had to surrender doctrinal positions and retreat from former 'entrenchments' has been that the area of ground she was defending was not legitimately hers to defend; it was ground God had not seen fit to give her but which she had felt he ought to have given her. If our present thesis is anywhere near the truth there may be yet other ground that the *Churches* will have to surrender, if not to the world, at least to one another and to God – the ground which at present creates and maintains denominational barriers. The ease (and indeed the desire) to make confident distinctions between 'the true Church' and the rest sprang from the older view of the nature of the Church and of her authority as teacher. In terms of that view, 'truth', in the sense of agreement about the precise way in which the Christian experience shall be or has been formulated in words, could be the only basis of Christian unity; but is it perhaps the case that the unity of the Church *is* the truth, the fact to which even our divisions cannot give the lie? If so, it is high time Christians began to live this truth, to do, as one, those things which express and realise the Church's true nature and in which therefore she cannot fail. The unity which is truth, the atonement which is not a theory but a living experience, the 'wholeness' (catholicity) which is true manhood and not just a complete system of doctrine, these are surely the things the Holy Spirit brings to 'remembrance' (realisation) in the Church as he leads her into 'all truth'.

FURTHER READING

J. BAILLIE, *The Idea of Revelation in Recent Thought*, Oxford 1956

J. KNOX, *The Church and the Reality of Christ*, Collins 1963

H. D. LEWIS, *Our Experience of God*, Allen and Unwin 1959

E. L. MASCALL, *Christ, the Christian and the Church*, Longmans 1946

H. R. NIEBUHR, *The Meaning of Revelation*, Macmillan 1960

A. M. RAMSEY, *The Gospel and the Catholic Church*, Longmans 1936

A. SNELL, *Truth in Words*, Faith Press 1965

CATHOLIC WORSHIP

SIX

The Sacraments
and Personal Faith

THEODORE SIMPSON C.R.

'The main difference, therefore, between the English and foreign Reformation, lay in this – that *we* retained, and *they* lost, the sacramental system. The name Priest, which they have consistently rejected, and we as consistently have preserved, is the token and seal of that system, and so of our distinctiveness.' So T. T. Carter, Rector of Clewer, summed up *The Doctrine of the Priesthood in the Church of England* in his book of that title. Here then is the quintessence of nineteenth century Anglo-Catholicism. There is the familiar contrast between the glories of the English reformation and the unfortunate errors of *foreign* reformers; the stress on the 'sacramental system', regarded as an infallible means of delivering grace to those fortunate enough to have been enrolled in the ranks of *Ecclesia Anglicana*; the characteristically romanticised view of Anglican history – everything that Anglo-Catholicism stands for in the popular mind.

It is the 'fatal influence' of the 'Swiss Reformers' which is the main target for Carter's criticism – the hideous poison of foreign Protestantism which, he implies, has been unscrupulously introduced into the Anglican system. By the late nineteenth century the Oxford Movement was in danger of becoming a movement *against* Protestantism, a movement of rebellion from within a Church which, it was held, had come perilously close to selling its birthright. The whole armoury of scholastic and Counter-Reformation theology was brought to bear upon the enemy.

It is not enough, however, to ask what a movement is

against: it is much more important, especially for its ad-
herents, to ask what it is *for*. Superficially, what the Oxford
Movement appeared to stand for was the idea of the Church
as a mysterious supernatural institution. It was inevitable
that this kind of teaching would very quickly foster the
kind of ritualism which very soon became the hallmark of
the 'Catholic' party in the Church of England. But the
movement was always very much more than the expression
of a romantic taste for bells and incense in preference to the
decent sobriety of Sung Mattins. It is strange, but hardly
accidental, that many of the leaders of the movement came
themselves from an evangelical background – like Newman
himself, Ronald Knox, or Raymond Raynes – to mention
just three figures who between them span the whole of the
first century of the movement. Paradoxically enough, they
had more in common with Evangelicals than they had with
their high and dry predecessors who stood in the eighteenth-
century tradition of high churchmanship. In spite of their
party warfare, their extravagant disagreements and flam-
boyant propaganda (Knox's 'Latimer and Ridley Votive
Candle Stands'!), Evangelicals and Catholics were united in
a common belief that the Christian faith was about God's
initiative in the redemption of man. If Evangelicals tended to
look primarily to the cross, and Catholics to the Incarnation,
what they had in common was a burning conviction that
God had come to search out man, and that in Christ the
divine initiative was fully and completely displayed.

It is impossible to begin to understand the teaching of the
Oxford Movement unless we recognise that this was its
motive power. Pusey's attempts to maintain what would
now be regarded as a fundamentalist position in regard to
holy Scripture; Neale's labours in the cause of ritualism
through the Cambridge Camden Society; Henry Scott
Holland's devotion to Christian socialism; Gore's attempts to
'put the Catholic faith into its right relation to modern
intellectual and moral problems' in *Lux Mundi*; Dolling's
labours in the slums of Portsmouth – all these varied activities

were pursued under the inspiration of a common faith that Christ was, and they were called to be, (in poor Francis Thompson's phrase) 'The Hound of Heaven'.

For such men, sacramental religion was not the antithesis of personal faith in the living God: on the contrary it was its very heart and spring. It was the passionate conviction that God was at work in and through his Church that sustained them. Yet, to say the least, it was unfortunate that the only Church which they knew which still spoke as if this were true was the nineteenth-century Church of Rome. And what they heard as they listened at the key-hole of the Vatican was talk of the authority left by Christ to his Church, of the powers bestowed upon her priesthood, and of the grace committed to her charge. All too often they were led to think and to speak as if the Church had in some way *replaced* Christ. In the words of Neale's hymn quoted in the last chapter:

> '*So age by age, and year by year,*
> *His grace was handed on;*
> *And still the holy Church is here,*
> *Although her Lord is gone.*'

Christ is gone – but the Church is here!

On the theological front, they found themselves almost always on the defensive. In the face of the Englishman's traditional claim to the right to find his own way to heaven, they reacted with strident affirmations that the Church, and only the Church could land us safely on the other shore. Without a valid ministry and valid sacraments they claimed, we should be lost – left without certainty of grace in this world or salvation in the next. But this was a battle they were destined to lose. As more and more of their fellow-countrymen moved out of the orbit of the Church of England, the possibility of recovering England for the Catholic faith as they understood it became an ever more distant dream.

Yet, curiously enough, this very process of withdrawal served to set in train another kind of movement among Christians which has radically transformed the situation in which we find ourselves. Their increasing isolation made Christians increasingly conscious of their common heritage. It was the missionary societies who were the first to become sensitive to the new spirit which was abroad, as they began to see that the traditional competition, and indeed warfare, between different Christian communions was very damaging to the Christian cause – and that it was not a very suitable export for non-Christian lands. The societies took the first major initiative towards unity at the Edinburgh Missionary Conference of 1910. After this the Ecumenical Movement became increasingly a force with which all Christians had to reckon. New questions were asked of scholars and theologians, and the consequent rediscovery of 'biblical theology' and of the essentially corporate nature of the biblical Church, paved the way for further advances. On the Roman Catholic side, this kind of thinking, so long regarded as the province of eccentrics and heretics, achieved a dramatic breakthrough in the Second Vatican Council – where the theme of the Church as the People of God, the need for a generous and optimistic approach to the problems of reunion and to the non-Christian world, and the function of the Church as a 'sign of unity' for the whole human race were strongly stressed. In the light of all this, it has become apparent that a new assessment of traditional sacramental theology and ecclesiology is urgently required.

The weakness of the traditional Catholic theology of the sacraments lies in its tendency to translate the personal and dynamic terms of the New Testament into static categories like 'grace', 'power', 'matter', 'form' and 'validity'. More recently, Catholic theologians have made considerable efforts to escape from the strait-jacket of the traditional terminology – though it must be admitted that some of them seem to have escaped from the bondage of Thomist language only to fall captive in turn to the jargon of existentialism. I do not intend to try to summarise their work here. Instead I propose to offer my own more modest programme of re-interpretation, in the hope of showing how it is possible to safeguard the insights of the older theology, and yet to do justice to the demands of the new situation, without making use of any very complicated or technical vocabulary.

In their more unbuttoned moments, the Fathers of the Oxford Movement often spoke of the sacraments in dynamic rather than static terms. Carter, for example, speaks of the 'ministerial act' by which the sacraments are administered. And he also lays stress on the crucial importance of performing and accepting such an act in the context of faith. There is need for a 'mutual concurrence' between priest and layman: '. . . as no man can ordinarily by an act of his own mind obtain the promised blessing' (so much for 'Protestantism'!), 'so neither, without a corresponding fitness in the receiver, can the act of the priest impart it.' It is, then, an act imparted and received in the context of faith – and he rightly says that this safeguards the 'cardinal truth of justification by faith'. And yet, as it stands, this won't quite do. For what he understands by a 'sacramental act' is an act performed by the priest *in the place of Christ* and directed towards some kind of material object, conveying grace as though it were the product of a spiritual mechanism.

Carter just falls short of saying that the sacramental act is a personal act of the risen Lord himself, addressed to each one of us personally and individually through the ministry of the priest. Curiously enough, the bolder claim has very much more liberal implications than the narrower one – and perhaps this is why they shrank from making it. It seemed to them that to admit that wherever two or three were gathered together in the name of Christ, there Christ was in the midst, at work among us, would open the door to every kind of schism and sect. It might seem reasonable to claim that the Church had the exclusive custody of grace: it was scarcely credible that it could claim the custody of Christ himself.

At first sight, the doctrine that sacramental acts are simply personal acts of Christ is alarming just because it seems to leave no place for the institutional Church at all. It may be true that Christ is present in the sacrament of the

altar, but is it not also equally true that he is present –
perhaps more 'authentically' present – whenever a man
feeds the hungry or visits the sick: inasmuch as you do it to
one of these, you do it to me? We need not be afraid of such
questions. Indeed, it is only by asking this kind of question
that we can begin to see just what are the distinguishing
marks of the traditional sacramental acts, and what differen-
tiates them from those ordinary human acts of charity
which are the stuff of genuinely human living.

The good Samaritan finds an enemy lying in the ditch.
He carries him to the inn, and takes care of him – no doubt
washing his wounds and feeding him. The washing and
feeding are ordinary enough: but they speak of an extraordinary compassion. For it is his *enemy* whom he serves. In
the context of the Jewish claim to be the People of God and
their bitter rejection of the Samaritans, these simple acts
take on a new meaning. In the more particular context of
Jesus' own ministry, the story takes on a deeper meaning still.
For Jesus too was a friend of sinners, reviled as the com-
panion of gluttons and drunkards – himself no better than a
Samaritan by Jewish standards. Yet he claimed the right
to act authoritatively on God's behalf. Behind his story of the
good Samaritan lies the ironical question, 'If a man, even a
Jew, is left for dead in a ditch, perhaps you would agree that
even such a man as myself has the right to go to his rescue?
How can you deny that this is the work of God?' The more
we explore the context in which Jesus' own acts of compassion were set, the deeper their significance is seen to be.
The teaching of Jesus, his claims, his signs, reveal the
deeper meaning of what he does – for those who have eyes
to see and ears to hear.

In itself, every sacramental act is just an ordinary human
act – washing, breaking bread in fellowship, forgiving,
anointing; hands extended to admit to fellowship or to
appoint to office; promises mutually given and accepted.
There is no reason why we should end the list at this point.
The supernatural structure of sacramental action is built

upon the whole network of those human acts through which a man enters into relationship with other men – grace does not destroy nature, but perfects it.

But some kind of selection is necessary, for not every act of this kind is a suitable vehicle for the more specialised activities of the Kingdom. Every good act is an act of Christ: but there are some which are more characteristic of him than others, and better suited to his deeper purpose. We are not commanded simply to feed the hungry, but also to bring them to our table and to break bread with them in fellowship – and furthermore, to do this 'for a remembrance' of Christ's death; nor just to wash the feet of the poor – but also to bring them into the fellowship of the Church where the mysteries of Christ's death and resurrection are celebrated and appropriated. The selection of particular human acts as the basis of the sacramental acts, and their stylisation (even, dare one say, ritualisation?) is inevitable if they are to fulfil this deeper purpose.

A sacrament, then, is just such a *personal act*, but an act set in a *context* which gives it a new and deeper significance. Because it is a human act, it shows us how to find Christ at work wherever we see men loving and caring for one another. But this kind of act becomes a Christian sacrament just because it is set in a Christian context – in the context of the words and deeds, death and glorification, of Christ, and of the biblical imagery which formed the background to his own ministry. In this way a new dimension is revealed which remains hidden in those anonymous sacraments of the gospel which are to be found wherever compassion for others and respect for others can be seen at work.

In the sacraments, then, we come to know God. Not theologically, as though they gave us additional information about him; nor at second-hand, as though we received a report about him; but personally and directly, as we know a friend who comes to serve us. We know him through the acts of love and compassion he performs. And just as any human act of love can take on a deeper meaning when we know the context in which it is set – as the Jew in the story must have found a new significance in what was done for him when he learnt that it was a *Samaritan* who had rescued him – so the sacramental acts take on a deeper meaning when they are set in the context of Christ's redeeming work. Nor is this knowledge something external to us, as though it were something that could be described or catalogued. Recent studies of the way in which a man reacts to his environment, like Maurice Merleau-Ponty's *Phenomenology of Perception*, have shown that we react to what happens to us by changing the whole 'orientation' of our minds and bodies – by responding as a complete organism, rather as when the whole shape of the springing of a bed is modified by placing a weight upon some part of it. Someone raises a hand to us. If this act is set in the context of a violent quarrel, we flinch back, changing the whole stance of our body, and adopting an attitude of aggression. If it is an old friend we meet in the street, we stretch out our own hand to grasp his, simultaneously parting our lips in a smile and offering a conventional form of greeting. If it is a lover, a husband, a child, we will respond in quite other ways. The sacraments too are human acts, acts of Christ directed towards us personally and individually. We find a particular significance and a special meaning in them because they are acts set in a specific context. And they change our own inner 'orientation' – they effect a change within us, just like every other human act. But this particular change is such that it makes a new mode of union with God a possibility for us – to give it its traditional title, it is 'created grace', a real interior change which makes possible a new relationship to the Father in the Spirit. To use the current philosophical jargon, the sacraments give us knowledge of God 'by acquaintance', interior knowledge produced through direct personal contact, not knowledge 'by description', formal and abstract knowledge of his properties.

This knowledge of God by acquaintance becomes ours just because we are able to discover in the sacramental acts a personal act of Christ towards us, set in a context which gives it a special significance. This context may be a complex one, made up partly of the social grouping within which the act is set and the agent by whom the act is performed, and partly of what is said about it. Certainly, the verbal context is extremely important – and here as Catholics we are on familiar ground. For it is precisely in the conjunction of words and deeds that Catholic tradition finds the essence of the sacraments. In a famous comment on baptism, St Augustine said, 'Take away the word, and what is water but water? The word is added to the element, and it becomes a sacrament, itself, as it were, a visible word.' Yet even here we can see the beginning of that process by which the sacraments were slowly transformed into quasi-mechanical operations upon objects, instead of being seen as intelligible acts directed towards people. It is not the immersing into water, but the water itself which Augustine takes to be the visible or material element in the sacrament (the 'matter'): and it is not the word of the gospel, or even the visible structured Church (as Cyprian's arguments implied) which is the context which turns immersion into the Christian sacrament of baptism, but the words actually uttered at the moment of baptism (the 'form').

Augustine's intention was to make it plain that some kind of sacramental life, however tenuous and notional, was possible outside the Church. But we can now see that this purpose would have been better served by a sacramental theology based on the interpretation of the sacraments as acts of Christ in his Church rather than as operations upon material substances. And unfortunately the traditional view has had the effect of depersonalising the sacraments – so making possible, and indeed inevitable, the subsequent Protestant devaluation of them in favour of preaching. What I am suggesting, therefore, is, to put it in traditional terms, that we should look for the 'matter' of the sacrament in the sacramental action itself (not in the material element used in the action), and that we should extend the notion of 'form' to include the whole context within which that action is set. Because it requires an act of discernment, an informed faith, to see in such an act the act of Christ himself, the context will be of great importance. But there is no reason to deny that wherever such an act is performed with the intention of doing what Christ did, there Christ will be at work.

Behind Christian baptism there lies both Jewish proselyte baptism and the eschatological baptism of John, to which Our Lord himself submitted. These Jewish baptisms had, of course, the character of a washing away of sin, but in addition they served to admit the baptised to the new life of a 'chosen' community. The fact that the Christian at baptism was immersed rather than merely washed makes it plain that for Christians also baptism was as much an act of adoption into a community as a washing away of sin. Indeed, in Galatians 3:24, St Paul brings together justification, baptism and adoption in such a way as to suggest that he held that the Christian knew God as 'Abba, Father' (Rom. 8:14; Gal. 4:6) just because he had been claimed by Christ for sonship within the family of God through his baptism. It was in and through this act that he was 'justified'. By it he was delivered from the burden of sin, and admitted to the holy People of God (*cf.* the comparison between baptism and circumcision in Col. 2:11ff). By it the Christian has been claimed once and for all by the Christ who came to claim all sinners once-for-all for himself upon the cross. If we see the baptismal immersion as an adoption ceremony whose wider meaning is revealed by the biblical images of God's election of Israel (through the waters of the Red Sea, 1 Cor. 10:2), of circumcision and admission to the People of God, of new birth (Titus 3:5–7), of adoption to sonship, and of dying and rising with Christ (Rom. 6:4; Col. 2:12), we shall no longer be tempted to ask what is the precise 'effect' of baptism – as though this could be measured in terms of certain kinds of sin washed away or certain quantities of 'grace' bestowed.

Baptism inaugurates a personal relationship to God in Christ, and a relationship of a particular kind. What this relationship means for us is revealed in the wealth of images which are used to describe it in the New Testament. To find its fullest and deepest meaning, however, is the work of a lifetime of prayer, repentence, and faith – and for many 'conversion' or a first confession will be a significant milestone along the road.

Once baptism is understood as an act of adoption – an adoption with other, wider implications – it is possible to set the hoary old controversies about infant baptism, and the relationship between baptism, conversion, sacramental confession and confirmation in a new light. Indeed, as far as infant baptism is concerned, this venerable practice only begins to make sense in so far as we discount the traditional emphasis upon baptism as a washing away of sin, and instead stress its other (and, I would argue, primary) aspect as an act of adoption. It is sad that the theological ingenuity which has been mis-spent in trying to discover what kind of sin, 'original' or actual, is absolved in infant baptism, was not instead employed to explore the implications of baptism understood as an act of adoption. The important point, however, is that adoption inaugurates decisely and once-for-all a relationship within which further initiatives of love and forgiveness are possible, and indeed necessary. It is a relationship, too, into which the adopted child has to grow. It can precede a conscious and willing acceptance by the adopted child: and yet without some such response at the appropriate stage it remains a purely formal act which is 'external' to him. Our baptism, therefore, becomes 'real' for us just when, and in so far as, it becomes an inner reality for us – in so far as it effects a change in our inner 'orientation'. It has already happened to us – Christ has once and for all claimed us as his own: yet before the meaning of that claim can come home to us, we must respond to it and accept it. And this response is not our own work, but the work of the Spirit, who helps us to discern its meaning;

and the work also of the Son, who comes to us again and again in new initiatives of love – in the proclamation of his gospel, in his gift of absolution, in his pledge of fellowship given to us through the eucharist. Thus our baptismal adoption is progressively renewed and deepened within us through the sacramental action of the Son, and by the discernment which is the gift of the Spirit.

It is encouraging that the services of Baptism and Confirmation published by the Church of England Liturgical Commission (S.P.C.K. 1967) lay stress upon the images of adoption and new birth at the expense of that of the washing away of sin. It is also to be hoped that the custom (which they encourage) of administering baptism at the main service of the parish – ideally of course at the parish eucharist – will become very much more widespread. This is important not only because it helps to display the corporate aspect of baptism, but because it also helps us to see that in accepting a child for baptism the congregation also acknowledges its responsibility for that child. The congregation, in fact, functions as the divine adoption society. It is hardly satisfactory, therefore, to lay the whole burden of responsibility for the child's Christian upbringing upon the sponsors or the parents. If we are, and rightly, concerned for baptismal reform, we ought to ask ourselves what *we* are prepared to do. It is not enough to bully the parents into sending their children along to a Sunday School run by a few untrained adolescents. Nor is it satisfactory from a pastoral point of view to greet parents who ask for baptism with a series of rather incomprehensible demands. We must, therefore, face the fact that if we intend to continue the practice of infant baptism, we must also make sure that some members of the Christian body are prepared to make themselves personally responsible for the Christian upbringing of every child who is baptised. This would be a mammoth task. It would mean that many of the clubs and societies, which now absorb so much of our time as Anglicans, would probably have to disappear. But it is only in the context of this kind of personal concern for the child that we have any right to begin to lay down conditions for baptism. We must face the fact that if, for most of the citizens of this country, their baptism is a formal and meaningless affair, this is largely because *we* acquiesce in a situation which obscures its meaning.

In the first fine careless rapture of the Christian life, it is difficult to believe that we shall 'sin wilfully after that we have received the knowledge of the truth' (Heb. 10:26). Yet, regrettably, experience leaves no room for doubt about this. That Christ's renewed forgiveness was a possibility even for those who had known the joy of a deliberate and conscious acceptance of baptism was a lesson which it took the Church a long time to learn. From the point of view of later developments perhaps the most interesting passage in the New Testament is 2 Cor. 2:5–11. Here St Paul exhorts the Corinthians to receive the penitent sinner with love and forgiveness – and his rather obscure words, 'If I have forgiven anything, for your sakes I have forgiven it in the face of (or in the person of) Christ' suggest that he saw a connection between his own and the congregation's acceptance of the sinner, and Christ's gift of forgiveness.

There has been both loss and gain in the institutionalisation of this process in the form of sacramental absolution. The gain lies in the fact that it is now plain that this is not merely something done by the congregation or by the priest, but rather by Christ acting through the priest. Furthermore, the machinery employed guarantees the secrecy of the penitent's confession. Against this, it must be said that where this practice is not widely accepted and understood (and there are relatively few Anglican parishes where it is) confession before a priest is apt to look like a rather hole-and-corner devotion for the specially devout (or the specially neurotic). For this reason, and also because so many penitents need much more help in discovering their own true condition, there is a great deal to be said for the introduction of some kind of liturgy of penance. Even a private self-examination is likely to be a much more fruitful affair if it is done in the presence of our brethren, and if it is prompted by some kind of corporate meditation upon the gospel. In this way it would be possible to make provision for the whole congregation to deepen its penitence and to recover its vision and commitment, while still ensuring that those who wish to go on to make a private confession of their sins have the opportunity to do so. This would require a certain amount of co-operation between priests from different parishes, so that the service would not be unduly lengthy – but that may in fact be another point in its favour.

The distinctive feature of sacramental absolution is that it is not merely a proclamation of God's love, but also a personal act of forgiveness directed towards the particular penitent. It is important to see that it is our baptismal adoption which provides the context for this. It is just because we have been claimed by Christ already that we can turn to him with the confidence of those who look to an old and trusted friend for forgiveness and understanding. It needs the discernment of faith to find in the absolution of the priest the forgiveness of Christ, but those who have really understood the meaning of their baptism will not find it impossible.

The relationship between baptism and confirmation is much more problematical. In an essay of this length I can do no more than to offer my own opinion that none of the various layings on of hands which are described in the New Testament corresponds exactly to confirmation as we know it, and that St Paul's teaching that it is our baptismal adoption which initiates our relationship with the Spirit must be taken as the final word on that subject. What does seem clear is that the laying on of hands in the New Testament is understood either as a form of commissioning (e.g. Acts 13:2), or as an act of acceptance. The ceremony mentioned in Acts 8:17, the key text for the older Anglican High Church view, may well fall into the latter category.

That is the evidence; but what we are to make of it is quite another matter. Everyone would agree that confirmation is a suitable occasion for an adult and public proclamation of our faith – though whether it is realistic to ask this of a child of twelve is another matter. If confirmation is postponed, as perhaps it ought to be, then it will probably be necessary to separate it from admission to communion. Again, everyone would agree that confirmation can be seen as a public commissioning to adult witness and adult responsibility within the Church – though it is nonsense to say this unless we are prepared to attempt a much more realistic training programme for confirmands with this in mind. The difficulty lies in the dispute about the 'gift of the Spirit' in confirmation. But if we see our baptism as a personal act of Christ which inaugurates a new relationship with the Father in the Spirit, we shall no longer be tempted to speak in these impersonal terms. Within a relationship of this kind, new developments are always possible. It is precisely because confirmation marks a new stage in the relationship of the confirmand to the whole Body of Christ that it also marks a new stage in the relationship between the confirmand and Spirit.

Ordination, in contrast with confirmation, sets a man apart for a *special* ministry within the Church. It is not therefore, in the same sense as confirmation, a completion of baptism: all adult Christians ought to be confirmed – but it would be ludicrous to suppose that they all ought to be ordained! Nevertheless, there are similarities between confirmation and ordination. Like confirmation, ordination is done in the context of baptism. It establishes a new relationship between the ordinand and the whole body of baptised Christians, by licensing him to perform certain functions within and for the Body. And that Body is not merely a sociological entity, it is the Body of Christ: the ministry for which he is ordained is Christ's ministry: and the new relationship to Christ which is established at ordination involves a new relationship with the Spirit.

In recent years there has been a tendency to define the

ministry in terms of its functions instead of speaking of some 'gift' or 'power' which is handed over at ordination. In so far as this enables us to escape from a rather crude view of the Spirit, it is a welcome step forwards. On the other hand, it is vitally important that we should see that the function of a priest, like that of every Christian, is to be the agent *through whom Christ acts*, and through whom he acts in a particular way by the power of the Spirit. If the priest is not the deputy of Christ – his 'stand-in' – nor is he the deputy of the Church either: he is rather the *minister of Christ*, a man through whom the risen Lord continues his work. This is why the priesthood is such a central issue for Catholics. For the real heart of the Catholic tradition is to be found in the conviction that the risen Lord is still at work in his Church – he is still *active*. It is the same Lord who still baptises, still makes eucharist, still absolves.

In some sense, of course, every Christian is *alter Christus* – another Christ. And Catholic tradition witnesses to this in so far as, for example, it has always acknowledged that a layman may baptise, that he must and should bear witness to the gospel, that he must be Christ to the world. But that certain specific functions should, in normal circumstances, be reserved to specially appointed ministers is essential if the visible and ordered structure of the Church is to be maintained. It is just because the specific function of the bishop in ordaining new ministers for the Church, and that of the priest in presiding over the eucharistic assembly of the local church, serve the purpose of giving to the Church a structure and an articulation that their ministries are so important. Furthermore, because the visible order of the Church which was first established by Christ in the call of the Twelve, has as a matter of history been maintained through these particular ministries through the whole period from early patristic times to the Reformation, the Church cannot now discard them without discarding her past. If Catholics must insist that the heart of the Christian faith is that the Lord is active still, they must also insist that it is the *same* Lord who is active, and that the Church of the future must be recognisably the same Church as that to which our fathers in the faith belonged.

By his call of the Twelve our Lord established the Church as a visible society, an intelligible sign of the Kingdom. Traditionally, the visibility of the Church has been maintained through the structure of Catholic order, with the bishop as its centre and focus. Behind the principle of Catholic order there lies the profoundly evangelical doctrine that it is Christ who has chosen us for union with one another and with him, not we who have chosen unity for Christ. It is for this reason what we cannot disown the visible Church, in spite of all her weaknesses and her failings. The Catholic priest, therefore, has a dual role: he is Christ's minister, one through whom the Lord acts – but also one through whom he acts *as the Lord of the Church*. The visible Church is, therefore, the context within which the ministry of the priest is set. It is in the name of the *same* Lord of the *one* Church that he absolves, that he gives thanks, that he breaks bread.

When a man is ordained to any ministry within the Church, Christ acts through the ordaining minister in order to appoint him to a particular ministry. The 'matter' of the sacrament, then, is just a simple act of appointment through the laying on of hands. But that this is a sacramental action, and what kind of sacramental action it is, is determined by the context within which this act is performed. There is no reason to doubt, therefore, that wherever such an act is performed with the intention of doing what Christ did, there Christ is at work. But the *kind* of ministry that is bestowed is revealed by the total context within which this act is set. Where the ordaining minister is a 'valid' bishop, for instance, it is clear that the ministry for which he is ordained is a ministry within the visible Church, and that he is being set apart for the same ministry as that enjoyed by the ministers of the undivided Church of the past. To this extent he has a different ministry from that bestowed upon those ordained at the hands of presbyters, or by some other

F

method. The context must also include some kind of definition of the functions for which he is ordained. It is a welcome
feature of the ordinal put out by the Anglican-Methodist
Unity Commission (*The Ordinal*, S.P.C.K. and the Epworth
Press 1968) that it includes, for the first time in Anglican
history, a specific mention of the duty of the bishop and of
the priest to preside at the eucharist. But the climax of the
rite is the prayer to the Holy Spirit which accompanies the
laying on of hands. This is of course the traditional 'form –
and it is of crucial importance.

The revised ordinal makes a large break with Anglican
tradition at this point. Instead of the rather verbose, 'Receive
the Holy Ghost . . .' with the mention of the retention and
forgiveness of sins (a formula borrowed from John 20:21–23),
we have the precatory formula, 'Send down thy Holy Spirit
upon thy servant *N*. for the office and work of a presbyter in
they Church'.

The advantages of this change are obvious enough. There
are many respectable precedents for the use of the precatory
form, and it has the merit of making it quite plain that what
is envisaged is the establishment of a new and permanent
relationship with the Spirit for the performance of specific
functions in the name of Christ, without giving the impression that the Spirit is parcelled out at the command of the
bishop. Since the duty of the priest to absolve in the name of
Christ is mentioned elsewhere in the ordination prayer, its
omission here is not important. By avoiding the term priest at
this point (it is mentioned in the title to the service), many
Methodist consciences will be eased – but, to judge from
reactions in Catholic Anglican circles, rather at the expense
of burdening the conscience of many Anglicans.

It is not difficult to see why this should be so – indeed, the
quotation from T. T. Carter with which I began this essay
is sufficient to illustrate the point. In my view, however,
this is a kind of test case for Anglican Catholics precisely
because it represents a challenge to them to abandon the
party slogans of the past and to make a real effort to dis-

tinguish between those genuine Catholic principles to which we and in our view also the Church of England are (implicitly or explicitly) committed, and the traditional rallying cries to which, as a party movement within the Church, we have given our allegiance in the past. The fact is that most Free Churchmen, and many Anglican Evangelicals, have an 'invincible ignorance' about the word 'priest'. No amount of explanation, it seems, will convince them that it does not mean the same as *sacerdos* – *sacerdos* understood as the proper title of a sacrificing priest who puts a victim to death. But the question is, if we are agreed that *sacerdos* is in *some* ways a misleading term, which can be applied only analogously to the Christian priesthood, is it any longer desirable to insist on the use of the word 'priest' at this point? My own answer to this would be 'No'. 'Presbyter' is the kind of neutral word which arouses no distressing associations of this kind. It is found in the New Testament, in the Fathers, and is still the word used at what is now generally agreed to be the crucial laying on of hands in the Roman ordinal. Against this, one might argue that *sacerdos* is used elsewhere in the Roman rite. But again, we are faced with the question as to whether what we *mean* when we use the word 'priest' is not sufficiently covered by the sentence which is found in the ordination prayer in the Anglican-Methodist ordinal after the laying on of hands: 'Make them worthy to offer with all thy People spiritual sacrifices acceptable in thy sight, and to minister the Sacraments of the New Covenant.' In my view this safeguards everything for which the Fathers of the Oxford Movement fought, and I think it would be a mark of our self-confidence and of our willingness to search for a positive way forwards for the whole Church to abandon our objections to this ordinal.

Rather similar questions arise about the question of the 'Service of Reconciliation'. It is really a tremendous step forwards that the Commission has been able to agree that whatever happens in the future, Catholic order must, in some form, be maintained. This is not to say, of course, that the present administrative structures of the Church of England must be preserved intact. In fact, it is much to be hoped that Catholics will clearly acknowledge that these structures – huge dioceses, the parochial system and so on – are related to the principles of Catholic order only in the most haphazard and unsatisfactory way, and it may be that a Methodist-Anglican union would force upon us some much needed organisational changes. It is rather a pity therefore that the Commission has chosen to recommend the establishment of parallel episcopates for a limited period. If there is to be a real hope of genuine union between us, this can be achieved, I suggest, only by setting the bishop free to do his real work of bringing the local churches together by being the bond and the link between them. What we really need is very much smaller dioceses, and a bishop who is free to devote himself to his proper task. For what we should be seeking is *reconciliation* with our Christian brethren, rather than the absorption of one Church by another, or some kind of loose federalism. Here the bishop has a crucial role to play, a role very like that of St Paul in dealing with the churches under his care. We must seek to re-establish the only kind of context which can bring out the full meaning of Christ's presence among us, a genuine union in love embracing all Christians, recognisably one with the undivided Church of the past, and here and now a genuine sign for the whole human race of the unity we have in Christ.

It is for this reason also that I would hope that Catholics would not wish to imply either by word or deed that Christ is not present and active among all those who call upon his name. To speak of the 're-ordination' of free Church ministers seems to imply that their present ministry is in some way unreal. I have argued elsewhere that the best way in which our ministries and our Churches could be knit together would be by some form of mutual ordination. The implication of this is, of course, that on both sides there are ministries which are genuine ministries of Christ, but that they are not in fact the *same* ministries – they have similar functions, but they are set in different contexts. But it is important here to distinguish between means and ends: as Catholics, we are clear enough that the end must be one visible episcopal Church, with a universally recognised ministry. But whether we achieve this by mutual ordination, by the means proposed in the Service of Reconciliation (which also admits of the interpretation that what is happening is a mutual ordination), or by some method like that employed in South India, is comparatively unimportant. What is important is that there should be a coming together in love, with respect for one another's consciences – a genuine reconciliation at every level of Church life. And this is important not only for us but for the world. For if the Church is to be once again a *credible* sign of the Kingdom of love, it must be the visible expression of a genuine union in love, based on mutual respect, embracing men and women of every race and colour, founded upon our common loyalty to the gospel of Christ. The search for this kind of unity is a quest which we can never abandon, however difficult the road, however incomplete the results, for we are driven to it both by our loyalty to Christ and by our love of our fellowmen.

This kind of union in love with all other Christians alone can provide the proper context for the celebration of the sacraments. To this extent, we cannot be surprised if the sacramental life of all our Churches is impoverished at the present time. But it is at the eucharist that we must feel our divisions most keenly. For at the very heart of the eucharist we find a simple act of fellowship – the sharing of a common loaf and a common cup. This act becomes a sacrament precisely when it is set in the context of Christ's unitive work, the ministry of reconciliation achieved upon the cross and ratified in the resurrection. Of this work, the union in love of Christians is the sign and the fruit. But the real significance of the eucharist is bound to be lost whenever it is done outside the context of genuine Christian community – which is why, as Dom Gregory Dix pointed out some years ago, the quiet 'eight o'clock' is really the least satisfactory expression of the eucharist. Furthermore, this context will always be in some sense defective until the time comes when it is possible to celebrate the eucharist both as the expression of the union of all Christians in a particular place, and as the local manifestation of the unity of the whole church of God – and before that can come to pass we shall have to recover a ministry which can act in the name of the Lord of the whole Church, past and present.

Meanwhile, however, we celebrate the unity which we have, incomplete though it may be. And the meaning of this unity is brought out by the images with which the central act of fellowship is surrounded. One of the advantages of the 'thanksgiving' of the experimental service now authorised for use (*Alternative Services, Second Series: An Order for Holy Communion*, S.P.C.K. 1967) is that it makes a much fuller use of the biblical imagery than does the prayer book service. Thus, the eucharist is an anticipation of the Messianic Banquet: so we eat and drink as those who 'look for the coming of his kingdom' – and yet as those who are already 'in the presence of thy divine majesty', and who worship with 'the whole company of earth and heaven (*cf.* Luke 22:18, 30). We come to share in the feast of the new covenant – as those who celebrate and give thanks for Christ's sacrificial death, and who rejoice in his pledge that his life was given for us so that we should know beyond all doubt that he came to claim *sinners* for God (Mark 14:24 and parallels; 1 Cor. 11:35). We come as the People of God, a 'people for thine own possession', so that through the renewal of our fellowship with Christ and with one another, we may know the joy of union in love with the Father through the Spirit. We come therefore to offer a 'sacrifice of praise' (Heb. 13:15 *cf.* 1 Pet. 2:5) – a joyful and thankful proclamation of his saving acts in Christ, and a sacrifice which neither replaces not rivals Calvary, but rather celebrates it.

The eucharist, however, unlike the other sacraments, involves a *double* action, so that the second action is set in the context of the first. First of all the priest identifies the bread and the wine with the body which was given for us and the blood which was shed for us. Only after this does he minister the bread and cup to the congregation. It is this first action which distinguishes the eucharist from any other kind of common meal held by Christians. The distinction between the eucharist and the other sacraments has often been noted by Catholic theologians, and Aquinas among others draws attention to it. I think that we can now see, however, that they did not make this distinction sufficiently sharp. As we have seen, there was a tendency in the past to speak as if the sacramental actions were primarily directed towards some kind of material substance, and only then towards the recipient of the sacrament. I have argued that it is more helpful to see the sacraments as personal acts of Christ directed towards the individual. The *second* of the eucharistic acts is itself of this kind: Christ comes to us with bread and wine and with the words 'My body, given for you', 'My blood, shed for you'. But this second act is set in the context of a previous act by which the bread is identified with the body offered for us and the blood shed for us. The act of communion therefore presupposes a change in the status of the elements. The act of fellowship is set in the context of this previous act of identification.

The eucharist is therefore a celebration of, and a renewal in, our fellowship in the Lord's death. It is a proclamation of his resurrection and glorification. It looks to the coming of the Kingdom. At its centre there are two very simple acts: taking and blessing; breaking and giving in fellowship. It is through these acts that Christ makes himself known to his people day by day and week by week as their personal Lord and Saviour. Here then personal faith and sacramental religion find their true union and fulfilment. It is, of course, a matter of faith that Christ is really active here (*ex opere operato*) – but it is not our faith that brings him here (*ex opere operantis*). This faith is an *informed* faith, a faith illuminated by the great biblical images of our redemption: by our awareness of our union in Christ with all our fellow members of the Catholic Church living and departed – a union of which the priest is the living symbol: by our union in love with all those who love the Lord – tragically obscured though this may be by the fact of Christian disunity: but also by our union with all those who consciously or unconsciously, and in however anonymous or incoherent a way, share in Christ's redeeming work of love. It is here that the Church becomes what it is, and anticipates what it will be, until he who once came in humility, and still comes secretly in the power of the Spirit, shall at last come in glory to claim his people. And then the work of love will be complete, and we who now know in part by sacrament and through faith, will finally know as we are known.

FURTHER READING

BERNARD LEEMING, *Principles of Sacramental Theology*, rev. edn. Newman Press 1960. Indispensable source-book for the theology of the sacraments. Particularly valuable is the full discussion of confirmation, pp. 185–223.

E. C. F. A. SCHILLEBEECKX, *Christ the Sacrament of Encounter with God*, Sheed & Ward, Stagbooks 1963. Broke new ground by translating the terms of sacramental theology into the language of personal encounter.

JOHN GUNSTONE, *The Liturgy of Penance*, Faith Press 1966. Gives a great deal of useful information about the corporate aspect of penance, and makes some suggestions as to how it might be restored.

KARL RAHNER, *Studies in Modern Theology*, Burns Oates 1965. Includes a valuable essay on the corporate aspect of the sacraments.

o. CULLMANN and F. J. LEENHARDT, *Essays on the Lord's Supper*, Lutterworth Press 1958. Shows a welcome readiness to reconsider Protestant objections to the traditional understanding of the sacraments in the light of biblical theology.

H. BENEDICT GREEN, C. R., 'The One Baptism,' *Theology* LXVIII, October 1964, pp. 458ff. Breaks new ground in his discussion of the relationship between baptism and the cross.

E. M. B. GREEN, 'Essay on the Eucharist', *Guidelines*, J.I. Packer (ed), Falcon Books 1967. An important contribution to the debate about the relationship between the cross and the eucharist. His conclusions are often closely parallel with those reached by the present author in 'The Priestly Ministry', *Church Quarterly Review*, October-December 1966.

E. L. MASCALL, 'Eucharistic Doctrine after Vatican II', *Church Quarterly Review*, Pt. I, Vol. CLXIX, Jan-March 1968, pp. 19 ff; Pt II, Vol. CLXIX, April-June 1968, pp. 141 ff:

JAMES QUINN, 'New Thinking on the Real Presence', *Faith and Unity*, Vol. XII, July 1968, pp. 69 ff:

JOSEPH M. POWERS, 'Mysterium Fidei and the Theology of the Eucharist', *Worship*, Vol. 40, Jan. 1966, pp. 17 ff: 'New Thinking on the Eucharist', *Herder Correspondence*, Vol 5, July 1968, pp. 197 ff.

These four essays give a comprehensive account of the controversy which has surrounded the proposal of Schillebeeckx and others that 'transubstantation', should now be reinterpreted as 'transignification'. Mascall, Quinn and Powers argue that it is not sufficient to speak of a 'real presence' of Christ in the eucharistic elements through a change (even a divinely authorised change) in their *meaning*, but that it must in addition speak of a change of *substance*. Hence they argue that we must accept *both* transignification and transubstantation. The implication of the article in *Herder Corres-*

pondence however is that transubstantation must now be *re-interpreted as* transignification—Christ is present because the bread and wine have become symbols of this redeeming work of love and because he has appropriated them to his own use in order to create a new kind of fellowship through his death and resurrection. There can be no doubt that some such re-interpretation will be necessary if we are to escape from the older quasi-materialistic interpretation of the sacraments.

SEVEN

Tradition in Worship

JOHN WILKINSON

There was a time when all that mattered in British foreign policy could be implied in a prayer for 'Christian kings, princes, and governors'. It is still a good phrase if you are thinking about Belgium and Holland, Portugal, Spain, and Tonga. But it has its limitations. If liturgy is to be alive, it must alter quickly enough to relate realistically to the world, but not so radically that it loses touch with the tradition of Christian worship. Any change therefore involves tension and risk, and the tension is that of the familiar double meaning in the word 'apostolic'. What does it mean? Stretching back in continuity to the apostles? Stretching out in witness to a neighbour? Surely it means both, and this is the area of tension.

Since common prayer is one of the ingredients essential to the life of a Christian community, this tension matters to everyone. It can arouse strong reactions to change, and they are by no means confined to Anglicans. Indeed English Anglicans share with Roman Catholics a factor of history which aggravates their difficulties, since in both Churches the development of liturgy has been accidentally hindered for nearly four centuries. Roman Catholics since 1588 and English Anglicans since 1662 have seen hardly any alterations in their services until the present decade. There were minor changes – we left out the service for The Fifth Day of November, and they added a few collects, epistles, and gospels; and there were changes of emphasis. But the limits of change were soon reached.

The fixed texts, hedged about by legal interpretation,

came to occupy a false position. Not only did they fossilise at the heart of public worship a set of sixteenth-century assumptions and phraseology which needed regular re-appraisal, but also, since the use of the texts was legally required, the main question left to ask about them was, 'How do we use them?' So far as the Roman Missal is concerned, this approach could hardly be better illustrated than by a book like Knox's *The Mass in Slow Motion*, whose basic question was not, 'How ought Christians to pray together?', but, 'How, given the Mass we have, can we make the best of it?' Pastorally the question could not be avoided. But too often the answers could be little more than the rationalising of a situation which it was fruitless to criticise. Anglicans were in the same boat as they expounded the Prayer Book, and while some were busy proving it evangelical and others proving it was Catholic, many more basic questions had to wait.

Among Catholic Anglicans there have been three main lines of reaction. Some continued to maintain the position adopted by the leaders of the Oxford Movement, and to hold that the fullness of Catholic worship was available through the proper use of the Prayer Book as it stood. This position was maintained by men like the redoubtable T. A. Lacey, and is today held by the so-called 'Prayer Book Catholics', though this title has lost its meaning.

Beside this tradition, and often merging with it, is the reaction of 'enrichment'. For some Anglicans it was clear that the provisions of the Prayer Book were too meagre: and among the most obvious needs were those of the religious societies which began to be founded in the mid-nineteenth century. Mattins and Evensong were not enough for those who wished to pray the full choir office, nor the Prayer Book Calendar to meet the needs of a daily Mass. Such needs drew attention to the gaps in the Prayer Book, and to fill them Anglicans turned principally to Latin or Greek sources. Thus, half a century later, Charles Plummer collected his *Devotions from Ancient and Medieval Sources* (1916) not only from the pre-Reformation English books of Sarum and York but also the early Roman Sacramentaries and the Gallican, Mozarabic, Ambrosian, and Roman Missals 'to supply materials which may possibly be serviceable to those who are engaged in the problem of what is called "Prayer-Book Enrichment".' The influence of such work is today to be seen not only among Anglicans, but in many collections of prayer material intended for use in the Free Churches.

T. T. Carter had been engaged in a comparable research on behalf of his Clewer nuns. In 1866 he printed for them a collection of litanies, both medieval and Counter-Reformation in origin. They were not only translated for the nuns, but considerably edited and purified. Partly this was a mere matter of translation, but partly too it was an effort to make use of Roman Catholic forms of prayer without bringing in with them doctrinal positions not accepted by Anglicans. It is interesting to compare Canon Carter's versions with those which J. M. Neale printed three years later for his Sisters at St Margaret's, East Grinstead, which were less accomplished as translations and less scrupulous over doctrine.

'Enrichment' started as an effort, often successful, to supplement the Prayer Book. But at an early stage it divided into two movements: the one producing such collections as Plummer's, which omitted anything 'at variance with the teaching or practice of the English Church'; the other finding the supplementary material so far preferable to the Prayer Book that gradually the Prayer Book was submerged. Thus priests began by interpolating the Roman Canon as a private devotion, as suggested in Orby Shipley's *Ritual of the Altar* (1870). But there were soon some who came to regard the 1662 prayer not merely as second-best, but as inadequate. For them the Canon was the essential, whether they said it silently or aloud, in English or in Latin.

Of these three schools among Anglican Catholics, 'Prayer Book', 'Enrichment', and 'Western Rite', each in its way was appealing to tradition in worship. The 'Prayer Book' men, realistically acknowledging the limitations of 1662, were none the less able to use it. They saw it not merely as a beloved and expressive form of common prayer, but as an adequate vehicle of Catholic worship, and indeed many of them felt that, unless this were true, the whole basis of Anglicanism was imperilled. To 'enrich' the Prayer Book was not to deny its implicit catholicity, but rather to see this catholicity as giving freedom to use, beside the provisions of 1662, the classic devotions produced in the ages of faith. Sometimes the resuscitated treasures were worthy of the name. But the zeal for ancient sources often produced material which was merely indigestible and obscure. This criticism too often applies to Neale's translations of office hymns, and to much of Plummer's collection as well. English parishioners are rare who would of themselves use such phrases as, 'Purge our labours from evil works, and confirm our endeavours after good'.

The 'Western Rite' school, therefore, had some justification in its complaint that such enrichment was often no more than antiquarianism. As they came to use the Roman Missal in its completeness, with text, ceremonial, and vesture as closely as possible in accordance with the Roman requirements, they often said and did things which were not obviously intelligible. But at least they were things which had survived, and were in use the world over.

Looking back on the growing years of the Anglican Catholic movement from the standpoint of the present day, we may be surprised to find it so derivative. There are two main explanations. The first was the belief that to be Catholic it was necessary to stand in a tradition, whether this happened to be the living tradition of the current Book of Common Prayer (or Roman Missal), or a wider and more ancient tradition admitting anything valuable that could be found in Catholic history. The second was the acceptance of fixed texts as the normal instrument of prayer, an attitude which is easy to condone in the light of the centuries when they had remained unchanged. In such a situation, and with no real hope that it would change, what seemed more natural than to look outside the authorised body of texts to other fixed texts which were (or had been) authorised in some other part of the Catholic Church?

Since those days three developments have taken place. The narrow area of choice which lay before the early Anglican Catholics has lost its landmarks, and many questions are open. The first of these developments has been the Liturgical Movement, a fifty-year period of pastoral study which inspired new questions about the given liturgy. Near the beginning of the movement, among Roman Catholics, and essential to it, was the raising of a question about the Roman Mass itself. Was this *par excellence* the Catholic rite? One of the founders of the Liturgical Movement, Dom Lambert Beaudouin OSB, drew attention to the equal importance of the Eastern rites in his own communion, and arranged that some of his own monks should use them. To take such a step in Belgium seemed at the outset to be pure eccentricity, but it had wide consequences. It showed that, at least by Roman standards, the Roman rite had no monopoly, and gave a new context to questions which before had been answered with reference to the West alone.

The second development, which was hastened by the Liturgical Movement, was a reassessment of history, and therefore of tradition. Questions of the origins of Christian worship received renewed attention, and their practical bearing was discussed. The names of Justin, Irenaeus, and Hippolytus came to be known in a liturgical context, and the names of Alcuin and Durandus were less in evidence. A new historical effort led to a re-evaluation of the fixed texts, and a new emphasis in their interpretation.

The third development, closely connected with both the others, came with the Vatican Council, and its *Constitution on the Sacred Liturgy* (1963). The Liturgical Movement which began as a pastoral study among a few (sometimes rebellious) pioneers ended as a revolution affecting the whole Roman Catholic Church. For it is the voice of Dom Lambert Beaudouin and his colleagues, which echoes in the Constitution.

The Constitution is a positive document. But it rests on two principal criticisms of the existing Roman rites. First, that they were hard to understand. Some of the things to be said and done were obscure in themselves, others had become obscured by unsuitable additions, and others were archaic. The second criticism is that it was hard to take part in the services. Some were over-long and repetitive. Often people lacked instruction, and better teaching was needed both in parishes and in seminaries. In the case of the eucharist participation was seriously hindered by the habit of non-communicating attendance. To meet these criticisms the Constitution proposed rehabilitation along three lines:

'Elements which have suffered injury through accidents of history are now to be restored to the vigour which they had in the days of the holy Fathers'.

'Provision is to be made . . . for legitimate variations and adaptations to different groups, regions, and peoples'.

And there should be 'communal celebration involving the presence and active participation of the people'.

Although the Constitution contains some detailed practical proposals, it is essentially concerned with basic principles, and not with the exact ways in which they are to be applied. Nor does it foreclose the many questions it raises. Indeed there are times when it seems to sit on the fence, as in the section which states both that 'the use of the Latin language is to be preserved in the Latin rites' and also that local authorities are to decide 'whether and to what extent the vernacular language is to be used'. The question is not decided in the Constitution, but at least it is raised, and the Church is left to seek an answer. This is not the same as sitting on the fence.

The Vatican Council also passed on to the local Churches some questions about tradition. The Constitution states that the liturgy is 'made up of immutable elements divinely instituted, and of elements subject to change' (art. 21): 'sound tradition' is commended: but it is to be retained in such a way that 'legitimate progress' can be made (art. 23). Elsewhere it it made clear that the tradition stretches from the scriptures themselves right up to the latest liturgical reforms. Tradition is not to be abandoned: 'there must be no innovations unless the good of the Church requires them; and care must be taken that any new forms adopted should in some way grow organically from forms already existing' (art. 23).

The criticisms and suggestions contained in the Constitution have already led to alterations in the liturgy, alterations which 'Western Rite' Anglicans have been swift to adopt. But the principles of the Constitution apply in equal measure to those who have so far stuck to the Prayer Book. A new effort of analysis is required if Prayer Book services are to be easier to understand and take part in. One departure made by the Constitution is of particular interest. Whereas the Roman Missal was promulgated for use by everyone (with very few exceptions) who used the Latin rite, the new situation encourages local orders and local decisions. The concept of uniformity – sometimes raised to the status of an ideal – has been set aside in favour of adaptation to local circumstances and cultures. We are likely to hear less of the Catholic traveller, comforted to find an identical Mass in Kamloops and Khatmandu, and more about the needs of the regular local congregation.

Roman and Anglican ideas of uniformity were never identical, but they gave rise to a mentality which still persists in both communions. As lately as in 1948 a Lambeth Conference was able to suggest that the Book of Common Prayer was one of the chief factors which contributed to the unity of the Anglican Communion. This was a surprising statement. The different Churches of the Anglican Communion had had other books since the early eighteenth century. Even within the Church of England the wide variety of usage had long made it clear that, as a means to uniformity, the Book of Common Prayer had failed. Yet, if we admit that uniformity is not the ideal, we are still faced with problems, for we must still create the new material which will authentically express

and sustain the worship of the apostolic Church. We are back
to the word 'apostolic'.

What people are to understand in liturgy, what they are to
take part in, must be Christian: it cannot be detached from
the tradition of the historic community which is to use it. Yet
the retention of historic elements must not hinder understanding or participation. Here is the tension, but in recognising it we must not over-simplify. It is all too easy to treat
the traditional and the modern as if they were in opposition
to each other, but the culture and the society we call modern
is in fact a mixture which includes both. Take a visitor round
London, and you will show him Carnaby Street and the
Post Office Tower. But you will also make sure he sees the
Tower of London. To be modern is not to be confined to the
newest of the new, but to observe and appreciate a mixture of
styles and customs. Carnaby Street itself is not so much an
invention as a revival.

Thus the principle expressed by the Vatican Council, that
liturgy should be understandable, is not a demand that it
should be in the English of a radio instruction-manual. The
aim is not simply to pass on facts, but to invest the facts with
the power and the depth which traditionally they have had
among Christians. The principle forbids language that is un-
necessarily complicated, but not language which deals
poetically with personal relationships. It praises what is in
tune with modern times, but it does not condemn what is old.
To be true to modern society the liturgy can and should
preserve the treasures of its past, though the urge for pre-
servation must never become an escape from creativity.

To use historic Christian material is to acknowledge the
reality of a continuous Christian community stretching back
to the time of the apostles. But because the successive centuries in which the material was produced were peopled by
human beings, never long remaining fixed in one social
structure, there is comparatively little of the old material
which does not demand some adaptation. This is obvious in
the case of single words whose meaning has now become

changed, like the old chestnut 'Prevent us' in the collect or
'hell' in the Apostles' Creed. It is a matter of controversy
with words like 'thou' which have survived only in a liturgical
context, for it is clear that present-day Christians are divided
between those who have for so long used 'thou' as a reverent
address that they find 'you' disrespectful, and those who see
'thou' as evidence that the Church still regards itself as a self-
contained system set apart from a profane world, and is un-
willing to move out of its cocoon. But the demand for
adaptation goes deeper still. We live today in a society in
which such an idea as kingship has lost much of its pictorial
quality. Crowned heads are rare, yet the liturgy is coloured
by royal language, and prayers like the collects reflect a vivid
picture of an imperial Roman court, where suppliants present
their petitions. Even the phrase 'thy divine majesty' could
have been applied to the Roman emperor. How far is our
egalitarian society to go in removing such language, and the
associations it carries? What is the point beyond which the
revisers must not venture?

Royal language was expressive in the days when kings
were part of a living experience. But to re-read the eucharistic
prayer of Hippolytus, is to see how free it is from the royal
language of Rome. Its phraseology is far closer to that of
the New Testament, and loses nothing of its grandeur or
intelligibility for that. We could lose a great deal of royal
language without being the less Christian. But we could not
lose it all.

The Liturgical Movement rediscovered the primitive
Church and the origins of Christian worship. But its lesson is
not simply that we should revive the earliest prayer-texts.
Hippolytus and Serapion were as much men of their age as
the writers of the Gallican liturgies or Thomas Cranmer himself, and their work is in no way too sacrosanct to be adapted.
To respect the primitive is not to reject every later development, and such things must be judged on their merits, and
not dismissed because they are 'late', 'medieval' or 'accre-
tions'. The advantage of the earliest witnesses is that they

show, as no later witnesses can, how the Christian community interpreted the apostolic faith and life at a time when it was still fresh. If they are uniquely important, it is because they speak for the Church at a uniquely formative stage in its existence.

Justin's evidence is unique. But we have the writings of some of the apostles themselves. They do not solve all the questions we wish to ask, but they carry a still higher authority, since those who wrote them were the immediate witnesses to Jesus Christ and his teaching. We cannot find more of the incarnate Christ than what is given in the pages of the New Testament. Here is, in some sense, the sticking-point for the innovators. The New Testament and the Old, can never be set aside. If the Church is to be apostolic it must ponder, reflect, and express the message of the apostolic writings.

To stretch out to the world as well as back to its earliest documents, the Christian community will often have to transpose the language of the documents into modern forms, since even the Bible took shape in a society with its own temporal peculiarities and limitations. But deep inside the tradition of Christian worship is the practice of reading the Bible itself to the people, and of encouraging the ordinary Christian to read it for himself. It is recognised that the understanding of the Bible presents difficulties. But the Christian solution has been to ensure that readings are accompanied by sermons, to ensure that the texts are understood in the Christian sense (how else could one possibly stand up and read the Song of Songs in church?), or in other words to equip Christians with a means of handling their foundation documents.

To return to the question of royal language: it is clear that this has an important place in the Bible. It appears in Isaiah and the Psalms, and the tradition is continued in the New Testament with the phrases, 'the King eternal, immortal', or, 'him that sitteth on the throne'. Christians faced with this language must either explain it or else avoid reading such passages altogether. But if they must explain the Hebrew understanding of kingship, they need not for ever pray with Collects which reflect a Roman version of the idea. It may well be that a tradition which was deeply expressive to the first users of the Collects will convey little to is, or even be misleading, and, where this is so, no one is compelled to stress this particular strand in the tradition when there are so many others. The only proviso is that those who reject royal language must first find some alternative and more effective expression of formal reverence. And such expressions are uncommon in the civilisations of the twentieth century.

Efforts in 'Prayer-Book Enrichment' were valuable, not least because they restored to currency so many prayers and phrases which revealed the Christian community's awareness of God. Often the prayers were not suitable for use in their original form, but they can still inspire those who write new prayer material. Beside these sources, and even more important, are the prayers recorded in the Bible. Here again the exact prayers which are recorded are seldom suitable for word-by-word repetition, but, taken together, they reveal a variety of emphases which is sadly lacking in many Anglican services – particularly 'after the third Collect'. Christians may not know God by ninety-nine names, but he is addressed by over forty in the Bible, each of which reflects insight into his character and the covenant-relationship. The Collects are content with very few. When you have said the words 'Almighty', 'everlasting', 'merciful', 'eternal' and 'blessed' the list of epithets is almost complete. Only one Collect addresses God as 'Father'. Again the Bible provides a constant reminder of the importance of praise and declaration in worship. Here, on the whole, the Collects are satisfactory. But there are still too many prayers both in formal and informal use which contain little else but a succession of petitions balanced only by the most formal expressions of trust and adoration. Such petitions are to be found in the Bible, but they are not the norm.

Two current problems illustrate the place of tradition in

worship. The first concerns the recent proposal that the words 'we offer unto thee this bread and this cup' should form part of the Thanksgiving or Prayer of Consecration in the new form of the eucharist of *Alternative Services, Second Series*. The second is the problem of prayers for the dead.

The words which the Liturgical Commission proposed for inclusion in the eucharistic prayer were hardly a novelty. In fact they first eucharistic prayer in which they were used was that composed by Hippolytus early in the third century (the earliest eucharistic prayer certainly known). These words, or words very like them, are implied by earlier documents, and had a place in every early eucharistic prayer. They are clearly in the mainstream of Christian liturgical tradition. Nevertheless one member of the Commission in a note of dissent wrote that 'Inquiry has shown that the phrase . . . is unacceptable to many Anglicans'.

Anglican Catholics could hardly pretend to be surprised at this objection. They were well aware that the proposal restored phraseology which had deliberately been excluded from the English Prayer Books. But they were equally aware that it had been restored in other parts of the Anglican Communion (e.g. in South Africa and the West Indies). They felt that misunderstanding of the words, which was forgivable at the time of the Reformation, was no longer necessary, and this feeling was strengthened by the fact that some Free Churchmen were proposing to use similar phraseology.

There was no doubt that the new phrase added a concept which was lacking in the English Prayer Books. The 1662 Holy Communion rite treats explicitly of three offerings: the first is Christ's one sacrifice, once offered on the Cross, the sacrifice which the eucharist represents and commemorates; secondly what is done in the service is described as a 'sacrifice of praise and thanksgiving' (*cf.* Ps. 50:14; Jer. 17:26); thirdly in the eucharist the Christians' response is a sacrifice, the offering of 'ourselves, our souls and bodies' (*cf.* Rom. 12:1). There is everything to be said for the mention of offering in such terms. But it is the Christian conviction that they are not simply three separate offerings. In the eucharist they are somehow united: through the eucharistic action with the bread and wine we show forth Christ's death; through the sacrifice of his self-offering we are enabled to offer our praise and thanksgiving, every aspect of ourselves, in a way which is acceptable. The Anglican Catholic may well hesitate to try and define the exact way in which all the sacrificial elements in the eucharist are drawn into a unity, and welcome an open-ended statement of the kind made by Dr Mascall when he says that in the eucharist, 'The Whole Christ offers the Whole Christ'. But the question is not whether there is a sacrifice in the eucharist, but whether the words, 'We offer unto thee this bread and this cup' help to express the sacrifice.

The eucharist is so simply (and so little) described in the New Testament that it cannot conclusively be decided whether such words as 'communion' (1 Cor. 10:16, *cf.* 21) or 'do this' (1 Cor. 11:24) have a restricted technical meaning as sacrificial words. They could have such a meaning, but both are words with so wide an application that no appeal based only on them could carry conviction. But the idea of sacrifice was so central to Jewish religious thought that it is not surprising to find Christians taking it into the vocabulary of their faith. Thus in Hebrews 13:15–16 'offering the sacrifice of praise' is a phrase immediately followed by a statement that 'to show kindness and to share what you have with others' are the sacrifices which God approves. This wide use of sacrificial language continues among the earliest Christian writers after the New Testament, and is applied to martyrdom and to virtuous conduct.

Clearly too the sacrificial language covers the eucharist. Clement of Rome is already speaking of Christian 'High priests' and their 'offerings' before A.D. 100 (1 Cl. 40:1), and within twenty years Ignatius of Antioch uses 'place of sacrifice' e.g. *Trall.* 7:2, *Philad.* 4 as a standard word in contexts where we would use the word altar (its synonym). And within this general use of sacrificial language in the context of the eucharist we soon find a mention of the offering of the bread and wine. Justin Martyr, writing in about A.D. 155, says they are 'offered' 'for a memorial of the passion' (*Dial.* 41), and parallel phrases from his contemporaries and successors abound, and can be found in any outline of eucharistic doctrine. But in evaluating this use of language it would be a mistake to imagine that Justin is using his words in the precise way they had come to be used in Reformation controversies. He uses the word 'offer', but we do not know how much he meant by it. Indeed it is possible to regard his words (and those of Hippolytus) as referring simply to the external sacramental action, by which the president of the eucharist 'gives thanks over' the bread and wine which have been set before him, and in doing so dedicates them to God's service. Cyprian in about A.D. 250 certainly seems to have been using the word in this sense when he mentions Christ at the Last Supper 'offering the cup' (*Ep.* 62:9). In this case 'offer' and 'give thanks over' would indicate the same action, even though one expression occurs in the gospels and the other does not.

The language of Serapion's eucharistic prayer is equally definite in stating that the bread and wine are being offered. 'To thee have we offered this bread, the likeness of the body of the only-begotten . . . we have also offered the cup, the likeness of his blood' *Sac.* 13, 4:1. It is the visible elements which are being offered, even though they are invested with the special significance which Christ gave them at the Last Supper.

This use of the word 'offer' is applied to bread and wine which are to be received in communion as the body and blood of Christ, according to Christ's institution. Even before, Serapion Cyprian already exchanges the word 'blood' for 'wine' in a discussion with those who wished to use water instead of wine in the eucharist: 'We discover that it was a mixed cup which the Lord offered, and that it was wine which he said was his blood. So it appears that the blood of Christ is not offered if the cup has no wine in it, nor is the

Lord's sacrifice celebrated with the due hallowing if our offering and sacrifice does not correspond with his passion' (*Ep.* 63:9). This development in language opens up new possibilities. A century later Ambrose is saying that 'even if Christ is not seen to be offered (sc. in the eucharist), yet he is offered on earth when Christ's body is offered' (*Enarr. in Ps.* 38:25), and such language forms one strand in the extremely varied vocabulary with which the Fathers come to speak of the eucharist. But it does not drive out all other ways of describing what is done, and the clearest evidence appears in the liturgy itself, where the bread and the cup are indeed qualified by adjectives or phrases like those of the Roman Canon ('the holy bread of eternal life and the cup of perpetual salvation') but are never replaced by such a phrase as 'we offer unto thee the body and blood of thy Son'.

The early evidence for the use of the phrase, 'We offer unto thee this bread and this cup' is therefore plentiful. The phrase, or one like it, has a regular place in the liturgies of East and West alike. But are Anglicans bound to use the phrase in revising their liturgy simply for this reason? Charles Davis at least is a theologian who thinks not:

> 'More proof is required than is usually cited for the thesis that what the Church did in the past must now be regarded as unalterable ... The data show what happened in the past' (*A Question of Conscience*, pp. 130–131).

And if the phrase is in the category of 'elements subject to change', it would be alterable today.

For Anglicans (though not in the same way for Roman Catholics) the phrase can be, and was, changed. None of the English Prayer Books contained it. And though it formed part of the eighteenth-century liturgies of the Non-Jurors, it was not officially approved by Anglicans until it was reintroduced overseas during the present century. If Anglican Catholics wished to teach doctrines of eucharistic sacrifice, they were well able to do so out of the Prayer Book of 1662. For in fact the idea that 'The Whole Christ offers the Whole Christ' does not depend on the words in the disputed phrase. Indeed they are thoroughly inadequate as a means of expressing it. Thus if Anglicans seek a liturgy which grows, organically from forms already existing' and 'expresses more clearly the holy things which it signifies', there is a great deal to be said against the phrase. For every Anglican who knows that 'we offer this bread and this cup' need mean no more than 'we give thanks over', there are fifty who see the word 'offer' in the context of later controversies.

If 'apostolic' meant only 'stretching back', all the pre-Reformation evidence would argue for the retention of the phrase, however it were to be understood. But if we are to 'stretch out' as well, to other Anglicans and to the non-Christians of the present century we are faced with a task of analysis. The things which are essential must be kept, and some if these may be difficult and need explanation. But there are other difficult expressions which can well be re-expressed or dropped altogether.

Re-expression involves risk. The idea of offering sacrifice, so familiar to Jews and Gentiles of the first century, has no literal equivalent today, for we use 'sacrifice' only to mean 'self-sacrifice', or in some other transferred sense. It is one of the words which has to be explained, for every Christian should be led to understand the sacrifice once offered by Christ, and to use this language about it. But this understanding is hardly likely to come through the use of the words 'we offer unto thee this bread and this cup'.

Not many Anglicans outside the Convocations were deeply concerned whether these particular words were accepted or rejected, but there are many more who are affected by questions about prayers for the dead. This is not so much because there have always been Anglicans who used such prayers, though they had a place in the Elizabethan Primers and in the devotions of the Caroline Divines, as because they have been in general use for the last half century. Prayers for the dead were unfamiliar to the large majority of Anglicans till the end of the nineteenth century, and it was with the

Boer War that the change came. In 1900 an official 'Form of Intercession' for the troops in South Africa included a prayer for the dead. And when war returned in 1914, bringing a toll of human life beyond any previous experience, such prayers became increasingly common, till by 1918 their use was widespread.

The mere fact that the prayers answered a psychological need does not prove that they are legitimate. Prayers for the dead were used by Tertullian in the second century A.D. (as they had been by Judas Maccabaeus a century before Christ's birth) and appear on the earliest epitaphs of the Christians. But none of this is a guarantee that they were rightly used, and it is certain that by the time of the Reformation these prayers had been seriously misused. When Reformers objected to prayers for the dead in the context of chantries and indulgences, they bore witness to a deeper dissatisfaction with the unreformed Church in which they had been brought up: that it had intruded itself as an institution standing between men and God. But by no means all English Christians saw prayers for the dead in such a context at the time of the Reformation, and even for those who disliked them they were not so urgently in need of reform as other elements in the life of the Church. In the event two expedients were adopted by the Church of England.

The first was to adopt the policy, consistently applied by 1552, of altering prayers for the dead into prayers which contrived also to mention the living, or changed asking into thanksgiving. So in the burial Collect of the 1549 book there is the phrase, 'We meekly beseech thee . . . (that) at the general resurrection . . . both we and this our brother departed . . . may obtain eternal joy'. But even this could be interpreted as a prayer for the dead man, and in 1552 the prayer was simply that 'we . . . may receive that blessing . . .' Thus public prayers that had been direct petitions for the dead, if they remained petitions at all, became prayers in which the emphasis was on the living, even though the dead were mentioned. The second expedient was to avoid outright condemnation of prayers for the dead. The *Homily on Prayer* is indeed a strong dissuasive, but it dismisses prayer for the dead not as wicked, but as fruitless: and *Article XXII*, which was finally published at the same time as the Homily, and had in an earlier draft condemned prayer for the dead in the same terms as the Romish doctrine of Purgatory, finally appeared in a form which made no mention of such prayer.

The *Homily* presents prayer for the dead as pointless. It states, correctly enough, that such prayer is not commanded in the scriptures. With most contemporary writings it assumes that prayer for the dead is inevitably bound up with a doctrine of purgatory, but points out that 'the scripture doth acknowledge but two places after this life', heaven and hell. If God's judgment immediately followed death the dead man would thus already be in one or the other, and it was useless to try and alter what God had irrevocably decided. 'Therefore let us not deceive ourselves, thinking that either we may help other, or other may help us by their good and charitable prayers in time to come.' Such an argument, if pursued very far, would rule out the value of all intercessory prayer.

Christians who wish to consider the state of those who have died, must search the Bible. But the Bible presents this part of its teachings not in a single, logically coherent scheme, but in a rich variety of analogies, some timeless and lucid, and others in the remoter language of contemporary Jewish expectations. The different analogies are held together by the assumption that God is to judge his creatures, and that his judgment determines their final state, either heaven or hell. Heaven is described in a cluster of images which illustrate the theme of joy in God's presence, the joy of God's people in his finally-accomplished salvation. It is the fulfilment of many particular aspects of the revealed will of God, like the ordinance of the sabbath rest, or the ideal of a holy city. Above all it is the fulfilment of the covenant, for only in heaven are God's people securely his, and he manifestly theirs.

Already 'now' there are partial fulfilments of the covenant.

Even on earth Christians begin to enjoy the worship and fellowship of heaven, and to glimpse the wonders of God's nature. But this 'now' stands in contrast with the 'then' when we hope for the direct and unhindered enjoyment of these privileges. Heaven is still for us in the 'not yet', despite the finality of Christ's mighty acts, and the assurance they bring.

As human beings we are not able to use words like 'now' and 'not yet' without thinking sometimes of the period that must elapse between them. But we must beware of becoming too literally attached to such thoughts, since time itself is to be fulfilled and transmuted in heaven. Time-language has a use if it serves our belief that our individuality will remain when we are 'changed' and made 'like the angels'. But time-expressions used about a timeless 'then' can only be accessories to the main truth, that heaven is the final enjoyment of God's presence and glory.

Still looking for the teaching of the Bible, let us ask who is to enter heaven. Our answer is affected by two beliefs which are not reconcilable in terms of secular logic: the first a belief in Christ's total victory into which he incorporates those he has saved, and the second a belief that God is our Judge, a judge who knows completely the quality of our faith and conduct. God alone knows us at this depth. Thus if I speculate on the state of a Christian friend who has died, I cannot arrogate to myself the judgment only God can make. I have grounds for hope when I consider the completeness of Christ's victory and love. But I am also aware of plain biblical teaching about the reality of judgment: I have to regard both these strands in the biblical teaching, even though logic will not enable me to subordinate one to the other, or to reduce the two to one.

Attempts have often been made to soften the abruptness of this logical difficulty. There is the theory of an 'intermediate state' in which the person who has died is progressively purified until he is fit for heaven. But such a theory raises as many logical puzzles as it purports to solve, not least since it is hard to see how any created being could be 'fit' to enter the presence of the Creator. Or there is the theory of a 'second chance', as if entry to heaven was like entry to a university. The Bible teaches neither of these compromises. The biblical hope lies in the revelation that God 'desireth not the death of a sinner', but rather the full life which Christ came to impart.

As Christian people it is our duty to pray, but our prayers are to be 'in Christ', in the context of God's revealed charac- ter. In the Bible praise is blessing God for being what he is, and petition is asking him to act in accordance with his revealed character. So Solomon speaks to God as the One 'who keepest covenant and mercy with all thy servants' and goes on to pray. 'Therefore . . . keep with thy servant David my father that thou promisedst him'. Solomon is asking God not to change his mind, but to perform what he knows to be in his mind. Nor indeed is such a petition as, 'Take not thy Holy Spirit from us' an attempt to make God change his mind, for we pray in the context of the knowledge that God is a God who constantly sends his Spirit on his people. Abraham was not trying to change God's mind when he prayed for the deliverance of Sodom (Gen. 18). Rather he was seeking to enter into and test God's mind and will. Christ himself taught us to pray 'thy will be done', and in prayer we wish to align our wills with God's, confident that it is a will for mercy and loving-kindness.

'Thy will be done on earth' – these are, of course, the words. We are commanded to pray for those on earth. Should we also pray for the dead? Prayer clearly has a subjective value, enabling us to see more clearly what is God's will, and to set ourselves to obey it. But prayer is more than this. It is also a way of 'bearing one another's burdens', and Christ consistently encouraged the belief that faithful prayer is answered, and not only through a change of heart in the one who prays.

If we pray for the dead, what can we ask? We have no knowledge of their needs (if any), and our prayers are limited both by our ignorance of 'where they are' and our unreadiness to anticipate God's judgment on them. Yet we are acquainted with God's final purpose for his people, and we pray that it may be accomplished every time we say 'thy kingdom come'. When a son prays for his dead parents he is not only satisfying his own psychological need to find an expression for his love, but also praying that God's revealed will may be accomplished in them. This prayer would certainly be wrong if it involved doubt in the sufficiency of what Christ had achieved for them. But, quite apart from the fact that such a danger is no greater in intercessions for the dead than for the living, prayer is an expression not of fearful doubt, but of faith in Christ's purpose and power. It is, moreover, clear from many instances in the Bible that Christ acts in power on one person in response to the expressed faith of others. Thus four men brought him the paralytic (Mark 2:1–5), and 'seeing *their* faith' he forgave and healed him. Without such examples there would be little hope in intercession, but to intercede is to place a particular case trustingly into the context of Christ's purpose. Prayer for the dead might also be wrong if its contents were not based on what is implied in the biblical revelation about the life after death (or, for some Anglicans, if they could be seen to fall within the extremely vague limits implied by *Article XXII*) and there are many such prayers in Christian, and indeed in Anglican, tradition. But it is not hard to find prayers which are firmly attached to biblical foundations. Every Christian is justified in praying for the dead in the language of refreshment, light, and peace – the rest of the fulfilled sabbath, the unending light of the Lamb, the peace of salvation, and the refreshment of the messianic banquet.

The point at which the Catholic and Evangelical traditions part company is in the mention of individual names in the prayers. Evangelicals are prepared to mention names in a context of thanksgiving. But the dead are more than happy memories, and the Christian faith teaches that they are alive. If thanksgiving is inadequate by itself, the Evangelical will concede that names can be mentioned so long as they are linked with some mention of the living: it is legitimate to pray, 'Hear *us* as we remember those who have died in faith, and grant *us with them* a share in thy eternal kingdom': and wrong to pray, 'Remember those who have died in faith, and grant *them* a share in thy eternal kingdom'. But such a view would force us to pray 'Thy kingdom come' as an abstraction. If the fulfilment of the prayer is to have any reality for me, it must involve many of the persons I have known in this life, and especially those I love. If I pray directly for them I am doing what every Christian felt free to do until the Reformation. Only with the Reformation Prayer Books was it felt necessary to change this direct and natural form of prayer into (what is different) a prayer for myself-and-the-deceased, or the-deceased-and-all-the-elect.

Prayers for the dead have had a chequered history, and their abuses have been notorious. But when they contain nothing contrary to the scriptures there is no reason to prevent their use, and every historical reason to use so understandable and primitive a form of prayer.

If Anglican Catholics seek, with the Vatican Council, to revive a 'sound tradition' in worship, they will read their history. But they will seek in it something more than the static orthodoxy which finds its goal in correctness, or the restoration of primitive wording. This may well be what is required, as in the simple petitions for rest and peace which appear on the walls of the catacombs. It may have lost its clarity, like 'we offer unto thee this bread and this cup', and have to be replaced. But in seeking and contending for what they value, they need above all to remember that orthodoxy is valueless until it is transmuted into the dynamic force behind the Church's witness.

FURTHER READING

The present Anglican discussion on the sacrificial understanding of the eucharist should be studied against the background of the important articles by J. L. Houlden, Arthur Couratin, Michael Moreton, and Geoffrey Cuming collected in *Theology* LXIX, October 1966, and the essays by Austin Farrer and Geoffrey Lampe in *Eucharistic Theology Then and Now*, S.P.C.K. Theological Collections, No. 9, 1968.

The best short account of prayers for the dead in the English Books of Common Prayer is that in the article on the subject in *The Prayer Book Dictionary*, G. Harford and M. Stevenson (ed), 1912, pp. 274–275.

The extent and substance of current conservative evangelical disquiet on these two topics is revealed in *Prayer Book Revision and Anglican Unity*, a pamphlet by R. T. Beckwith, 1967.

EIGHT

Catholic Spirituality Today

CHRISTOPHER BRYANT, S.S.J.E.

Mircea Eliade tells the story of an obscure and poverty-stricken Jewish rabbi, Isaac son of Jekel by name, who lived several hundred years ago in Cracow. Sleeping in his single-roomed house, one night he dreamt an extremely vivid dream of a treasure which was buried underneath the bridge leading to the royal palace of Prague. Three nights running he dreamt the same dream. He could not stop thinking about it. In the end he decided to make the 300–mile journey on foot to Prague to see if he could get the treasure. Having arrived at Prague, however, he found the bridge guarded by soldiers and the treasure, if there was a treasure, completely inaccessible. As he stood there the captain of the guard, a kindly man, asked him what his trouble was. So the rabbi related his dream. The captain of the guard laughed. 'You shouldn't pay any attention to dreams. Why, only the other night I had a dream about treasure. I dreamt of a treasure buried in the house of a man I never heard of, a rabbi called Isaac son of Jekel, who lived in Cracow. The treasure was buried in the corner of his house behind the stove. But only a fool pays attention to dreams.' The rabbi listened with inward astonishment; he bowed low to the captain of the guard and thanked him. Then he set off back to Cracow. On his arrival home he went straight to the corner of his house behind the stove and began to dig. Eventually he unearthed a treasure sufficient to end his poverty.

The treasure the rabbi discovered in this parable was the treasure of his ancestral faith. He had grown up with it. It

163

had been within his reach all the time; but he did not recognise it. To discover it he had to make a long journey and learn from a stranger: he had to enter into dialogue with the guardians of a tradition other than his own. Many Christians today are in the position of that rabbi, for the treasure which will revitalise our faith and enrich our life is within our reach, buried in our own tradition. But the trouble with tradition is that there is so much of it, some of doubtful, some of negative value. We need guidance where to dig; and this guidance will come through dialogue.

A spirituality for today must be sought through dialogue with contemporaries – true representatives of the contemporary world; and it will begin to take shape as men sympathetically but critically open themselves to the beliefs of those whose outlook is strange to them. Dialogue means not only face-to-face meeting and conversation but also the creative meeting with the mind of an author which comes through reading; for to read with understanding and to respond actively to what we read is true dialogue even though we may never see or even correspond with the author. If the spirituality is to be Christian as well as contemporary there will have to be dialogue also with the scriptures, and within the scriptures especially with the writings concerning Christ, his life and teaching, his death and resurrection, and the impact he made on his disciples both before and after Pentecost. To be Catholic a spirituality will also have been shaped through dialogue with the Christian past, with spiritual writers and thinkers, theologians and mystics, as well as the multitudes of unknown worshippers who have contributed to the development of the liturgy. In theory it is easy enough to distinguish the various strands of dialogue, scriptural, traditional, contemporary. It is more difficult in practice, for even as we attend to the words of Christ in the gospel our awareness of the contemporary leads us to value especially what seems significant today and to pass over other things which, though they may seem less directly relevant, have bulked larger in the minds of the first disciples.

I begin with a strand of Christ's teaching which has particular relevance today. The Sermon on the Mount describes human life as it is meant to be, open to God, open to man. Complete loyalty to God and total trust in him sets us free from all other cares; but this openness to God is bound, if it is genuine, to express itself in openness to our fellows. So man is meant to give (and to forgive) just as freely as God does. This description of human life sounds simple, but such a life in practice demands sustained heroism. It was the way Christ lived, but it brought him to the cross. To ordinary men it was impossible; but the heart of the gospel is that through Christ's death and resurrection the impossible began to be realised.

Within the community of the first disciples men began to live with the openness that Christ taught and lived. Baptism, the formal initiation into this community, symbolised and fostered a break with the past and the beginning of the new life in the community. Old values had to be dethroned, new values to be set up in their place, as membership in this brotherhood of believers made men aware of Christ, the unseen Head of the brotherhood. Those first Christians were far from perfect, as St Paul's letters make plain. There was no instant moral transformation. But when St Paul called the first Christians the Body of Christ, he was giving a name to an experienced reality, a name which explained, illuminated and deepened the experience. Through Christ they found themselves brought into a new relationship to the living God, as his sons. This liberating experience of sonship came through the Spirit, who both breathed the prayer 'Abba, Father', in their hearts and also bound them together in a shared faith and love. For the first Christians the experience of God, of Christ, of the Spirit was a community experience. Not all the disciples can have shared this experience at the deep level of St Paul. Within the community there were varieties of temperament and varieties of spiritual gifts; the more perceptive carried the less. The central act in which this corporate spirituality declared itself was the eucharist-union with God in Christ and with one another was expressed and cemented in the blessing, the breaking of bread and the sharing of the cup, by which the disciples represented and shared in the saving death and resurrection of Christ.

The starting point for a Christian spirituality must be the spirituality of the first Christians. In those little communities of Christians for whom St Paul wrote his letters we see in embryo a tension with which Christians have had to grapple ever since. Jews and Gentiles were mingled together and represent two distinct problems, since for the Jew the freedom of the Spirit meant freedom from the constraints of legalism, but for the Gentile it meant freedom from moral anarchy. For the one it meant a new liberty, for the other a healthy and liberating discipline. Without an element of law and discipline the liberty of the Spirit is liable to degenerate into licence. But law and discipline must be understood not as ends in themselves but as means to freedom. The history of Christian spirituality has as one of its great themes this tension between discipline and freedom, law and gospel, means and ends.

I shall consider three elements in a Christian spirituality: first, the prayer and worship that orients men to their true end; second, the radical repentance that this orientation demands; third, the element of law and discipline that both prepares for and underpins the rightly oriented life.

The Bible takes it for granted that the God we worship is the living God, the Author of the universe, who is active in every part of it, both within us and outside, the God who speaks and acts and loves and saves. He acts through the regularities of nature, but also in ways that are unpredictable. His will and presence is an ingredient in every event. He is also a God who is concerned for man and addresses him, so that when we orient ourselves towards God we turn (like St John on Patmos) to face One who has already spoken to us. He has been addressing us through our thinking and planning, through the events of our life, and also through our dreams, and the unaccountable ideas and impulses that invade our minds. He addresses us especially through people, their demands, their antagonism, their friendship, their love. He summons us not to be afraid, to be open, to trust. As God is addressing us all the time, the worship that orients us to him must focus and concentrate our attitude in every part of life. And because worship should express and foster a life which is completely responsive to God, the Bible has a unique importance in it. Reading and reflecting on the Bible and especially what bears more directly on Christ can provide a key to interpret God's purpose and action now. The exposition of scripture and the preaching of the Word in public worship is designed to enable a more complete response to the God who is addressing us through the details of our life and the events of our times.

Worship should foster a life responsive to God. Yet although God's action presses upon us in every event and all the time, there are certain pressure points, where God is more clearly seen and more intimately at work. These are of especial importance for the man who would respond to God. I will name three: the Christian community, a man's neighbour, his own being.

'Where two or three are gathered together in my name, there am I in the midst of them.' It was through membership in the Christian community, the Church, that the first Christians became responsive to Christ; for the Church is the sacrament of Christ, the sign of his presence, the means of his action in the world. This could be seen to be true in the first days of the Church. In the conditions of the modern world I believe this community responsive to Christ is best realised not so much through the highly organised national and diocesan structures of the Church as through its local embodiment in parish and congregation. And on the local level it exists most effectively in relatively small groups formed for some common aim or task. Such groups have an importance out of all proportion to their numerical strength.

For in a way impossible to larger bodies they can foster a community life responsive to Christ; their more fully personal relationships can make Christ more plainly visible.

If the first of these pressure-points of God's action is the Christian community, the second is a man's neighbour. Christ tells us to settle our brother's claim on us before we approach God's altar, for there can be no genuine approach to God that excludes or ignores the neighbour. To believe we love God while we hate our brother is to deceive ourselves. Our neighbour is both the person near us, the person with whom we are in constant contact in our home or at our work, and he is also the person in need whom we happen to be able to help. Our neighbour in either of these senses can be a major problem in our lives. We are often tempted to look the other way, to seal off our relations with him in a compartment of life undisturbed by our faith. But our neighbour is one of God's pressure-points, God's challenge to us. And if we would face God, we cannot ignore the challenge.

The third pressure-point is a man's own being. And since God addresses us through the whole of what we are, not only through our conscious thinking and planning but also through the nine tenths of us that is unconscious, lack of self-awareness will make us blind to what God is saying. 'Swink and sweat in all that thou canst and mayest for to get thee a true knowing and feeling of thyself as thou art'; writes the fourteenth-century author of *The Cloud of Unknowing*, 'and soon after that, I trow, thou shalt get thee a true knowing and feeling of God as He is.' Modern depth psychology has both underlined this insight and provided fresh tools for the task of gaining self-awareness. This is not the place to describe the methods and techniques of meditation and contemplation designed to help the awareness of God's action within. But a man's whole being is one of God's pressure-points and an important part of our response must be in a prayer that seeks to know both ourselves and God. 'When you pray go into your room, shut your door, and pray to your Father privately'. A Christian spirituality must find space for prolonged private prayer.

In worship we turn to face the God who is addressing us. Thus the most fundamental element in prayer is adoration, the acknowledgment of the reality of God. It has this in common with scientific research, that it is concerned with the recognition and exploration of a given reality. But its method of exploration is different, for whereas science selects from the concrete and the singular those aspects which it can measure, adoration explores reality in its wholeness and singularity, in order to acknowledge the Immeasurable, who addresses us through concrete events and particular people. Adoration demands the exercise of faith, for the God we adore is immensely beyond the capacity of our minds to grasp. The creed and other formulations of Christian belief are thus a means to adoration and faith. To make correct belief a substitute for a living faith in God is to misunderstand the function of the creed, which is not to limit the things it affirms but to rule out particular errors and to sign-post the way to God, the Unknown. Because faith seeks to acknowledge a reality, it needs as co-adjutors both the questioning spirit, to sift error from truth, and also the intellectual courage to venture out where the evidence points.

Among the obstacles to adoration (and to the openness to people and to events which it expresses and fosters) are false and one-sided ideas of God. One such idea still widely current today is of a father, tyrannical and condemnatory. Another is of a father, all-kind and all-tolerant but, alas, ineffective. The tenacity with which men cling to these ideas and the violence with which they sometimes reject them suggest their origin in part in childhood experience of father and mother. But whatever their origin such ideas hinder commitment to the real God and, therefore, their commitment to people which is the touchstone of true religion. God is not an idea but an active personal presence. He is neither tyrannical nor all-tolerant. What looks like unlimited tolerance is God's concern to foster man's freedom.

What looks like tyranny is his unrelenting opposition, like that of a doctor to the deadly cancer in his patient, to all that diminishes and enslaves man. The Bible contains the antidote to false ideas of God. But the uninstructed individual is apt to find in the Bible what he expects to find. The great corrective of false ideas of God is the worship of the liturgy with its great range of scripture readings, its prayers steeped in the ideas and images of scripture, together with the preaching of the Word. The liturgy, and especially the eucharistic liturgy, is centred in the crucified and risen Christ. And in Christ we see revealed both the character of God and the meaning of commitment. Commitment in faith to God means in some sense trusting ourselves to the world God has brought into being, over which he reigns. It means taking the risk of relying on our own God-created nature, on other people, on the way things happen. We do not need to have illusions about these things or to suppose that they cannot let us down; but our reliance is based on our reliance on God who is behind and within them. The crucifixion places the possibility of being let down at the heart of our faith. But behind the ignorance, fear, folly and wickedness of men God is at work, able to bring good out of evil, to turn tragedy into triumph. After the cross came the resurrection; behind death there is life.

The liturgy centred in the crucified and risen Christ both corrects false and one-sided ideas of God and points us God-wards. Yet at the same time the intellectual climate of our times is acting as a powerful solvent of all ideas of God. The scientific world-view frequently presents a universe without reference to God and our technological civilisation seems to leave God completely out of its calculations; and both look like a threat to Christian faith. I believe their final effect may be to purify and strengthen it, for it is our all too human ideas about God that are threatened, not God himself. Science is making us jettison much lumber that could hardly have been got rid of in any other way. We are being reminded that we cannot know God as he is; that we know him only indirectly through the created universe and through human history; that even in Jesus Christ, God incarnate, we only know as much of God as can be expressed in a human life. Thus Christians are being led to set a new value on the old tradition of imageless prayer. In their approach to God they lay aside all images and address him as the Unknown who mysteriously makes himself known. This is not to deny that we know God. But we know him as a small child knows the ocean after a single visit to the sea-side. He will know the look of the sea from the shore and the feel and taste of sea-water. But he won't know the ocean, its vast extent, its teeming life, its depths and its currents. So we know God and we don't know him; and our ignorance is often as significant as our knowledge. Sometimes a deep faith in God is expressed in the prayer, 'Lord, I don't know you, but I trust you and want to be guided by you'.

This profound sense that God transcends our understanding leads perhaps unexpectedly to a simple and human approach to him. We address him not as far away but as 'closer to us than breathing, nearer than hands and feet': to address him is to address our own depths. We need to express our faith, our gratitude, our repentance in order to focus these attitudes, to help them to grow, to make them more decisive in our life. Further the simpler the words of prayer the more effective they will be as a means of expressing these attitudes of commitment. Simple, childlike prayer speaks to and for the depths in us. It is able to enlist the whole of us in prayer in a way that a more sophisticated prayer cannot. For as we address what is deepest in us we address One who is deeper still.

Worship orients men to their true end. Its fundamental element is therefore adoration, and all the other kinds of prayer can be understood in the light of it. Thanksgiving is a form of adoration that acknowledges especially God's goodness and generosity. Petition adores God acting throughout the world of men and inviting us to co-operate in bringing about his will. Confession adores God in his righteousness and compassion. All these modes of worship are ways of acknowledging God and of fostering the direction of the whole of life towards him. It is plain that genuine adoration makes demands that ordinary human nature cannot face without profound change. This change is repentance.

The New Testament takes for granted man's thorough disorientation. He is a sinner, blind, lost, unable to escape from demonic powers. He is estranged from God and his fellows; he is divided within himself. His manhood is stunted for lack of the right relationship with God without which it cannot thrive. The trouble is a matter of sin rather than of sins, a condition in which man finds himself rather than the fact that he often does wrong. Man is haunted by a gap between his potential and his achievement that he is powerless to close. Today this condition is more easily understood as due to social conditioning than to genetic inheritance. It is a social fact as much as a personal one.

The gospel takes man's sin for granted and announces a remedy. 'Repent and believe': 'change your attitude and put your trust in God'. The Greek word, *metanoia*, repentance, means not penitence but change of mind or attitude. The three parables in Luke 15 illuminate Christ's teaching about repentance. There is a divine and a human factor in man's change of attitude. The parable of the lost sheep and the lost coin emphasise God's initiative in our repentance. The sheep and the coin have to be looked for and found. Man cannot by himself effect the needed change. He must be born again, he has to undergo a kind of death and resurrection, he has to pass from death to life. But neither is man passive in this turning to God; and the third parable, that of the Prodigal Son, concerns the human element in repentance. The prodigal in the story leaves home for a far country and after a time begins to be in want. Then he comes to himself. The prelude to repentance is the awakening from illusion, the facing up to reality. He realises that he need not be where he is. Change is possible, change is desirable. Repentance begins when hope is born, the hope that is awakened by the gospel of God's love for those estranged from him. Hope sets the imagination to work out practical ways and means for attaining the desired goal. Hope set the prodigal off on his journey home. Hope awakens the determination to turn from illusion to reality, from being shut in to being open, the determination to choose freedom. The real root of repentance is not penitence or sorrow for sin (which too easily degenerates into self-pity) but hope. Genuine penitence comes later, as the fruit of love.

Repentance is actualised partly through confession. The prayer of confession, since it expresses a sense of responsibility for sin is paradoxically an affirmation of human freedom and dignity. But there is more than one kind of responsibility. We are responsible, first, in the sense of being to blame for certain wrong acts or failures to act. In confession we acknowledge that we have freely and knowingly done what we ought not and left undone what we ought. We are the ones to blame and no other. But there is a second kind, our responsibility for doing our best to cope with a situation for which we are not to blame (or only so to a marginal degree). Over-anxiety, depression, feelings of resentment and self-pity are evils and can be very damaging. But they may be due to present or past circumstances for which we are only to a very minor extent to blame. If we blame ourselves for things we did not cause and cannot help we shall be taking the short road to the dungeons of despair. But we are responsible even for moods which we cannot help, not in the sense of being to blame for them but as having the duty of trying to find a cure for them, for managing them and mitigating their consequences. Feelings and moods such as these should be confessed more as a patient tells his symptoms to a doctor than as a wrongdoer seeks forgiveness for his misdeeds. It is hard to draw the line between the evil we are to blame for and the evil we suffer from, but the distinction is of great practical importance. Further, genuine repentance will lead to some sense of responsibility for the sin of the world as a whole, for the corporate selfishness that leads to war, to exploitation and a host of social evils. We are responsible in part for the kind of society in which these things take place, and we are responsible for doing something to reduce or alleviate the evils.

Genuine repentance issues in God's forgiveness, which means not the overlooking of our misdeeds but his acceptance of the whole of us as we are. But an obstacle to forgiveness is our fear of certain dangerous or destructive elements in ourselves and our desire to reject them. Thus we cannot wholly accept God's forgiveness and we partly exclude his healing, integrating, liberating action. Further, if we reject God's acceptance of the whole of us, we shall find it impossible wholly to accept other people. 'Forgive and ye shall be forgiven' states not so much a condition to be fulfilled as a truth about the very nature of forgiveness. If we have realised the completeness of God's acceptance of us we shall be unable to withhold acceptance from others. Many, however, cannot realise God's loving acceptance of them except through the mediation of people. Only because he matters to others or to one other can a man believe that he matters to God, can he believe that he matters absolutely. The Church is meant to be an accepting community in which men can realise God's love through the love of their fellows. One way in which this ministry is exercised is through the sacrament of penance. It can be misused as a means of getting rid of a sense of sin without genuine repentance. It can sometimes help to keep alive morbid guilt feelings that were better allowed to die. And these are serious objections. Nevertheless it remains a powerful means of reconciling men to God and bringing home to them the meaning of God's forgiveness. It meets a deep need in man to confess his sin and guilt before his fellow. It provides a man with an effective way of expressing his responsibility for his deeds. It gives the opportunity to a trained confessor of giving an individual the personal guidance and encouragement he may need. Through it Christ in his Church acts to restore and heal. And further the sacrament can reassure the sinner of his complete acceptance by

God, for it speaks to the whole man. The sophisticated intelligence may be able to tell itself of God's forgiveness, but the child in the depths of every man is glad of the assurance that comes in the words of absolution. It is a means to that radical repentance that a life oriented to God demands.

What, in conclusion, should be the place of law and discipline in the life open to God and man? It is clearly subordinate: discipline is a means to freedom, law must serve the gospel and be the instrument of love. Law and discipline must provide the communications and the civil service without which the rule of love is bound to be ineffective. The ground covered by discipline can usefully be marked out in terms of the cardinal virtues of prudence, justice, temperance and fortitude.

Man (under God) makes himself by his choices and decisions. It is of first importance that his decisions shall be taken after due thought: to be 'wise as serpents' as well as harmless as doves a man will need to reflect deeply, to make up his mind decisively, to act firmly. We need to consider before we can come to wise and firm decisions. Decision is difficult because it involves a choice between alternatives and therefore renunciation. If I decide to emigrate to Australia I have to let go the possibilities of emigrating to Canada and of remaining at home. Decision also involves the possibility of making a mistake. One of the problems of technopolis is that the possibilities of choice – in, for example, education, careers, jobs, holidays, entertainment – have been so multiplied as to make it hard for people to make up their minds. There can be a paralysis of the power to decide. But man makes himself by his decisions. To refuse or to be unable to decide will mean drifting under the pull and pressure of the winds and tides of the world around him; it will mean surrendering part of his humanity.

To make wise decisions men need times and places of withdrawal, times for reading, reflection and prayer. The tempo of life and the multiplicity of activities in a modern city make this withdrawal doubly necessary. But it will not come about by accident and good intentions are not enough. It needs to be planned with the foresight and the concern for detail with which the businessman plans a holiday. Some will aim at a time of withdrawal every day, some at a longer period carefully planned once a month, some at an annual retreat. The discipline to aim at may well include all three. Intelligence and forethought are no substitute for a life committed to God and to man, but they are that life's indispensable servants.

Reflecting and deciding are largely concerned with people and the society in which we live, for we depend on other people from birth to death. Our livelihood depends on a world-wide co-operative enterprise: we grow up, we become human with the help of others: we become educated, we assimilate culture through contact with the minds of a vast number of people alive and dead. What we receive from others constitutes a debt, an obligation to give in return, to promote the common good of mankind, of our own nation and neighbourhood, and of the smaller groups to which we belong. Not to pull our weight is to revolt against reality and thus to maim our manhood. The virtue of justice speaks of law, and law is meant to serve the gospel. The love generated by the gospel is greater than law, but it does not contradict it. Paying debts comes before donations to charity.

Love takes the weight out of law. It infuses an element of spontaneity and delight into the discharge of duty. And the claims of love and justice unite in the so-called golden rule, 'Do to others what you would have them do to you'. Strictly this is a rule of justice, but it could hardly be obeyed without the impulse of love. For to carry it out in the spirit demands an imaginative sympathy, a power to stand in another's shoes which only love could teach. A large part of man's growth to maturity consists in the development of wider understanding and acceptance of his dependence on others and his debt to them. Part of this debt is that of respecting their dignity and freedom. A life committed to God is a life concerned to recognise and enhance the dignity of men.

The virtue of temperance points to a third sphere where discipline is needed, that of the things we enjoy. Understood in a narrow and negative way temperance can be repellent. Yet some degree of moderation and restraint is part of mature humanity. Pleasure in itself is innocent. It is the reward that accompanies the activities which nature intends. But if we pursue it as an end in itself we tend to damage both our own interests and those of other people. The habit of moderation enables a man to live at peace in himself. The ability to say 'no' to inclination enables him also to live more intensely, just as reliable brakes enable a driver to travel faster without undue risk. William James, the American psychologist, used to give this advice: 'Do every day something you don't like doing for no other reason than that you don't like doing it.' He likened the practice to the regular payment of insurance premiums. The small regular payments give a sense of security by guaranteeing large compensation in the event of fire. In the same way small daily acts of self-denial build up a reservoir of strength with which to meet big crises should they come.

The most important field of discipline is that of the attention. The power within limits to attend to what we choose is the central citadel of our freedom. It can be strengthened by training: there is the positive training of the power to concentrate and the power to imagine: there is the negative refusal to let the mind be captured by every picture or idea that solicits attention; and there is bodily discipline, such as fasting, which plays an important supporting role to the discipline of the mind. But in this sphere of discipline the right motive is everything. The psychologists warn us of the unconscious motives that can sometimes underlie self-denial. It may be an unacknowledged fear of our own dynamism, our aggression, or our sex desire; it may be the desire of masochistic pleasure from punishing ourselves. And the strength which comes from self-discipline can be acquired in order to dominate others. These warnings are important; but there are also good and realistic motives for the practice of self-discipline. Moderation helps the growth of freedom and humanity. Strength is good even though it may be abused, and men often fail in their good actions and enterprises for lack of the strength that discipline would have given. As Christ said to his disciples in Gethsemane, 'the spirit indeed is willing but the flesh is weak'.

A fourth field of discipline is indicated by the last of the cardinal virtues, fortitude. To live humanly in the world demands courage. Fortitude is the bodyguard of the other virtues, because they all need fortitude to make them secure. It may take as much courage to decide on and adhere to the right course when it is unpopular as it does to combat the tyrannies that ought to be resisted and the injustices which should be fought. Courage is needed to face the fears that unman us: the fear of unpopularity or hostility, the fear of ridicule or failure, the fear of loneliness, of boredom, of physical discomfort or of danger. Unfaced any of these fears (perhaps without my realising the fact) might lead me to evade my duty. Fortitude has also a close affinity with faith. The element of venture, of risk-taking, implicit in faith, requires and elicits the fighting spirit proper to man. 'Fear not, only believe.' 'Why are ye so fearful, O ye of little faith?'

The cardinal virtues point to four fields in which human life requires a certain discipline: the over-all direction of life, the debt owed to other people, the sphere of the enjoyable and the sphere of life's difficulties and dangers. The discipline of the cardinal virtues provides the sub-structure upon which the life of openness to God and man can rest. But it is no substitute for that life. It is by grace we are saved, not discipline. Yet discipline prepares for grace, and also provides the element of law and order both within our own beings and in our relations with others which grace can penetrate and transfigure.

Law and discipline are a means to the life open to God and to man that Christ taught, lived and makes possible for his disciples. But a fresh vision of Christ in relation to mankind is needed, if this possibility is to be widely realised today.

The New Testament acknowledges Christ as the Word of God who is the Light of all men everywhere; and Raymond Panikkar has written of the unknown Christ of Hinduism.[1] Christ must be seen not only as the fulfilment of Hindu aspirations but as the unknown inspiration of all that is true and valid in Buddhism and Islam, in Marxism and scientific Humanism. The new vision will be born, I believe of dialogue. Television and jet-travel are forcing world-wide dialogue upon us. Though this can be seen as a challenge to faith it is better understood as an opportunity to gain a larger vision of the universal Christ, the Word who addresses every man in his own language. A fresh vision of the universal Christ can awaken hope in the man of today, can instil a sense of new possibilities and a fresh purpose, can turn him in openness to God and to his fellows and to the community of faith in which this openness can best be realised, can indicate the worth-while goals to which he can direct the giant strength which science and technology have put at his disposal.

[1]Raymond Panikkar, *The Unknown Christ of Hinduism*, Darton, Longman & Todd 1965.

IN A CHANGING WORLD

NINE

Catholics in the Church of England

JOHN GUNSTONE

'The White City stadium was a great and inspiring sight on Sunday morning. I walked round the arena about eleven o'clock (half an hour before the service was timed to begin), and I calculated that forty-five thousand people were already in their seats. They had been pouring in from all parts of London for an hour. The tube trains were filled with men, women, and children, with modest badges on their button-holes or pinned to their dresses, and happy smiles of expectation on their faces. Never have I seen such a crowd so courteous and considerate. Owing to the skill and good humour of the army of stewards, seats were soon found, and while they waited the worshippers sang hymn after hymn with "go" and fervour, for Catholics have all the Englishman's love of hymn-singing. The threatened Protestant interrruption happily did not eventualise. Half a dozen "loyal Churchmen", with an entire disregard for decency, had secured badges and found places on the unreserved stand; but they were recognised by a steward of long experience, who dealt with them promptly and properly. He told the people in the adjacent seats who they were, and why they were there. He warned them that they would be carefully watched, that there were policemen on duty to prevent any brawling, and that unseemly conduct would not be tolerated. Three or four Protestant kites, with texts on them that I could not read, were flown over the Stadium, but the strings were cut by the White City authorities; and, while the choir was singing the Introit, a gentleman outside the White City protested through a loud-speaker. But he could have been heard by only a very few, and he was soon "moved on". And all was peace and unity and joy. At half-past eleven the singing ceased, and a great silence fell on the assemblage as the processions entered the arena. . . .'

So reported the *Church Times* on 21 July, 1933. The High Mass had been arranged at the White City to commemorate the centenary of the Oxford Movement; and for those who were there that Sunday morning it must have seemed that at long last the strife was o'er, the battle won. In spite of opposition from bishops, congregations and Kensitites, in spite of desertions to the Church of Rome, Anglo-Catholics, terrible as an army with banners, had risen up within the citadel of the established Church and within a hundred years claimed it for their own. Key parishes and important posts had fallen to their leaders, and the ancient faith was once more being proclaimed in England's green and pleasant land. No wonder the *Church Times* correspondent, swept up in the exuberance of the moment, saw the Bishop of St Albans' canopy-bearers in the procession as representatives of the 'thousands of young men and women, earnest, eager, sometimes not a little impatient, the living assurance of victory in the future'!

Like the rhythm of the tide, Anglo-Catholicism had surged through every nook and cranny of Anglican thought and life, cutting and shaping the Church of England and her sister Churches into the form they are today.

It recalled Anglicans to a more vivid awareness of themselves as one with that holy, catholic and apostolic community which they acknowledged in the creeds. The Church is more than merely an institution created by the gathering together of Christians; it is a sacred mystery, inaugurated and indwelt by God for the salvation of men. Anglo-Catholics believed passionately that their Church was in these islands the true successor to the Church of St Columba of Iona and

St Augustine of Canterbury, and much of their scholarship was directed towards demonstrating that the Prayer Book and Anglican formularies have maintained the orthodoxy of primitive and undivided Christendom. If the doctrine of the Church as the Body of Christ has dominated Anglican theology in the first half of the twentieth century, this is because that doctrine was revived by the Tractarians in the second half of the nineteenth.

As far as the ordinary layman of the Church of England was concerned, Anglo-Catholicism affected his quest for personal holiness, his taste in corporate worship, and his attitude towards the clergy.

Like other renewals, the Oxford Movement was inspired by a desire for holiness; but although this sprang from the devout evangelical background of the early Tractarians, it eventually took as its model the post-Tridentine spirituality of the Roman Church. A rule of life was its foundation, and on this was built up a system of set prayers and offices, formal meditation, spiritual direction and frequent confession, and regular attendance at the eucharist on weekdays as well as on Sundays. Retreats, devotions before the reserved sacrament, the veneration of Our Lady, vigils and fasts, pilgrimages and Stations of the Cross – such was the pattern of Anglo-Catholic devotion as it unfolded through the Church's year. Prayer manuals were legion, purchased from the tract-case at the back of the church. The Anglo-Catholic knew the Rosary and the *Angelus* by heart, and the Anglo-Catholic godfather bought his godchild the *English Missal* as a confirmation present.

The layman's taste in corporate worship was stirred by the ceremonial introduced by the High Churchmen to their services. When the disciples of the Tractarians began to interpret their principles in terms of parochial worship, robed choirs, surplices, vestments, ornaments and incense appeared, and everything was done to make the eucharist the focus of the cult. Anglo-Catholics became liturgical buccaneers, plundering the venerable treasuries of other

Christians for the adornment and enrichment of their own. The result was often bizarre, varying from the 'English' use of Percy Dearmer and the Alcuin Club to the Roman use of Adrian Fortescue and the Congregation of Rites, but it gave ordinary Anglicans a new vision of worship. The devout soul who was taught to look up when the bell rang for the elevation of the host, and the boy from the poorer household who served conscientiously Sunday by Sunday at the eleven o'clock High Mass, learnt what it means to adore a transcendent and glorious God; and the Church of England and the Anglican Communion would have been a very much impoverished community without their devotion.

Once the ritual squabbles had lost their bitterness, the Church came to realise the need for liturgical renewal, and it was the research of Anglo-Catholic scholars like F. E. Brightman and W. H. Frere that prepared the way for Prayer Book revision at home and overseas. A generation later Gabriel Hebert and Gregory Dix popularised the liturgical movement with *Liturgy and Society* (1936) and *The Shape of the Liturgy* (1954), books that can be found on the bookshelves of almost every vicar's study. If we are critical today of some aspects of older Anglo-Catholic ritual – the mock baroque and the neo-gothic settings, the non-communicating High Mass and the priest-centred performance of the rites – yet the experience we have gained has been invaluable. We should not be in a position to move on from *Series Two* towards authentic liturgies for modern man if it had not been for these experiments in reviving traditional ritual.

The layman's attitude towards his clergy was affected by the Tractarians. A Catholic view of the Church brought to the ordained ministry a professionalism and a priestliness unknown to Church of England parsons in recent ages. Then they had been family men with their own accepted and beneficent place in English society. Now they began to copy Roman clergy in outlook, manner, dress, and – in some cases – celibacy. The tremendous stress on the doctrine of the apostolic succession buttressed their authority and, with their training and disciplined life, the clergy acquired the character of professionals. Their business was to lead people to holiness, their cassock was their uniform. There was nothing amateurish in the way they conducted worship, instructed the young, ministered to the sick, and counselled the penitent. To be a member of an Anglo-Catholic congregation was to belong to a paternalistic yet dictatorial régime: what 'Father' said was gospel. When he presided at a solemn High Mass, the Anglo-Catholic priest symbolised his role in the life of the faithful: he was their mediator and intercessor, confessing for them, pleading for them, and – in the days before the parish communion – receiving holy communion for them.

But his position was sometimes self-contradictory. Claiming obedience to the Church from others, he occasionally had to disobey lawful authority himself. Perhaps the clergy – or, at any rate, the Anglican clergy – have never been as submissive to their superiors as canon law expects them to be, but Anglo-Catholicism brought with it an extreme form of casuistry in matters of worship and discipline which endeavoured to justify almost any innovation or policy. It may have been understandable in the circumstances of the past, but when every excuse has been made, it was hardly consistent with a Catholic doctrine of the Church. Some felt this acutely – and were received into the Roman fold.

Beyond the experience of the layman in the parish, Anglo-Catholicism has had far reaching effects on the Church at large. The ecumenical implications of the revived doctrine of the Church are yet to be worked out in our own times. While the vision of a reunited Christendom cannot be credited solely to the Anglo-Catholics, their interest in other 'branches' of the Catholic Church gave a decided impetus to the ecumenical movement from the Anglican side. The concern for reunion which has marked all Lambeth Conferences since they first met in 1867 was largely due to moderate Anglo-Catholic bishops from overseas, and it led in 1920 to the famous *Appeal to all Christian People*. The so-called 'Lambeth Quadrilateral' embodied in this Appeal was the product of that same moderate Anglo-Catholicism and, generally speaking, all the current schemes of reunion involving Anglicans and other Christians are attempts to put into practical effect the principles set out by it. There is some justification for the Evangelicals' complaint that the Anglican image in the eyes of other Churches is very largely an Anglo-Catholic one.

Anglo-Catholicism full-blown loved the sanctuary. But it loved also the world beyond. The experience of its priests in some of the worst slum parishes in England gave birth to a social awareness that was more than Christian good-neighbourliness. It ran like blood under the skin of Catholic theology. The doctrine of the Incarnation revealed the glory of the Church, but it also revealed the glory that is in man, whose nature has been united with the divine. From a practical concern for social justice – translated in recent years to the stand against apartheid in South Africa – Anglo-Catholics were led to a study of society as a lesson in God's ways among men. Sociology and its related studies were taken up by High Churchmen, such as the Christendom Group, and demonstrated in the Church Union's summer schools of sociology as means through which the Church could be more effective in her ministry and mission. It is not an exaggeration to say that the scientific approach to matters concerned with Church structures and strategy in the reports published by various official committees since the war, owes nearly everything to the pioneering work of Anglo-Catholic priest-sociologists in the first half of this century.

It was out of this social concern that the religious communities were founded in the Church of England. The first sisterhoods were established in the 1840s for work in poor parishes in London and Plymouth, and in 1868 B. F. Westcott preached a sermon at Harrow calling for 'a discipline which shall combine the sovereignty of soul of Antony, the social devotion of Benedict, the humble love of Francis, the matchless energy of the Jesuits, with faith that fears no trial, with hope that fears no darkness, with truth that fears no light'. One of his hearers was the youthful Charles Gore. Although the communities looked to the religious orders of the Roman Catholic Church for models – variously interpreted by the scholarship of John Mason Neale or the romanticism of Joseph Leycester Lyle – they contrived to give a distinctly Anglican ethos to their lives. Once targets of abuse, the religious communities have an honoured place in the Church of England, and many feel that they are the most important contribution made by Anglo-Catholicism to the witness of their Church.

The Church of England's parochial system is a walled garden in which movements and parties may prosper. The Tractarian appeal was to the parochial clergy (the first tract was called *Thoughts on the Ministerial Commission respectfully addressed to the Clergy*), and the appeal was highly successful. Guarded by the freehold and an antiquated machinery of clerical discipline, Anglo-Catholic vicars were virtually bishops in their own parishes. The curates and nuns were their diocesan staff; the parochial church council was regarded as an unnecessary evil. In his *Sociology of English Religion* (1967) David Martin has a pen sketch of the typical High Church clergyman: 'sartorially correct even down to the biretta and the kind of rimless glasses favoured by cardinals . . . combining the priestly turbulence which terrorises bishops with an unblinking assertion of ecclesiastical authority.' The official diocese was viewed with indifference, suspicion, or even hostility. If the bishop was invited to visit the parish, it was only to administer confirmation (with cope and mitre if he could be persuaded to wear them). No preachers were allowed in the church except those who could be trusted to teach the faith – members of the religious communities for missions and Holy Week, friends of the vicar from the Federation of Catholic Priests, and visitors from overseas vetted by a reliable missionary society (more often the Universities' Mission to Central Africa rather than the suspiciously comprehensive Society for the Propagation of the Gospel!) As a form of congregational connectionalism of a dissenting vintage, it would be difficult to find a more efficient example than the High Church parishes of the Church of England.

To serve this Church-within-the-Church there were the voluntary societies and the theological colleges. The societies, like the Society of SS. Peter and Paul Ltd, the Society for the Maintenance of the Faith, and the Church Union, proliferated to promote Catholic causes and to defend victimised members. Arranging retreats, publishing pamphlets, overseeing elections for the Convocations and the Church Assembly, providing Catholic answers to current questions, financing the installation of tabernacles and aumbries, organising conferences – these and many other projects initiated by the societies wove the Anglo-Catholic network and toughened its fibre. The 'Tractarian' theological colleges maintained the supply of deacons. The working party which produced *Theological Colleges for Tomorrow* (1968) has identified twelve in England, the first – Chichester – being founded in 1839. As independent bodies (like the private patrons of parishes) they could choose whom they wished and train them more or less as they liked. Mirfield and Kelham provided young men from the poorer areas with a training for ordination in the days before grants were available.

The system made it possible to be a certain kind of Christian in the established Church. With an ear to the Anglo-Catholic grapevine, or armed with the *Church Traveller's Directory* which classified churches like hotels ('DSCR' was four-star rating: 'daily mass, sung eucharist on Sundays, confessions and reservation'!) the High Church layman could spend the whole of his worshipping existence in the parishes of his own tradition. As for the Anglo-Catholic ordinand, he joined the Anglo-Catholic society at his university, went to an Anglo-Catholic theological college, prepared for his ordination examinations by reading Anglo-Catholic books, served his title under an Anglo-Catholic vicar, was appointed to Anglo-Catholic parishes, and, when he died, benefited from all the last rites that Anglo-Catholicism was able to offer him. Comprehensiveness was anathema. He was a party man through and through. Not even the Church of Rome in its most illiberal, ultramontane days shielded its children more efficiently from Evangelicalism, modernism, radicalism, or whatever other -ism was threatening the peace of the Christian fellowship.

Such, then, was Anglo-Catholicism in its triumphalist phase. But not any longer. The movement has lost its momentum in the muds and eddies of post-war life and theology, and the call to 'Catholic loyalties' no longer rallies an identifiable body of Anglican opinion that can speak with one voice. Older priests and laymen who remember former days say that a glory has departed from the Church of England. The design on the covers of the latest batch of Church Union pamphlets tells its own story: a fat question mark squats behind the puzzled title, *What's Happening . . .?*

At its simplest level it has been the very success of Anglo-Catholicism that has absorbed so much of its interest and verve. When they had to fight to do the kind of things that they thought a Catholic ought to be allowed to do in the Church of England, then a spirit of rebellious righteousness drove zealous supporters to extreme lengths. Many suffered a long exile in a downtown parish because of episcopal disfavour. Now those prejudices have gone. The Church of England has become a permissive society. When Ian Paisley comes over from Ireland to parade his anti-papalist banners as anti-ritual Anglicans did in the latter half of the last century, every Church of Englander dismisses him as a psychopathic case. We have lived so close to the changes of the past two or three generations that we have not realised how remarkable they have been.

Furthermore, Anglo-Catholicism has never been so united a party as it is sometimes assumed. From the edge of the movement where priests and congregations have considered themselves but half-a-step removed from Rome, there has spread out a very broad variety of High Churchmen, the majority of whom have thought of themselves first as Anglicans and only secondly as Catholics. It is these moderates who have exercised a greater influence than any other group in parochial, diocesan and provincial affairs. Aided by such agencies as the *Church Times* and the Parish and People Movement, they have sponsored nearly everything that has been achieved in the Church of England in the way of administrative reform, pastoral reorganisation and liturgical renewal. Indeed, it might be argued that the energies of Anglo-Catholics have been exhausted in trying to haul the Church of England into the twentieth century by means of the committees and commissions that have littered the ecclesiastical scene since the formation of the Church Assembly.

But there have been other factors in the decline of Anglo-Catholicism; and one of these is the increasing mobility of English society. As we have noted, the strength of the party was in the stability and inviolability of the parochial system. During recent years, however, the population of this country has become more fluid. Urban slums have been pulled down and rebuilt with all the consequent dislocation of family life; the expansion of industry and the spread of the civil service has meant that people have to move their homes frequently; the social trek along the commuter roads and railways leading out of London and the big cities has caused a whole series of local congregations to disintegrate. Then there was the destruction caused by the winter of the bombs, 1940–41. During the blitz London boroughs like Stepney lost more than half their parish churches – many of them famous Anglo-Catholic centres – and few of them have been rebuilt. The people who worshipped in them have either died or gone to live elsewhere.

One might have thought that the new estates and the new towns would have provided the opportunity for an Anglo-Catholic revival, for the Church of England has embarked on a massive church extension programme in these areas; but this has not been the case. The younger clergy who were sent to work in such places found that it was futile to try and transplant the paraphernalia of Anglo-Catholicism into the temporary church or the dual-purpose building they used for their services. It was one thing to convert a flourishing town parish into an Anglo-Catholic community; it was something quite different to draw together into Christian fellowship the small band of Anglicans from varying backgrounds who gathered together for the parish communion on a new estate. In this situation the congregational connectionalism on which the Anglo-Catholics depended broke down. For the first time in their lives, High Churchmen in the new towns found themselves obliged to worship with families from Evangelical or Broad Church traditions. Some could not face the challenge and took the bus or car elsewhere. Others opted out of Church life altogether. But many stayed, discovering a domestic ecumenical movement within the Church of England; and it is from such situations that many of the most fruitful experiments in the Church's ministry and mission have sprung. Attempts have been made to seek afresh what it means to be baptised into the Christian fellowship, to assemble for the eucharist, and to manifest the life of a Christian in the midst of secular society. As a result, the concern of the priest and the layman in the new area has been for things like house meetings and projects of neighbourhood involvement rather than the elaborate sung mass and the High Church society. Theirs is a truly Catholic witness, but not in the forms associated with Anglo-Catholicism in the past.

Another factor is the change brought about by the flowering of biblical theology, historical criticism and liturgical research. These studies have led Anglo-Catholics (together with nearly all other Christians) to re-examine their assumptions and to embark on radical revisions. While it was the work of Anglo-Catholics like Sir Edwyn Hoskins to teach that the gospel and the Catholic Church are one, yet this was

H

not done without a mollifying effect on accepted Tractarian dogmas concerning the Christian community, its ministry and its sacramental signs. Book like G. W. H. Lampe's *The Seal of the Spirit* (1951), S. L. Greenslade's *Schism in the Early Church* (1953) and Francis Clark's *Eucharistic Sacrifice and the Reformation* (1960) have made it impossible for Anglo-Catholics to be so doctrinaire about the necessity of confirmation, the error of intercommunion, and the interpretation of the Prayer Book Communion service as a sacrificial rite. Nor has the *Apostolic Ministry* (1964), the last *magnum opus* in the Tractarian tradition, escaped undamaged. Only recently Frans Josef van Beeck, a Roman Catholic scholar, after summarising Gregory Dix's famous contribution on the ministry of the early Church, to that symposium concluded that the Anglican Benedictine only 'arrives at little more than a most interesting hypothesis.' No wonder we sometimes feel that we must either give up or begin all over again!

Changes in attitudes outside the Church are also telling against Anglo-Catholicism. Since the advent of television and the increase in mass advertising, ordinary people tend to be more critical in their approach to topics in which they feel every man has a right to his own opinion – notably religion. Anglo-Catholicism presented Christian teaching logically and with conviction: yet dogma expounded lucidly and correctly today so often sounds dead, and the questions people ask are not answered so easily from the textbooks of doctrinal and moral theology. Anglo-Catholic concern for ceremonial seems unrelated to the Jesus Christ so many want to find and serve. The authoritarianism of the Anglo-Catholic clergyman clashes with the independence of the contemporary mind, and modern man is much more at ease with his vicar if he calls him by his Christian name than if he addresses him as 'Father' (which is why the cassock is worn less in the street nowadays and the clerical collar is being replaced by a tie). Our image of the Church, it seems, must change.

And yet another factor is the advance towards Christian

unity. In the former ecumenical scene, dominated as it was by Churches of the Reformed tradition, Anglo-Catholics could always be expected to take a stand on certain essentials of faith and order. No matter how far liberal or evangelical Anglicans were prepared to waive the Prayer Book requirements on episcopal ordination and episcopal confirmation, a solid Anglo-Catholic block barred the way to any compromise.

Then came the inauguration of the Church of South India. The debates in the Convocations in 1955 were a moment of truth for Anglo-Catholics, creating the same kind of crisis which the proposals for the Jerusalem bishopric had created for their Tractarian forefathers a century before. The question was put abruptly to them: How far were they prepared to stand by their principles against the undoubted wishes of their brethren in India who formed a tiny proportion of a small Christian witness in an overwhelmingly non-Christian country? The solid Anglo-Catholic block cracked. a contingent from the 'Annunciation Group' (which had formed originally to protest against a united act of worship in Hyde Park!) was lost to the Church of Rome, but the majority accepted with varying degrees of uneasiness the proposals for limited intercommunion. Although the crisis affected the Anglican-Methodist negotiations which began a few years later (and started them off on the assumption that the 'C.S.I. method' of reunion would not be acceptable in England), Anglo-Catholics had been forced to compromise. They had had to acknowledge that Anglicans could be in communion with a Christian community which recognised (even temporarily) ministers who had not been ordained by a bishop; and that acknowledgment made their former stand illogical.

While the Roman Catholic Church remained aloof and immobile, Anglo-Catholics always entered ecumenical discussions at a grave disadvantage, because they tended to feel that they must carry the burden of Catholic witness alone. It is true that the involvement of the Orthodox with the

World Council of Churches did something to relieve this pressure; but the Orthodox do not represent the great Christian Church of the West, and in every move in the ecumenical game Anglo-Catholics were acutely aware of the cold, critical eye of Rome upon them.

It was a foster-mother-fixation, a curious love-hate emotion, for Anglo-Catholics have to some extent depended on Rome's aloofness and immobility as a means of self-identification. Post-Vatican I Catholicism enabled High Churchmen to take their bearings, and, comparing papalism with their own form of Catholicism, to demonstrate how and why theirs was a more excellent way. The promulgation of the dogma of the Assumption during the Marian Year of 1951 seemed to confirm their position. This, they could say, is what happens when you over-rationalise and over-centralise ecclesiastical authority: you are left with nothing but papal infallibility.

Shortly after this came the first signs that Rome was beginning to move. It was not much to begin with – simply the constitution *Christus Dominus* (1953) relaxing the eucharistic fast – but suddenly Anglo-Catholics found their compasses going crazy. Fasting communion had been their eleventh commandment, and they could hardly believe that it was lawful to receive communion after tea. The Confraternity of the Blessed Sacrament, the watchdog of Anglican eucharistic discipline, was smitten with paranoia, with some members wanting to keep the high road of tradition and others wanting to take the low road with Pius XII. But if *Christus Dominus* was a shaking of the foundations, Vatican II and its aftermath was a veritable earthquake. Many of the problems now being faced by Roman Catholics as they seek to find God's way for their Church in the modern world are similar to those faced by Anglicans, and the inability of Roman Catholics to provide infallible answers to those problems has stripped Anglo-Catholics of the reflected security that they once enjoyed. What can we say, for example, about the Free Churches and their ministers when

Pope John had called non-Roman communities *fratres separati* and Pope Paul *communiones christianae*? If we share with them a common baptism, why cannot we share in a common eucharist? If a Christian group is in some way an *ecclesia*, then surely its ministers are in some way apostolic?

So what of the future? Will an old guard soldier bravely on into the 1970s and 1980s until the last six candlesticks are sold to the collector and the last edition of the *English Missal* lies forgotten at the back of the sacristy cupboard? Was Anglo-Catholicism after all just another phase in English culture which, like romanticism, is fading into history?

Certain expressions of Anglo-Catholicism are certainly dead or dying – its sense of exclusiveness, its finical legalism, and its demand for a type of theological and liturgical conformity. But, valid and necessary though they may have been at the time, these were only expressions: the true spirit of the movement is still very much alive. If *Catholicity* (1947) is acknowledged as the authentic voice of the party in the post-war period, then the last two decades have seen a growing response to its authors' appeal for a *wholeness* of Christian faith and practice. One only had to read the *Statement* issued by the National Evangelical Anglican conference at Keele in 1967 to see how Catholic attitudes are reflected in the ideas of that vigorous group. Anglo-Catholics owe this concern for wholeness, not only to our reverence for what is 'Catholic' and traditional, but also to our experience of living in a Christian community where we have to accept the tensions between ourselves and Evangelicals and others in charity, and seek to make them creative in the Church's life. The difference between ourselves and our High Church forefathers – if any – is that we find our feet set in a larger room than many of them imagined.

With such a heritage Anglo-Catholics should, like the men of Issachar, have an understanding of the times to know what Israel ought to do. There is more than a breath of prophecy in the ancestry of our party. As members of a Christian community which, despite its comprehensiveness, is learning to grow together, we are in a strategic position to be used even further by God, provided we are open-eyed and open-minded to all that is going on around us. The other essays in this book illustrate various ways in which Anglo-Catholics react to this situation. I will simply indicate two or three areas of Church life where I think Anglo-Catholics have particularly important contributions to make, bearing in mind what I have sketched about their recent past.

As the frontier between the Church and society is being shortened and more clearly defined in the progress of secularisation, the Church herself has become more aware of what Vatican II called 'her solidarity with the entire human family', and this in turn has brought about far-reaching changes in her understanding of her mission. The Church is seen less as an empirical institution set up over against the world and more as a sacrament of Christ's presence within the world – a sacrament which crowns the Christian presence in society itself. As a result, the focus of Catholic attention has shifted from assertions about the ordained ministry to questions about the ministry of the men and women who make up the local congregations. These have now become the foremost figures in the Church's mission as they fulfil that prophetic, priestly and royal task for which they have been anointed by God.

In seeking answers to these questions the Anglo-Catholic is able to draw on wide and varied resources to supplement the studies pursued by his fellow-Anglicans. Out of habit he looks first at the Roman Catholic Church. There he sees in the crucial chapter on 'the new people of God' in Vatican II's *Constitution on the Church* the scriptural and theological truths of Church membership and of the laity as gifted by the Holy Spirit for the building up of the Christian community. He looks next at the Free Churches and learns from their forms of a priesthood of the laity exercised in different structures. He also ponders on the phenomenal success of the Pentecostal Churches and the emphasis they place on the *charismata* (it is, incidentally, significant that the 'neo-pentecostalism' of the older Churches in the U.S.A. has attracted sympathetic interest among High Church Episcopalians). And he relates all this to his own situation in the Church of England and to ecumenical planning for mission. Here is a wholeness of outlook that seeks to include all in dialogue and that is typical of true Catholicism.

The questions that are being asked about the role of the ordained ministry in the Church might be interpreted as a negation of Anglo-Catholic teaching; but in fact these are questions which beg for distinctly Catholic answers. The great stress High Churchmen have given to the apostolic nature of the ministry has to be applied to the search for more varied and flexible forms of ministry needed in the contemporary Church. The Vatican has recently taken steps to revive a permanent diaconate and to give to catechists and lay leaders a wider responsibility. The 1968 Lambeth Conference adopted similar measures. In the Church of England there are many interesting experiments, from the lay elderships to the schemes for part-time and worker-priests in various parts of the country. To these experiments Anglo-Catholics can bring their own insights into the nature of the ordained ministry and from the past recover precedents which will help us revise our institutions on scriptural and traditional patterns. Fortunately most Anglo-Catholic colleges seem to be joining in the discussion about the shape of clergy training for the ministry of tomorrow.

Anglo-Catholic teaching on the nature of the episcopate and the priesthood exalted the status of the diocese and the parish to an undue degree just at the time when these medieval institutions were becoming increasingly irrelevant to modern society. The fact that Anglo-Catholicism took firm root in the parish added to the tendency. This must now be modified. Pastoral theologians have in recent years re-shaped the theology of parish and diocese, demonstrating that the *paroikia* must not be thought of in geographical terms and that *episcope* and *diakonia* are not necessarily restricted to men (or women) holding particular kinds of offices. Furthermore, sociological studies substantiate what many are discovering through practical experience – that the small group, with leaders and members sensitive to the dynamics that activate its life, is the most effective unit for many of the things that Christians should be doing together. If the local congregation is to pray together, learn together, serve one another, and engage in charitable and evangelistic enterprises, then the small group will become the basic unit of the local Church. In moving away from the traditional structures to the more complex and multiform groupings of the local Church needed in modern society, AngloCatholics from their understanding of the ministry will be able to give invaluable assistance in guiding these new 'parishes' in matters such as their discipline, their eucharistic assemblies, their clergy, and their relationships with each other and with the universal Church.

Inspired by the example of the Roman Catholic orders, the religious communities are embarking on radical reviews of their lives, to reinterpret B. F. Westcott's picture of an Antony, a Benedict, a Francis and a Jesuit in contemporary terms; and this may mean shedding much that they have valued in the past (including, in some cases, the religious habit!) But more significant feature of Church life today is the rapid spread of another kind of religious community, a more informal affair modelled in the simplest way on the apostolic fellowship described in Acts 2. These new communities generally consist of groups of families and friends who want to be more committed to Jesus Christ and a common life and who set themselves up in large vicarages or country houses, living under a simple rule as a venture of faith. Lee Abbey and Scargill are the largest and most well-known, but there are many others, often without a thought of an official title or a formal foundation. Like the older communities, they are also indicative of a silent rebellion – a rebellion against the transitoriness of ordinary parish life and against the disintegration of the extended family in modern society. Here, then, is a movement which is very close to the heart of Anglo-Catholic aspirations.

Whatever its form, the local Church is called to proclaim the gospel to the world around it, and so she must take note of the work done by those pioneers whose lonely and often dangerous task it is to spy out the land ahead and around the main body of the Christian army. The paperback views of these radical theologians frequently disturb the traditionalists and the outcries against the 'new Reformation' reveal how their role is misunderstood. The Anglo-Catholic's concern for wholeness must lead him to promote the dialogue between the progressives and the conservatives, a dialogue which sidesteps denominational boundaries and in which the participants find allies in unexpected quarters. This is, or should be, a familiar role for Anglo-Catholics. Concern for tradition is not the same as anti-radicalism. *Essays Catholic and Critical* (1927) was a successful attempt to bring together the critical-liberal movement of the 1920s with the 'keener discernment of the supernatural element in religion' which the contributors detected among their contemporaries (the preface of this book is worth reading if one believes that 'the spectacle of a disordered and impoverished Christendom' is something new). Similar Catholic bridge-building is necessary now. Between the theology of the secular city and that increasing unsteady corpus of doctrine known as 'orthodoxy' there is a great gulf fixed; but it is not the same gulf as that which separated the rich man from Lazarus, and it is not so great that Anglo-Catholics find themselves on one side only. The fact that many of the present-day Anglican radicals come from a High Church background (*Prism* begat *New Christian*!) is encouraging. At least our *avant-garde* should understand the kind of questions we want to ask!

And we must not feel rejected if modern Christians find less inspiration in the traditional Anglo-Catholic spirituality. Our response to the Crucified can be demonstrated in other ways besides taking part in the Stations of the Cross, and for many today Malcolm Boyd's *Are You Running With Me,*

Jesus? articulates a more meaningful devotion to Our Lord than the twelve o'clock *Angelus*. If we sometimes dig our toes in, it will only be to remind our progressive brethren that, if God is immanent in his world, he is still transcendent over it; that there is a time for contemplation as well as activity, for retreat as well as involvement; and that we can never really resolve in this life that other tension which comes from Christian commitment, the tension between the joy of freedom and the acceptance of ascesis. But there will be nothing new in these reminders: they are necessary in every generation, and they are as old as Abraham.

Contemporary Anglo-Catholicism, therefore, has a mediatorial and interpretative role to play in the Church. If Anglo-Catholics are to fulfil this role adequately they will need the assistance of one independent society with some full-time staff. Free of the limitations inevitably imposed by ecclesiastical officialdom, such a society could feed information into the movement and initiate projects for the benefit of its members and for the benefit of the Church as a whole. In recent years the Church Union, through its conferences, committees and publications, has developed into this kind of an organisation, and if other High Church societies could be persuaded to accept a merger with it, then a good deal of unnecessary wastage and duplication would be avoided.

This is not, perhaps, the role we have known in the past, but the principle is the same – the proclamation of the whole gospel of God. Though the liturgy may be different and the style of pastoral authority may change, yet the Anglo-Catholic will insist on the primacy of worship and the necessity of obedience, for it is still God's world we live in and it is still in God's Church that we are saved. If the High Mass at the White City stadium is seen in retrospect as an unwitting requiem for the end of the Anglo-Catholic triumphalist era, we can reflect that there is no resurrection without a death, no reconciliation without a sacrifice. As the Catholicism of Charles Gore and Henry Scott Holland was different from that of the Tractarians, so contemporary Anglo-Catholicism is different from theirs. It just takes a little time for all of us to realise this.

In July 1967 Hugh Bishop, Superior of the Community of the Resurrection, Mirfield, gave the inaugural address at a conference on the religious life held in Oxford. The conference was summoned to discuss the implications of the times for the members of the older Anglican religious communities, and his final words might well have been addressed to any Anglo-Catholic today:

'In one sense, of course, we must treasure the past and carry it with us into the future, for the past is part of us and it has made us what we are. But we must never cling to the past or try to live in the past, when the Spirit is leading us on. So the word of God spoken through Moses to the children of Israel at a turning point in their history is the word of God to us today: *Speak unto the children that they go forward.* They obeyed, and out of their obedience their deliverance and the fulfilment of all God's promises to them came. But the fact remains that the journey across the desert was still a hard one and often a wearisome one and there were times when they became *much discouraged because of the way.* Yet we are told that as they journeyed, when night came *they pitched their tents towards the sun-rising.* So, please God, will we pitch ours.'

FURTHER READING

ROGER LLOYD, *The Church of England 1900–1965*, S.C.M. Press
1966

HORTON DAVIES, *Worship and Theology in England: The
Ecumenical Century 1900–1965*, Oxford 1965

GEORGE TAVARD, *The Quest for Catholicity*, Burns Oates, 1963

A. M. RAMSEY, *From Gore to Temple*, Longmans 1960

NICOLAS MOSLEY, *A Life of Raymond Raynes*, Faith Press 1961

ROSE MACAULAY, *Letters to a Friend, Last Letters to a Friend*,
and *Letters to a Sister*, Constance Babington Smith (ed),
Collins 1961–1964

Fr Bishop's address to the 1967 Oxford Conference for
Religious is printed in the Community of the Resurrection's
journal, *CR*, No. 258 (Michaelmas 1967)

TEN

Catholics in the World Church

MARK GIBBARD, S.S.J.E.

Challenge of the Present

When a high Anglican friend of mine heard that I was preparing this chapter, he wrote, 'To be a Catholic is to be committed to ecumenical action and thus to enduring a situation of anomalies and risks.' He was right; for, if we are engaged in mission in the world of today and the swiftly changing Church, we are bound to be faced with 'anomalies and risks'. This is because our outlook has been moulded by systems of theological thinking and by patterns of Church and ministry, which were formulated to meet needs far back in the past. Christopher Butler, the Roman Catholic auxiliary Bishop of Westminster, for example, has declared that 'a problem for theological developments which have become overdue' has been sharply raised by the Vatican Council II's recognition of the ecumenical movement as 'fostered by the grace of the Holy Spirit'[1] Students of Christian thought, both Catholic and Protestant, can recall in the history of the Church other periods of theological reconstruction. There have been times, when the setting of Church life has been altered and when the implications of God's disclosure in the scriptures have been freshly grasped. We may be living at the dawn of such a time.

But perhaps my friend did not choose the right word, when he wrote, 'enduring anomalies and risks'. It may be wise for the sake of some greater future good to 'accept'

[1]B. C. Butler, *The Theology of Vatican II*, Darton, Longman & Todd 1967, p. 116.

anomalies and risks, but to speak of 'enduring' them smacks of nostalgia for the past and of a general deploring of the present. I for one could never share this mood. The founder and inspirer of my religious community, Richard Meux Benson, said:

'A member of this community needs to be specially a man – not simply of the day, but a man of the moment, a man precisely up to the mark of the times. This makes him – so far from being the traditional imitator of bygone days – most especially a man of the present moment and its life. His duties throw him entirely into the interests of the present moment. Eternity is in that moment, and all the energies which are given to eternity are given through that moment. He therefore reviews calmly, dispassionately, dutifully, all the phenomena of the age in which he lives. He does not review them as things to deplore, but as things to rejoice in, and as things to be acted upon.'[1]

Nor does any '*enduring* of anomalies and risks', which is a consequence of undue attachment to the past, ring true to the New Testament. Paul wrote of his past attitude to the law and his former legal rectitude:

'All such assets I have written off because of Christ. I would say more. I count everything sheer loss, because all is far outweighed by the gain of knowing Christ Jesus my Lord, for whose sake I did in fact lose everything. I count it so much garbage, for the sake of gaining Christ and finding myself incorporate in him'

(Phil. 3:5–9).

This was how the apostle in his day gained that flexibility essential to his mission as he moved from a rather static Judaea into the shifting cosmopolitan world of the Mediterranean. Catholics and Protestants in our day remind us that we are a pilgrim Church; we need now the audacity of Abraham.

[1] R. M. Benson, *Instructions on the Religious Life*, Mowbray 1951, iii, p.88.

'By faith Abraham obeyed the call to go out to a land destined for himself and his heirs, and left home without knowing where he was to go. By faith he settled as an alien in the land promised him, living in tents.'

(Heb. 11:8–9).

Mission now seems to involve 'living in tents', not cluttered up with needless impedimenta from the past, learning from precedent, but never bound by precedent. 'Christ sets us free, to be free men' (Gal. 5:1). This language about 'enduring of anomalies and risks' hardly fits in with what Christ himself said about mission:

'Come with me, and I will make you fishers of men. And at once they left their nets.' . . . 'Nothing for the journey beyond a stick: no bread, no pack, no money in their belts.' . . . 'You neglect the commandment of God, in order to maintain the tradition of men.' . . . 'Anyone who wishes to be a follower of mine must leave self behind; he must take up his cross, and come with me.' . . . 'Go, sell everything you have, and give to the poor, and you will have riches in heaven; and come, follow me.'

(Mark 1:17; 6:8; 7:8; 8:34; 10:21)

Granted Christ said these things to individuals, yet Churches are composed of individuals; so what does all this imply for our Churches today and for movements within them? What in particular is our Lord saying through these words to that Catholic movement, which has for a century brought strength and devotion to many parts of the Anglican communion? This is for some of us a very personal question, for it has been through that movement that we have received our knowledge and love of Christ himself.

I can only put up a *ballon d'essai*, which commits no one except myself; nor are these more than very tentative suggestions about our mission today. How can we 'live in tents', *treasuring what is 'of faith'*, and letting if necessary the rest go? Committed to Christ, crucified and risen, but not to much else.

'The cross is the place where the unity of the Church is a deep and present reality, and where the Church is already showing the peace of God and the bread of heaven to the nations of mankind.'[1]

Contribution of Anglican Catholics

Anglican Catholics, followers of the Oxford movement, have already made a great contribution to the ecumenical movement by stressing that the ultimate aim must be the kind of organic unity of the Church we see in the New Testament. They stressed, long before the Orthodox and Roman Catholic observers came into the ecumenical discussions, that the mere federation and co-operation of Churches is not enough. This point has now been accepted on various grounds by many Protestants. Canon Max Warren, lately General Secretary of the Church Missionary Society, has paid tribute to what Anglican Catholics have done.

'The Oxford Movement served to present a timely reminder that co-operation alone leaves too many questions unanswered. The Oxford men asked the direct question, "What is the unity we seek?" The particular answer they gave is nothing like as important as the fact that they asked the question. It was a question which was to have the effect of a ricochet on the subsequent history of the ecumenical movement.[2]'

What further contribution can high Anglicans bring to the ecumenical movement and the Church of the future? Not, I think, 'Anglicanism' as an integrated coherent system (was it ever this?), but certain gifts, characteristically though not exclusively Anglican, which in experience have been found to bring men to Christ the redeemer and integrator of the world. I would single out three.

The first is a quality of pastoral care, varying in details with the centuries, but appearing in Chaucer's poor parson of

[1]'Through Mission to Unity', in P. Gardner-Smith (ed), *The Roads Converge*, Arnold 1963, p. 205.
[2]A. M. Ramsey, *The Gospel and the Catholic Church*, Longmans 1956, p 9

the town, in George Herbert, in Father Wainwright and in
Father Basil Jellicoe – a quality which has been rooted,
under Christ, in our understanding of the historic ministry.
This has been sensed by other Churches. In Australia, for
example, the Presbyterians, Congregationalists and Methodists proposed to come together into a Church having the
historic episcopate. Their negotiators did not suggest accepting bishops as a move in ecumenical bargaining to bring
the Anglicans into the plan, for the Anglicans are not at
present involved: rather the representatives of these three
non-episcopal Churches wished for bishops as *pastores
pastorum*, because they were agreed that '*episcope* (oversight),
exercised *personally*, is part of God's purpose' for his Church,
and that this personal oversight is vital not only in the local
congregations, but at all levels of Church life.

The second gift is certain insights into corporate worship.
These have always been potentially present in our Book of
Common Prayer, but we have recently rediscovered them.
The most notable of these is our understanding of the
eucharistic liturgy in which Christ, crucified, risen and
glorified, feeds us with his double feast of Word of God and
of the Bread of Life; and Christ does this, as we now see more
clearly, through the royal priesthood of all the faithful with
the set-apart ministry fulfilling its integral function and vocation. It is because the High Anglicans in Ghana are convinced
that they have these treasures of pastoral care and of worship
to share with non-Anglicans, that they have, after some
initial hesitation, undertaken to enter a united Church where
they will be greatly outnumbered by Presbyterians and
Methodists.

The third gift which Anglican Catholics have to share with
others is a theological freedom, which does not uproot itself
from religious tradition and experience. (The dangers,
spiritual and psychological, which such uprooting might
produce, are well known.) Along with a sane respect for
tradition, we have the possibility of a sensitive response to the
present leading of the Spirit; we do not have that over-

concern, which Roman Catholics, and even liberal Roman Catholics, often seem to have for the Church's reputation and consistency at almost any cost. This blending of freedom with tradition has been seen in *Lux Mundi*, in the works of Bishop Gore, and in *Essays Catholic and Critical*, to say nothing of our share in English biblical scholarship and in the more positive aspects of the 'new theology'.

These gifts are by no means ours alone; they are in other Churches too, particularly in parts of the modern Roman Catholic Church. Unfortunately we have a way of making our gifts look rather dull and dowdy, like jewels in antique settings. But if we are going to polish and reset them for the good of the whole Church, we shall best do so in dialogue with other Christians. For this we need some agility, the art of travelling light and of living in tents. This is part of our ecumenical vocation.

Anglican Catholics and the Ecumenical Movement

To join in ecumenical negotiations is another part of our vocation. We need wise judgment, but perhaps we have been over-cautious and too slow for our times.

An atlas of the modern world is soon out of date. The new maps of the Church began to be drawn on 27 September 1947, when in St George's Cathedral, Madras, the Church of South India was born. Anglicans united with Methodists, Presbyterians and Congregationalists. Senior ministers of these other Churches were consecrated into the historic succession of bishops. All future ordinations, they had agreed, were to be by bishops. But all present ministers went forward into the service of the new Church without any conditional ordination or any service for the unification of these ministries. There was indeed a 'gentleman's agreement' that any congregation could demand an episcopally ordained minister. Yet in the eyes of many Anglicans, and of the Orthodox and Roman Catholics, it was a strange anomaly to have in a Church episcopally ordained and non-episcopally ordained ministers side by side, even though the latter would obviously be a decreasing proportion. It was not surprising that High Anglicans like myself were uneasy, to put it mildly, about this anomaly: but our deeper concern was that some of the gifts of our Catholic tradition might disappear in what then looked like a pan-Protestant merger. At the 1948 Lambeth Conference one hundred and thirty-five bishops were ready to regard CSI as an integral part of the one Church and to urge that those who had been consecrated or ordained since the union should be accepted throughout the Anglican communion; but understandably ninety-four bishops were not ready for this. In 1950 the convocations of the English clergy were in a similar dilemma.

About this time a Benedictine monk in Rome, rather to my surprise, told me he thought that we Anglican Catholics should go out to CSI and make our contribution to it; I did not then realise what sensible advice that was nor how warmly our help would be welcomed in India. But a few years later many clergy with Catholic sympathies spoke in convocation in favour of recognising CSI and in 1955 a wide measure of intercommunion was agreed on between the two Churches. These clergy had changed their minds because they saw how the new Church was developing; and this is now even clearer. Of its eucharistic liturgy Père Louis Bouyer has written:

'It is much superior to the Prayer Book of the Church of England both on account of its traditional character and its theological soundness.'[1]

Of its ordinal the late Professor E. C. Ratcliff of Cambridge wrote:

'Any Church of the Anglican Communion proposing to revise its ordination rites will turn for guidance to the rites of the Church of South India.'[2]

[1] *Theology*, Jan. 1956, p. 4.
[2] *Theology*, Jan. 1960, pp. 7–15.

The synod of CSI in 1964 gave a warm welcome to a report on the episcopate by its theological committee, which stated:

'Our experience so far goes to show that episcopacy is not only an effective instrument for deepening unity within the Church, not only the form of ministry most likely to establish wider unity with other Churches: but a ministry blessed by God's grace with such positive good that we are determined to hold to its ourselves, commend it to others and preserve it in any union with other Churches.'

Time has proved the CSI has no desire to be a pan-Protestant Church and that the declaration in its Constitution is sincere:

'The final aim must be union in the universal Church of all who acknowledge the name of Christ; and the test of all local schemes of union is that they should express locally the principle of the great catholic unity of the Body of Christ.'

It was presumably because CSI wished to draw upon the Catholic tradition of the life of prayer that their bishops invited me to conduct in 1963–64 retreats for their dioceses. Incidentally when I stayed with Bishop Chellappa at Madras, I used each morning to walk across the lawns from his house for mattins and eucharist in the gleaming white St George's Cathedral where the new Church had been inaugurated; I could make my communion frequently in South India and I had no difficulty in going to confession; at the CSI synod I heard its liturgical committee being instructed to draw up a form for sacramental confession. By the time of my visit 84 per cent of their clergy had been episcopally ordained. Like other Churches CSI has its weaknesses and faults. We Anglicans with a Catholic tradition should, I think, look at it both realistically and generously, and also at future united churches, and see if we can give to and receive from them.

Ceylon is another place where some Anglican Catholics have taken up an excessively cautious and negative position. In 1949 a draft scheme was published for union between Anglicans, who in Ceylon are predominantly High, and Methodists, Baptists, some Presbyterians and the CSI diocese of Jaffna in the northern tip of the island. The extreme Anglo-Catholics strongly opposed the scheme and passed a resolution in the diocese of Colombo that they would enter no united Church unless from the start it was granted full communion with the Church of England, the province of India, Pakistan, Burma and Ceylon and a majority of the other Anglican provinces. The English convocations in 1961 refused by narrow majorities to promise this full communion: but afterwards some English Catholic scholars sent to Ceylon a discerning critique of the scheme. In the light of this the negotiating committee in Ceylon so modified their plan that it satisfied many of those who had led the opposition to it in the English convocations. Yet when I arrived in Ceylon in 1964 a group of Anglican Catholics were still opposing the scheme, apparently oblivious of the more generous line Anglican Catholics were then taking in England. It now looks as if within two or three years the new Church will be formed in Ceylon.

In 1965 ten theologians from the Anglican Church in Canada and ten from the United Church of Canada agreed unanimously on 'Principles of Union'. Their report has been accepted by the Anglican synod and the General Council of the United Church, and on its basis a plan of union is being drawn up. The report is Catholic, in fact surprisingly so, on the faith, the sacraments, and the nature of the Church. As so often, the unification of the ministries has raised difficulties. The sharpest criticism I heard in Canada was about a suggestion that the Holy Spirit might 'create new forms of order, when existing forms have ceased to safe-guard the apostolic faith and promote apostolic work'.

Yet the Church is a living body, not a legalistic institution. So its precedents are neither to be lightly disregarded nor to be blindly followed, rather their usefulness is to be studied in their original situation and their relevance to the present situation discussed. Thus, when faced with the Donatist problem, St Augustine was ready to depart from precedent and to modify St Cyprian's logical position that no sacraments at all could be administered outside the limits of the undivided visible Church. Similarly we should not be afraid to consider departure from earlier precedents and past formulations. The founder of our community wrote to an anxious churchman of his day, 'It is no use sticking to any particular phraseology as to a Quaker's dress', and he pointed out that even in the writings of the Fathers of the Church, 'Sometimes the wrong word of one age will become the right word of another.'[1] We should learn from, but not be bound by precedents.

Fear to depart from precedent has also characterised the reception in the USA of the report of the Consultation on Church Union, called from its initials COCU. Exploratory conversations go back to 1962, and at present the discussion is going on between Anglicans and seven non-episcopal Churches, not to mention the consultant-observers from other Protestant and Roman Catholic and Orthodox Churches. In 1966 the Consultation produced a slim, suggestive report, *Principles of Church Union*. This document was accepted unanimously by the General Convention of the American Episcopal Church at Seattle in 1967. Its resolution commended the report for local study, welcomed it as a suitable basis for a plan of union, and significantly set it in the context of our rapidly widening contacts with Roman Catholic, Orthodox and Lutheran communions. The criticism of the report in a small volume of essays written chiefly by Anglican Catholics and edited by Professor John Macquarrie was welcome and discerning. But again it was disquieting that the chief criticism I heard in the States from High Anglicans was directed against such statements as:

[1]G. Congreve and W. H. Longridge, *Letters of Richard Meux Benson*, Mowbray, 1916, p. 28.

'Our capacity to grow into what God desires us to be will depend on our commitment to the Church as the instrument of mission in the world. . . . Men can be slaves to the past because they cannot bear the unsettling of their foundations, or they can become pioneers on the frontier because this is where God calls them to be. To the bold he will provide the faith and courage to welcome whatever new forms of church life true obedience demands.'[1]

But perhaps it is from some new perspective like this that Anglican Catholics together with other Christians may discern the patterns for Church and ministry our times demand. The English Archbishops' recent commission on intercommunion in effect says this same thing and invites us all to look

'at the whole life and structure of the Church as at the service of the kingdom of God, which Christ came to proclaim. When the long established controversies about Church order are seen in this context many apparently irreconcilable differences appear in a new light. From the Catholic side it is recognised that the Church's structure of ministry exists for the service of the whole body. From the Protestant side it becomes possible to recognise the positive meaning of the historic ministry as a sign of the church's continuity in time. In both cases a more dynamic view of the history of Christian divisions make it possible to look forward to a reconciliation in which what is valued on both sides will be recognised and preserved.'[2]

Covenanting for Union

In practical ecumenism our pressing need is to find some method to do three things – to give solid expression to the considerable degree of unity already achieved, to focus the

[1] *Principles of Church Union*, p. 63.
[2] *Intercommunion Today*, Church Information Office, London, May 1968, p. 66.

mounting desire for unity, and to commit ourselves to an unrelenting joint-exploration of the way forward. Among such methods one now much discussed is 'covenanting for union'. In the past, as we have seen, many Anglican Catholics have begun by taking up unduly cautious attitudes towards some ecumenical proposals, often only to turn round later and modify their opposition. Perhaps without being precipitate we shall be able to adopt a more positive line towards these new methods.

'Covenanting for' or 'committing ourselves to' or 'declaring our intent to' union (what word we eventually select does not matter as long as all parties are clear and are agreed on its meaning) should probably be defined in some modest basic terms like these:

> 'a solemn undertaking to God and to each other to be obedient to the divine will for union in the foreseeable future.'[1]

Such a declaration would not commit the Churches to union by a particular date, but it would commit them to a mutually agreed amount of common action and of shared worship; and no declaration should be made until there has been full and free discussion at every level of the churches down to small local congregations.

ITS ADVANTAGES

First, it would enable Churches to go forward together in mission without having to wait for detailed schemes of union to be hammered out: in South India that took twenty-eight years – far too slow a process for the 1970s. Nor should we repeat what we have said too often in the past, 'Be patient. God has all eternity to work out his plans for our unity', because according to the Bible God calls us to make prompt

---

[1]*Covenant-Commitment before God*, report of English Standing Conference arranged by British Council of Churches. Church Information Office 1967. See also *Covenanting for Union in Wales*, an outstanding report by the Council of Churches in Wales

decisions in moments of history: 'Today, if you will hear my voice.' (To prevent misunderstanding I must add that, wherever a satisfactory scheme of union has already been worked out, I myself would urge its implementation and I would not divert attention there to this method of covenanting.)

Secondly, if a solemn public declaration were the result of discussion down to local levels, then subsequent mission and service in the world would be clearly seen as the concern of the great majority of active Church members, and not just of small minorities of enthusiasts. A declaration like this would have news value outside the Church, and would show to everyone that the Churches were serious in their desire for united service to the world. It would meet the kind of request put recently to an Anglican Synod by Dr Kenneth Kaunda, the President of Zambia:

Christ's compassion for God's creation should so occupy us that we have no time left to reflect on our differences nor on our power-status, but where – as the compassionately serving community – we simply become the Church. The world is not the Church's playground for selected charitable field exercises. Rather, the world in its totality is God's continuing challenge to the Church to lose herself. I repeat my appeal to you to become the Church, united with all the brethren serving the world for Christ's sake.'

Thirdly, it is when Christians have experienced this living together, this shared action and worship, that theological differences are likely to be more deeply explored and resolved. The dialogue, for example, between the Lutheran and the Roman Catholic scholars, Dr Edmund Schlink and Prof. Hans Küng, on 'the apostolic succession' shows us clearly the kind of advance we may expect.[1] In fact this is the kind of fresh perspective which seems to be coming into the ecumenical movement, as Bishop Oliver Tomkins has written:

[1]H. Küng, *Structures of the Church*, Burns Oates 1965, pp. 154–180.

'Unity must come by a process in which we all expect God-
to do radical things to ourselves as well as to others, in
stead of conceiving it as a process by which others are
drawn into conformity with ourselves. . . . At the level of
detailed scholarship there is good ground for hope that
the question of the ministry may be so formulated that we
are driven neither to make our affirmations in a way that
excludes others from grace nor to deny that something
more may be added without derogation to what we have
received.'[1]

Time is needed and reciprocal confidence for this theological re-exploration of Church and ministries, and yet we cannot wait for this theological work to be completed before
getting on with the job of deeply shared mission in the world.
A covenant could, I think, give us what we need.

ITS EXTENSIVE CONSIDERATION

This method of covenanting was raised in Britain at the
Faith and Order Conference in September 1964. In 1965 the
Anglican and some Presbyterian representatives in South
Africa proposed to their Churches that they should enter into
a covenant; this discussion is now going on with the addition
of some Congregational and Methodist Churches. In 1966
we discussed the same matter in the West Indies in our consultation with the Methodists, but we decided that the time
was not yet ripe for it. In New Zealand at Wellington
Cathedral on 10 May 1967 a solemn service of commitment
took place between the Anglicans, Presbyterians, Congregationalists, Methodists and the Associated Churches of
Christ. In Ceylon the Churches, which are planning for
union in a few years' time, have made a preliminary covenant
with one another, and this covenant has received the approval of the Church of India, Pakistan and Burma (1968).
In Rhodesia I was present at a meeting of the representatives
of the Anglicans, Presbyterians, Congregationalists, Metho-

[1] O. Tomkins, *A Time for Unity*, S.C.M. 1964, pp. 100, 110.

dists and of the Churches of Christ, when they all recommended that by 1970 their Churches should enter into a covenant as a step towards full union. It looks very much as if the Churches in Zambia and in Malawi will go forward to covenants, though there was objection in Malawi to the word 'covenant' or at least 'vow' its Nyanja equivalent. The Churches also in Ghana, which are hoping soon for union, are probably going to enter first into a covenant, promising to accept the final scheme as soon as it passes the synods of the Churches. This is presumably to avoid a last-minute breakdown of the kind which happened so tragically in Nigeria, where a few congregations refused at the last moment on legal grounds to join the union and so wrecked the whole scheme. This shows incidentally how vital it is to carry local congregations along with the planners in efforts towards union.

COMMON ACTION AND SHARED WORSHIP

The general implications of a covenant must obviously be agreed on beforehand. But one of the values of this method is that the details can be implemented at the pace suitable to each locality. The recommendations of recent inter-Church consultations in Malawi show the kind of shared work which might follow: Churches working together in local service-projects for national development, the merging of youth and of other organisations, joint action in pastoral care and evangelism, the sharing of church buildings, co-operative building of churches for common use, joint-action-for-mission committees wherever the Churches' work overlaps, the inviting of members of other Churches to all synods, retreats and refresher courses, and also joint theological training.

An increase of shared worship would naturally be part of the agreement, but again this could be adapted to each area, and it need not mean intercommunion. Perhaps the most prudent plan might be, quoting again our English report on *Covenant* (p. 14), to say that there should be that degree of participation in sacramental worship 'permitted by the corporate decisions of each church and by the conscience of individual members, both of which need continual submission to the Holy Spirit.'

After conversations with Roman Catholic bishops in Central Africa I am not without hope that if a covenant were proposed on such modest lines then in some parts of the world Roman Catholic dioceses might possibly be able to participate, particularly as it is said that nowadays when a national conference of Catholic bishops makes some responsible request to Rome the answer is usually 'Yes'.

Intercommunion[1]

Covenanting for unity does not necessarily involve intercommunion, but it is bound to keep the issue of intercommunion very much in Christians' minds.

The Reformed Churches in general wish for intercommunion. In most parts of the Anglican communion its priests are allowed in certain circumstances to give communion to non-Anglicans. For example in England since 1933 the bishops have permitted this at ecumenical gatherings, though this permission has not been a formal act of the English convocations.

But until recently it has been only one-way intercommunion, not reciprocal intercommunion, that is Anglicans have been able to give communion to non-Anglicans, but it has not been suggested that Anglicans should receive communion from non-Anglicans. The one exception to this was that the Lambeth Conference, which is an advisory not a legislative body, gave permission to bishops in 1930 to allow isolated Anglicans to receive communion in non-episcopal churches 'where the ministrations of an Anglican church are not available for long periods of time or without travelling great distances'.

But now there is quite a novel factor in the situation.

[1] *Editorial Note*: This essay had gone to press before the decisions of the 1968 Lambeth conference had been published.

Certain Roman Catholics are expressing a desire for inter-communion and indeed for some form of reciprocal intercommunion. This has not yet reached the level of clear theological articulation, still less of official approval. But to take an example, in its October number, 1967. *Worship*, the monthly of the great Benedictine monastery of St John's Abbey, Collegeville, Minnesota, warmly supported the suggestion made in America that there should be intercommunion in the week of prayer for Christian unity and also on some other occasions as a 'prophetic gesture'; and it added:

'From the Roman Catholic standpoint the problem of validity used to be regarded as the major obstacle to inter-communion, at least of Catholics with Protestants. It seems that this is no longer the case. Theologians argue compellingly, with texts from the magisterium, that we must not confuse validity with reality: traditional Pro-testant Churches, as components of the one Church, have a true ministry and celebrate a true eucharist.'

This is alluding to the work of contemporary Roman Catholic scholars who are pointing out the different usages of the term 'validity' in the history of Catholic theology and who are questioning its meaningfulness in much ecumenical discussion today.

To return to the Anglican communion, a new and bold step has been taken in the predominantly High Anglican dioceses of Central Africa. By a unanimous vote of their provincial synod at Blantyre in 1966 they have given per-mission for reciprocal intercommunion. This has to be implemented in each diocese. The resolution states the diocesan bishop may permit communion to be received from an authorised minister of another church when (a) 'an agreement of sincere intention to seek organic unity together has been publicly entered upon;' or more widely (b) 'at gatherings which have been specially arranged for pro-motion of church union, or for a special project of close co-operation.'

This departure from normal Anglican order is allowed, it says, 'in the hope of promoting the recovery of unity of order within the whole Church of Christ.'

This same resolution has been taken over by the province of West Africa; and it has been authorised for the strongly High Anglican diocese of Ghana, so that reciprocal inter-communion will there, it is hoped, be a part of the convenant for unity between the Anglicans and non-episcopal churches before the inauguration of full union.

In New Zealand the General Synod of the Anglican Church passed a measure in May 1968, which it will need to approve again after discussion in the diocesan Synods, welcoming to Anglican altars communicant members of the covenanting churches, and also allowing Anglicans to receive communion in negotiating Churches, with this rider:

'But frequent and habitual communion in other churches is to be discouraged both on pastoral grounds and in view of the persisting divisions within the whole Church.'[1]

In England itself the majority of the members of the Archbishops' commission in their 1968 report make the recommendation that reciprocal intercommunion be permitted for those who desire it 'in permanent close-knit communities such as schools, colleges, centres of prayer and conference, where Christians of differing traditions are regularly sharing together a common life and activity.' And also 'where local congregations or other groups of Christians are meeting together either in sustained efforts or on special occasions to promote the unity, ministry or mission of the Church.'[2]

THEOLOGY OF INTERCOMMUNION

So it seems time for Anglican Catholics to examine again the practice and theology of reciprocal intercommunion. We may not of course come to a unanimous opinion. I would suggest that we look afresh at the theology of the Church,

[1] *Church Times*, 24 May 1968, p. 8.
[2] *Intercommunion Today* C.I.O., 1968, p. 122, cf. p. 127.

of the ministry, and of the eucharist in that logical sequence. I can only indicate very inadequately the questions now being re-opened by Anglican and Roman Catholic theologians in these three areas.

First, granted that all individual Christians are by their baptism members of the Church, Anglican Catholics need to ask themselves the further question – in what sense can the major non-episcopal Churches, such as the Church of Scotland or the Methodist Church, be accepted strictly as Churches and as true entities within the one Church, the Church of Christ? The general Anglican position has been clear since the 1920 Lambeth *Appeal to all Christian People*, a document said to owe much to Frank Weston, a bishop outstanding among Anglican Catholics. It stated that not only were baptised individuals within the universal Church of Christ which is his body, but so also were 'the great non-episcopal communions, standing for rich elements of truth, liberty and life which might otherwise have been obscured or neglected.' And that in consequence 'we do not ask that any one communion should consent to be absorbed in another.'

In the same way all the delegates explicitly agreed at the opening of the present Anglican-Methodist conversations that they would regard 'the discussions between the Methodist Church and the Church of England as taking place within the Body of Christ.'

The documents of Vatican II now show a similar outlook, which marks a great advance on Pius XII's encyclical *Mystici Corporis Christi*, itself an advance on earlier papal statements. In the decree *De Ecumenismo*, to take one example, the title of its third chapter was deliberately changed from 'The Communities established since the sixteenth-century' to 'Churches and Ecclesial Communities separated from the Roman Apostolic See'. It is not exactly certain what an 'ecclesial community' means, but it is presumably a body with some of the essential structure of the one Catholic Church. Further if as is likely there is a distinction between 'Churches' and 'ecclesial communities', then the former will be regarded as having an even more satisfactory structure; and because this chapter of the decree is not referring to the Eastern Orthodox Churches, it is some of the non-Roman communions of the West that are described as 'Churches'.

When the position of the major non-episcopal Churches has been considered, the second and logical question arises – exactly how are their ministers to be regarded? They are normally chosen and trained with great care and set apart by prayer and the laying-on of hands to be precisely 'ministers of word and sacraments' of the Church of God. Among formal Anglican statements the Lambeth Appeal of 1920 acknowledged that 'their ministries have been manifestly blessed and owned by the Holy Spirit as effective means of grace.'

At the official conversations between the Church of England and the Free Churches in 1923 the Archbishops and the other ten bishops taking part stated about non-episcopally ordained ministers:

'Ministries which imply a sincere intention to preach Christ's Word and administer the sacraments as Christ has ordained, and to which authority so to do has been solemnly given by the Church concerned, are real ministries of Christ's Word and sacraments in the universal Church.'[1]

Similarly the recent report *Intercommunion Today* (p. 91) says:

'We recognise that such Churches are communities which minister saving grace to their members. This recognition must carry with it the recognition of their ministries, solemnly set apart with prayer and the laying-on of hands, as at least 'ecclesial' ministries, which have some share in the apostolic ministry. Many Anglicans would go further than this. It seems that few will not go this far.'

[1]Quoted in G. K. A. Bell, *Randall Davidson*, ii, 1120.

Some Roman Catholic theologians are today making a similar re-assessment of the ministries of the 'separated brethren'. The Canadian, Fr Gregory Baum, OSA, a *peritus* at Vatican II, wrote in the columns of an Anglican magazine *The Episcopalian* (Sept. 1967):

'If Roman Catholics take seriously the fact that the Vatican II Decree on Ecumenism acknowledges the ecclesiastical reality of other Christian Churches and the fact that non-Roman Christian Churches are used by the Holy Spirit to sanctify and save men, then it seems to me we can acknowledge the divine call of ministers in other Christian Churches inasmuch as they celebrate the good news and sacraments as they understand them.'

Another *peritus*, a professor at the university of Tübingen, Hans Küng, after a detailed exegetical study of New Testament passages on the ministry, continued:

'This raises further questions, as for example whether given the priesthood of all believers and the charismatic structure of the Church, the particular mode of apostolic succession we have, through the chain of laying-on of hands, should be regarded as exclusive. It represents the norm, and can be approved without reservation; but is it the *only* way into the pastoral ministry and into this particular apostolic succession? . . . There is surely no other way in which we can be just to the richness of the spiritual life and fruitful activity of the pastors of other Churches outside the Catholic Church; there is surely no other way by which we can overcome the divisions of Christianity and arrive at mutual recognition. The enormous theological, and in particular ecumenical implication of these questions is obvious. There is serious need for them to come under urgent discussion.'[1]

The French ecumenical leader, Maurice Villain, SM, has

[1]H. Küng, *The Church*, Burns Oates 1967, pp. 443–444.
J

also recognised that the status of Protestant ministers is no longer a closed question for Roman Catholic theologians and that this in turn raises the issue of reciprocal intercommunion:

> 'Will the Catholic Church ever recognise the ministries of the Churches born of the Reformation, so that this recognition may be the prelude to that bilateral intercommunion so much longed for today? These questions are not yet ripe, but it is already genuine progress that we can broach them in a spirit of serenity and keep them open.'[1]

So thirdly and consequently, the next question to be examined is – can we adequately describe the eucharistic rites of these non-episcopal Churches by the often repeated phrase 'God's uncovenanted mercies'? Can we go so far as to describe them not merely as eucharists of separated groups of Christians, but as 'real ministries of Christ's Word and sacraments in the universal Church'? We have just looked at some recent Anglican statements on these ministries.

We can now add to them recent Roman Catholic estimates. There are first official statements of Vatican II. Rome of course recognises the fullness of the eucharistic rites of the Eastern Orthodox. But it is about 'the separated Churches and ecclesial communities' in the West that it grants in the decree *De Ecumenismo* that:

> 'Though because of the lack of the sacrament of orders they have not preserved *the genuine and total reality* (amended from an earlier text 'the full reality') of the eucharistic mystery, nevertheless, when they commemorate the Lord's death and resurrection in the holy supper, they profess that it signifies life in communion with Christ and they await his coming in glory.'[2]

---

[1] M. Villain SM, 'Can there be Apostolic Succession outside the Continuity of the Laying-on of Hands?' *Concilium* April 1968, p. 52.

[2] *De Ecumenismo*, iii. 22 (my italics).

Also the decree *De Ecclesia* is speaking of 'separated brethren' in the West as well as of the Orthodox (or it would not have added the words 'ecclesial communities'), when it says of sacraments, in the plural, outside the Roman church: 'They are consecrated by baptism, through which they are united to Christ. . . . They also recognise and receive other sacraments within their own Churches or ecclesial communities.' (*De Ecclesia*, 2:15).

Individual modern Roman Catholic theologians have written more explicitly. Fr Bernard Cooke, an American Jesuit, in an article 'Eucharist: Source or Expression of Community' in the magazine *Worship* (June 1966, pp. 339–348), searched for a biblical and doctrinal basis for intercommunion and maintained that 'baptism establishes both the right and the obligation to participate in the eucharist' and expressed the view that 'We cannot expect Christian unity to take place apart from the influence of the eucharist. This would seem to suggest that some common celebration of the eucharist will have to precede our hoped-for union.'

Fr Gregory Baum, OSA, wrote in a Roman Catholic quarterly *One in Christ* (No. 4, 1967) about their priests giving communion to non-Catholics, 'there is no doctrinal objection to this' (p. 425); and about Roman Catholics receiving communion in a Church other than their own:

'Every worship service of a Church is, in some sense, a confession of faith and a sign of unity, and hence, if it is possible and commendable to share with dissident Christians in certain forms of worship, it would seem rather arbitrary to stop short at the eucharistic celebration and affirm that here participation is always doctrinally compromising.' (p. 427).

One more of the Vatican Council's *periti*, Fr Schillebeeckx, OP, has tried in terms of Catholic scholastic theology to write positively of the eucharist of the Reformed Church of his native Holland. He explained first that on the Catholic side it is recognised that the Reformed are through their baptism

orientated towards the eucharist of the Catholic Church;
secondly, that as the Catholic Church has always recognised
a 'baptism of desire', so it may well recognise a 'eucharist of
desire'; thirdly, if the Jewish rites genuinely foreshadowed the
Church's eucharist (as Catholic theology has always maintained), then the Protestant sacrament, *a fortiori*, does more
than this, for it directly commemorates the Lord's Supper
and it retains clear vestiges of the Church's traditional practice; hence he summed up:

> 'Celebrating the communion service and being firmly con-
> vinced that he is following Christ's will by so doing, an
> evangelical Christian undoubtedly possesses a 'eucharist of
> desire'; therefore in this liturgical celebration he really
> participates in the *res sacramenti* or in the effect of the
> sacrament, though not to the full'.[1]

This theological investigation has been carried further and
in more detail by Fr Frans Jozef van Beeck, SJ. He modestly
began a long essay 'Towards an ecumenical understanding of
the sacraments' in *Doctrinal Development and Christian Unity*[2]
thus:

> 'Our only concern is to find out whether Roman Catholic
> sacramental doctrine and practice warrant a few doors to
> be set ajar, in the hope that in this way we may catch a
> glimpse of sacramental reunion, the desire for which seems
> to become more widespread every day.'

Those, who are ill at ease with these scholastic distinctions,
are apt to ask – as that firm Anglican Catholic, Bishop Cecil
Alderson of Mashonaland, said perhaps a little naïvely to me
shortly before his death, 'If Christ in the Presbyterians'
Lord's Supper, for example, does not give them his Body and
Blood, what does he give them?' So it is not an entire surprise
that at their fifth meeting the official Joint Consultation on
Anglican/Roman Catholic relations in the USA concluded:

[1] E. Schillebeeckx, *Christ the Sacrament*, Sheed & Ward 1963, p. 241.
[2] Nicholas Lash(ed.), Sheed & Ward 1967, pp. 139–221.

'Whatever minor differences of understanding exist regarding the priesthood and its relation to the laity, they do not in themselves constitute a barrier to the Churches celebrating and receiving communion together;'

though the Roman Catholic and Anglican bishops present agreed that 'precipitate action' would not be for the good of the whole Church (*Intercommunion Today*, p. 93, n. 72).

More recently the Roman Catholic Bishops' Committee for Ecumenical and Inter-Religious Affairs in the USA and the Council of Christian Unity of the Christian Churches at the end of their third consultation have stated:

'We have found sufficient theological justification in principle for some eucharistic sharing. . . . We urge our communions to explore as rapidly as possible the circumstances and procedures for such responsible eucharistic sharing.'[1]

In view of all this Anglican Catholics may well face the question – are there compelling reasons why those Anglicans, who wish to do so, should not on occasions receive holy communion at least from those whom we may call the major Churches of the Reformation and also, should the invitation be given, from the Roman Catholic and Orthodox Churches?

Some Anglican Catholics would add the proviso that they would have to be sure that the other Church believed in some fairly articulate way in the doctrine of the real presence of Christ. Though this can hardly be called a scriptural requirement, there is long Catholic tradition behind it going back as far as the words of Ignatius of Antioch:

'The eucharist is the flesh of our Saviour Jesus Christ who suffered for our sins, which the Father raised up by his goodness.'

(*Ad Smyrn*, 7:6)

[1] *Tablet*, 18 May 1968, p. 512.

and of Justin Martyr:

> 'This food we call eucharist, of which no one is allowed to partake except one who believes the things we teach are true. . . . We have been taught that the food consecrated by the word of prayer is the flesh and blood of the incarnate Jesus.'
>
> *(Apol.* i, 66)

Yet this tradition can hardly be binding on Anglicans because for four hundred years many of our clergy and laity have held no doctrine of the real presence; and, as Dom Gregory Dix and others have shown, even our *Book of Common Prayer* has on this point been ambiguous. Perhaps it would be wiser to ask whether the Church concerned appears from its official statements to be intending to do at the eucharist what Christ at the Last Supper intended us to do.

Yet even if we have 'liberty' to receive communion on occasions outside the Anglican Church, we may sometimes be ill-advised to use this liberty. We may apply to our situation St Paul's words:

> '"We are free to do anything", you say. Yes, but is everything good for us? "We are free to do anything", but does everything help the building of the community? Each of you must regard, not his own interests, but the other man's.'
>
> (1 Cor. 10:23–24)

What then should be the limitations of our freedom? Clearly we should not go to communion where we know that it would cause embarrassment to the minister and congregation; nor should we go to communion in any Church in what might appear to be a casual way, seeming to imply that the traditions of that Church were matters of small importance. We should be careful not to give unnecessary pain to some of our fellow-Anglicans – even less to disregard the express prohibitions of particular Anglican provinces. Perhaps the time mainly to use this liberty would be when Churches have solemnly covenanted for unity, particularly when permission has been explicitly given, as in the provincial regulations of Central and West Africa.

Anglican Catholics may not be able to come to unanimity about intercommunion. The Church Union in its advice to its members, *The Problem of Intercommunion*[1] said:

'In the present theological ferment it must be acknowledged that Catholics themselves may conscientiously draw different conclusions in particular circumstances.'

Members of the Archbishops' commission on intercommunion also could not unanimously work out an agreed policy, but they declared explicitly their need to remain in dialogue and in joint exploration of these problems:

'Many of the questions we have faced are without precedent in the life of the Church, so that failure at certain points to agree in this commission, as in the Church of England at large, is understandable. We hope that by facing them afresh in a spirit of loyalty and mutual toleration the Church may find a greater agreement, which will serve its own members and their fellow Christians better than anything so far achieved.'[2]

It is well to remember that it was the decree *De Ecumenismo* (though the subsequent Roman Catholic Directory is more cautious and reserved), which seemed to hint by the word *communicatio in sacris* that some form of intercommunion might not be ruled out at least as an occasional help towards unity. Incidentally another Vatican decree, *On the Eastern Churches* (para. 26), certainly used this phrase to denote intercommunion. These are the words of the decree on ecumenism:

'Worship in common (*communicatio in sacris*) is not to be considered as a means to be used indiscriminately for the restoration of Christian unity. There are two main prin-

---

[1]Church Literature Association, 1967, p. 8.
[2]*Intercommunion Today*, p. 119.

ciples governing the practice of such common worship: first, the bearing witness to the unity of the Church, and second, the sharing of the means of grace. Witness to the unity of the Church very commonly forbids common worship to Christians, but the grace to be had from it sometimes commends this practice.'

(*De Ecumenismo*, 2:8)

A final *caveat*: if ever the time comes when we have full intercommunion with other Churches, we must be careful never to give the impression that we then have all that really matters. We pray and work for nothing less than the organic union of the New Testament Church, unity without uniformity. In stark reality it will only be when we work out organic union abroad and at home, in towns and villages, that we shall grasp what ecumenism and mission really are. It is then that we shall see how many of our Churches and clergy are no longer strategically placed. Only then shall we realise what full-co-operation between ministers, what an imaginative ministry of the laity, what new ways of expressing our faith, our worship, our life together and our mission really involve. Intercommunion without union might deprive us of this motive power for reform. 'Ecumenism is not a patching together of the past but a leap into the future'. William Temple said that, unless the Anglican Church reformed itself, it would be disastrous for another Church to be united to it. That may be true of other Churches also. It is time to be stripped for action together in mission.

FURTHER READING

W. M. ABBOTT SJ (ed), *The Documents of Vatican II*, Chapman 1966

E. M. B. GREEN, *Called to Serve*, Hodder & Stoughton 1964

A. G. HEBERT SSM, *Apostle and Bishop*, Faber 1963

H. KUNG, *The Church*, Burns Oates 1967

S. NEILL, *The Church and Christian Union*, Oxford 1968

A. M. RAMSEY, *The Gospel and the Catholic Church*, 2nd edn, Longmans 1956

K. SANSBURY, *Truth, Unity and Concord*, Mowbray 1967

M. THURIAN, *Visible Unity and Tradition*, Darton, Longman & Todd 1964
Le Pain Unique, Editions du Seuil, 1967

B. N. Y. VAUGHAN, *Structures for Renewal*, Mowbray 1967

Covenanting for Union in Wales, Council of Churches in Wales, 1968.

ELEVEN

Catholics
and Non-Christians

COLIN HICKLING

Some years ago Bishop Richard Rutt wrote a series of articles for a Korean newspaper on rural life in Korea as he had observed it during several years as a parish priest. In one of these articles (which were subsequently published in book form as *Korean Works and Days*) he describes a visit made with a Korean Christian friend to a Confucian temple. The Korean went inside the temple, made the sign of the cross, and prayed. He said afterwards, 'I was thanking God for the light he gave to the people of the East before they learned about Christ.'

The gesture and its implications may be set beside an exchange which took place in very different surroundings. Horst Symanowski, the pioneer of industrial mission work in the German Lutheran Churches, had been outlining to a young American minister the nature of his work in Mainz. With great enthusiasm the American said how much he himself longed to be able to 'take Christ into the factory'. 'Oh yes,' came the ironic reply, 'and then where would you take him next?'

Both incidents illustrate fundamental convictions about the nature of God and therefore about the nature of salvation. They reflect beliefs which are basic to an adequate Christian approach to those who do not believe in Christ or who do not believe at all. The speakers are men who, in very different contexts, have taken seriously the prevenience of God in every human situation: his active presence and his self-disclosure going ahead of the explicit confession of Christian faith. The God to whom the Christian gospel bears witness is the God whose nature it is to attract human wills towards himself in love, and to reveal himself in order that this attraction may be felt and answered. We may not think of him as absent from the world of human aspiration, achievement, and failure. The Christian can no more 'bring' the God of salvation and judgment to Korea than he can to an industrial centre in post-Christian Europe.

The words attributed to St Paul by the temple gates at Lystra and on the slope below the Parthenon at Athens must, then, be taken seriously as fundamental to the understanding of Christian mission: the more so if, as some have thought, these as well as the other speeches in Acts were set down, in part, as patterns for the Christian preaching. God has not 'left you without some clue to his nature'; he has made all men that 'they were to seek God, and, it might be, touch and find him' (Acts 14:17, 17:26, 27). There is room, indeed, for a variety of assessments of the degree to which non-Christian and post-Christian cultures can be seen as congruent with or pointing towards Christian faith. The vestiges of monotheism once confidently found in some primitive religions may indeed have been illusory. But the basic claim that outside Israel and the Church there exist a presence and activity of God which must be regarded as a saving presence and activity, is a claim resting on the Christian understanding of the very nature of God. The light which shines, indeed, in darkness, is still the light that enlightens every man.

Moreover, it is not only the understanding of the nature of God that is in question. The attitude towards non-Christians here indicated springs from the Christian belief – and more specifically the Catholic belief – about what it means to be human. At the heart of this belief lies the conviction that the extraordinary assertion of Genesis 1:27 – man is made in God's image – contains ultimate truth. The words translated 'image' and 'likeness', concrete and three-dimensional as they are, suggest indeed something naïvely physical in the intention of the writer or in the material he was using. But behind the primitive idea lies something much deeper; an assertion both of gift and of promise to which the Christian tradition has given great importance. Human nature is in its very essence related to God: to be human means to be created in order to mirror God's own being. 'Thou hast made us for thyself, and our heart has no rest until it rests in thee.' The audacity of the Catholic faith in man is astonishing, both when we reflect on human nature as we know it and on how little we know of God. Yet this faith is fundamental to the sense a Catholic Christian makes of himself, of the world, and of Christ. It is a faith which invites him to acknowledge and to reverence a real presence of God in every human being. The words of the Latin playwright are words which he hears, as it were, from the incarnate and exalted Christ, and which he knows he must echo: 'I am a man; I count nothing human alien to me.' The man on the 23 bus bears God's image. Whether he is a Cockney last seen in church at his christening, or a Pakistani who visited the mosque in the Commercial Road last Friday, or an embittered opponent of any form of belief in God – as a human person he reflects the creative will of God. If one came to know him, one might become aware of many ways in which, in and through his relationships with those around him, the redemptive grace of God is at work. And indeed this kind of belief about what it is to be human should prompt that sensitive awareness of, and respect for, another person, which are implied in Christian love. Whether in the context of mission, then, or in any other, the proper understanding of the non-Christian must be founded on reverence for the mysterious activity of God himself creating, sustaining, redeeming man who is made in his image.

It is interesting to find a similar view expressed by Karl Barth, who years ago did much to discourage us from thinking that we might be found by God anywhere outside the covenant revelation in the Bible. In a more recent book, he says:

'On the basis of the eternal will of God we have to think of *every human being,* even the oddest, most villainous or miser-able, as one to whom Jesus Christ is Brother and God is Father; and we have to deal with him on this assumption. If the other person knows that already, then we have to strengthen him in the knowledge. If he does not know it yet or no longer knows it, our business is to transmit this knowledge to him. On the basis of the knowledge of the humanity of God no other attitude to any kind of fellow-man is possible . . . We can meet God only within the limits of humanity determined by him [the limits referred to are not those of the covenant community of the Old or the New Testament]. But in these limits we may meet him.'[1]

The description given in this passage of the Christian's responsibility to his non-Christian brother is of the greatest value. It consists essentially in bringing to light, and to acknowledgment, what is already true. Baptism and the Christian life give authentic expression to what this man's humanity really means.

In some contemporary Roman Catholic writing, the claim to find a saving activity of God in non-Christians has been pressed very far. Karl Rahner has spoken of the possibility of the non-Christian, by virtue of his response as man to grace offered to him as man, being 'anonymously Christian'.

'It would be wrong to regard the pagan as someone who has not yet been touched in any way by God's grace and truth. If, however, he has experienced the grace of God – if, in certain circumstances, he has already accepted this grace . . . by accepting the immeasurableness of his dying existence as opening out into infinity – then he has already been given revelation in a true sense even before he has been affected by missionary preaching from without''[2]

Charles Davis took up Rahner's phrase and commented further:

[1] *The Humanity of God,* Fontana, pp. 52–54.
[2] *Theological Investigations,* Vol. V, Darton, Longman & Todd, p. 131.

'God's purpose for all mankind is one. According to that purpose, he intends all men to live in the order of that grace . . . he is present to [the unevangelised] by grace from the awakening of their moral consciousness.'[1]

And the Dutch theologian E. Schillebeeckx draws the conclusion:

'Wherever men make history, a history of salvation or of perdition is brought about, because the significance they give their life is always, in acceptance or refusal, a response to the anonymous grace of God, his call to salvation . . . If this freedom is confronted with Christ's salvation, though perhaps anonymously, in the universal and effective saving will of God, then this (implicit) confrontation with God's universal will to save – universal because it is concrete and individual with regard to *all* men – de facto causes a history of salvation or of perdition.'[2]

We notice at once that something is being said here which goes beyond the attitude commended by Karl Barth. We are being invited, as Christians working out a proper approach towards non-Christians, to note and value what is *potential* in every human being as though it were already more than potential. This line of thought is an extension of the teaching of St Thomas that all mankind is potentially the Church of God; and the word 'potential' covers so wide a range of possibilities as to be of rather doubtful value. More open to question than this, however, is the contradiction implied in the phrases 'anonymous Christian' and 'anonymous grace'. In one way, precisely the point of the self-disclosure of God in complete particularity in Christ is to *identify*, to give a more exactly recognisable form to, the goodness of God and the response it should evoke. The atheist Marxist, or the adherent of one of the sects in contemporary Japan, makes – let us say – some deliberate act of generosity because he believes, or in some intuitive way feels, that this is what he

[1]*God's Grace in History*, Fontana, p. 72.
[2]*Revelation and Theology*, Sheed and Ward, p. 4.

must do. Either or both may have made a quite explicit rejection of Christian, even of any theistic belief. In cases like
these it is one thing to say that God has been present in their
decision, that he and nothing else has attracted their will into
an unconscious conformity to his. Nothing less than this
interpretation will do justice to what we believe both about
God and about man. But it is another thing to say that such
individuals are in any sense of the word Christian. Even to
use the word 'grace' when this sort of inspiration is ascribed
to God is to broaden the meaning of the word so far as to
obscure part of its essential connotation. For we mostly use
the term in the context of an accepted relationship with God
in explicitly Christian obedience.

Nevertheless, we may value these statements as affirming
the universal activity of God already described: an activity
within the moral awareness of human beings as such beyond
the limits of explicitly Christian allegiance. They remind us
that the purpose of God spoken of in 1 Tim. 2:4 is not an
empty wish: his will it is 'that all men should find salvation
and come to know the truth.' This universal will of God for
the salvation of men – which the writer of 1 Tim. gives as the
reason why prayer is to be made for all men and especially
for the Roman authorities, a group less likely than most to
respond to the Christian preaching – does not wait for its
accomplishment until the missionaries' steamer arrives. The
non-Christian – and the post-Christian – are both already
open to the invitation of God at a moral and perhaps in
some way at an intellectual level. And both are capable of
response. Few of the Thirty-Nine Articles of Religion are so
much regretted by those who must give a general assent to
them as *Article XII* condemning 'Works before Justification' –
unless indeed 'the grace of Christ and the Inspiration of his
Spirit' mentioned in that Article are interpreted in the
'anonymous' sense already described.

In the non-Christian, then, simply as a human being
created in God's image, the saving will of God is to be discerned. The Fathers of the Second Vatican Council sum-

marise a whole chapter of Christian theology of man when they say that he is destined according to God's plan to be dignified 'with a participation in his own divine life.' He is present in a particular way in human moral decision, obscurely entering into relationship with the human will. *The Constitution on the Church*, from which the words just quoted are taken, goes on to say, in speaking of God's activity among men before the call of Abraham, that he 'ceaselessly offered them helps to salvation, in anticipation of Christ the Redeemer'; and what is said about the presence of God among the men of the ancient world must be affirmed also about those of any period in history who obey conscience, even though they have not been addressed by the biblical tradition or by Christ. Justin Martyr claimed that Christ 'is the Logos of whom the whole human race partake, and those who live according to the Logos are Christians, even though they are accounted atheists.' (*Apology*, I, xlvi, 2). Even if a good deal of Stoicism lies behind this doctrine, it is a Stoicism which has been legitimately baptised. For it echoes, not only the perception of Amos that Israel's neighbours and enemies were subject to the law and judgment of God as Israel was herself (Amos 1:3–2:3), and that they like her were the objects of his saving providence (Amos 9:7); but also St Paul's belief in a universal revelation of God to which men were capable of response (Rom. 1:19ff.).

Is it possible to go further and to say that, not only in the moral, but even in the religious aspirations and achievements of non-Christians, God has 'offered them helps to salvation'? The Second Vatican Council's *Declaration on the Relationship of the Church to non-Christian Religions* reminds us that 'men look to the various religions for answers to those profound mysteries which, today even as in olden times, deeply stir the human heart', and implies in its extremely brief review of the great religions of the world that these questions find in them answers which point in the direction of the gospel. 'The Catholic Church . . . looks with sincere respect upon those ways of conduct and of life, those rules and teachings which . . . often reflect a ray of that Truth which enlightens all men.' On the basis of this affirmative view, the Council Fathers urged those working among men of other faiths 'prudently and lovingly, through dialogue and collaboration with the followers of other religions, and in witness of Christian faith and life, [to] acknowledge, preserve, and promote the spiritual and moral goods found among those men, as well as the values in their society and culture.'

This type of approach, historically associated with Roman Catholicism, is also strongly affirmed in a speech by Canon Max Warren at the Toronto Congress in 1963.

'God has revealed himself in divers manners. We should be bold enough to insist that God was speaking in that cave outside Mecca; that God brought illumination to the man who once sat under the Bo tree; that the insight into the reality of the moral struggle and of man's freedom to choose the right, which was given to Zoroaster, came from God; that it was God who spoke to a simple Japanese peasant woman, a hundred years ago, of sin, of righteousness, and of judgment, and that God is at work among the four million Japanese who follow her teaching; that indeed, the God of a hundred names is still God. Thus boldly to believe is in no way whatever to hesitate in affirming what we believe, that in a quite unique way he revealed himself in Jesus Christ our Lord.'

On this view, pre-Christian and contemporary non-Christian religion is a real preparation for the gospel. It is one aspect of a 'general revelation' which is essentially continuous with the revelation in the incarnate Christ and the Church. Human aspiration towards the Divine has at every point in history been met by a divine response. And this response constitutes a genuine revelation in the full sense, not to be contradicted but completed and corrected by Christianity. Thus, for example, a writer like Masure could present the doctrine of eucharistic sacrifice as the fulfilment of a primordial human religious instinct. Some would go so far as to claim that the Vedantas should stand on a level with the Old Testament as prolegomena to the revelation in Christ.

This optimistic view of the non-Christian religions has received sharp criticism, notably from Professor Hendrik Kraemer. 'The Christian revelation', he writes, 'asserts itself as the record of God's self-disclosing and re-creating revelation in Jesus Christ . . . giving the divine answer to this demonic and guilty disharmony of man and the world.'[1] And in a more recent work he develops one particular reason for the discontinuity he sees between the world religions and the unique revelation in Christ.

'In the great Asian religious-cultural systems . . . the organic indissoluble unity, or to put it somewhat differently, the symbiosis of culture and religion belongs to their essence, and determines their fundamental character.'

In Christianity, by contrast,

'there is hidden a fundamental stubbornness and aloofness, which makes for an unavoidable tension; a detached "distance" in regard to culture as the field of human creativity.'[2]

And Professor Kraemer represents an element in Christian thinking about the other religions which has, like the more liberal one, a very long ancestry, beginning from those writers who saw, in features of the pre-Christian cults which appeared to prefigure the rites or teaching of the Church, counterfeits due to the ingenuity of the devil.

It would be foolish to disregard a judgment which rests, as Kraemer's does, on long experience of various Asian countries. Nevertheless, the great gulf which he sees fixed between Christian revelation and the other religions appears to be defined by some degree of over-simplification: the 'stubbornness' he refers to in the Christian tradition, for example, is hardly true of the evaluation of ancient philosophy in Justin Martyr; and a certain *a priori* view of the nature of the uniqueness of Christianity underlies much of what he says.

[1] *The Christian Message in a non-Christian World*, pp. 113–114.
[2] *World Cultures and World Religions*, p. 20.

Only by attention to the particular degrees of congruence or contrast in relation to Christian faith that may be perceived in each of the world's religions considered on its own, can we hope to appraise the extent of a 'preparation for the gospel' in them. And when we turn, for example, to J. V. Taylor's *The Primal Vision*, or to the books of Kenneth Cragg on Islam, we find ourselves encouraged to see real elements of divine revelation present both in the ancient religions of Africa and in Muslim belief and practice, which after all owe so much to the religion of the Old Testament. Thus Canon Cragg writes of the confrontation of Christianity with Islam:

'The earnestness of that *Hayya* [the muezzin's call] is also in the Christian Gospel. He invites men to a relationship with God and an attitude towards his fellows. He stands ideologically upon revelation. His concern is for a world of men in which the reign of God obtains. He acknowledges himself the trustee of what is greater than himself. In all these respects the elements of Christianity are not only and altogether contrasts.'[1]

Affinities between Christianity and Islam may be felt, too, on the Islamic side, as in the case of a group of Imams in Algeria at whose invitation a young Benedictine priest joined them in discussions of Christian belief which were of the most friendly kind.

In considering the non-Christian religions and cultures, then, the Christian is wise to keep his mind open to the great complexity of human experience which he will find there, expressed in myths or in ethics, in ascetic techniques and in more corporate ways of approaching God. Not that he would want – even were it practicable – to canonise all the sacred books of the world's religions, and create a vast Bible through which few would be skilled enough to find their way. Part of the reason why multi-faith services cause uneasiness to many is that (especially when they involve readings from

[1] *The Call of the Minaret*, p. 184.

the books of the various world faiths) they tend to give just this impression. The matter is not as simple as that, and the faith of the Bible – manifold as it is in expression and even to some extent in content, and gathering into itself at every stage elements from the beliefs and practice of its environment – remains always unique. But other religions are not mere anthropological phenomena having nothing to do with true religion. In dealing with another man's religion we are dealing with a profound aspect of *human* experience. And for that very reason we ought to be prepared to acknowledge that God has been and remains actively present and saving in them, in ways it may not always be possible to bring to light in the text of documents.

Even explicitly non-theistic systems ought to be approached in the same openness and humility of mind, in the expectation that here also the hidden activity of God has borne fruit. This applies in particular to the Christian's attitude to Communism. Formal meetings between Christians and Communists have taken place in recent years on the Continent[1] and have been initiated in this country. On the latter occasion the common ground between the two faiths, in ethics, and in the doctrine of man and of history, was set out at some length; and it was striking to notice how, in talking about the educability of human society, some of the Communist speakers seemed to be feeling after something remarkably like a doctrine of grace. Both eschatology – in very different forms – and hope have an important place in both systems. There is no room for a Christian dismissal of Marxism as the supreme anti-Christianity. Rather the Christian needs to be shown to what extent Marxist practice underlines the failures of Christians to embody the gospel in action. Once again, nobody would be so rash as to think that only minor issues divide us. The Marxist and the Christian views of freedom and of human capacity for moral growth may indeed be closely comparable; but only the Christian doctrine of God

[1] Cf Paul Oestreicher's description of the 'dialogue' in *Theology*, Dec. 1967.

can make it possible to think explicitly in terms of grace. And grace is one of the essential Christian differentials in reflecting about the human condition. But conversation is, in this as in every case, a better approach than controversy or apologetic, if we accept that God has not been absent from the thinking behind the ideals and efforts even of godless men.

In the light of this approach to the non-Christian – an approach of humility, of respect, of listening for what God is saying in their belief and in their conduct – what becomes of the Christian preaching? Certainly we cannot think of it in a simple way as a shining of light in the darkness. Or, if we are to think of darkness, it is in a relative sense and not as though the world outside the Church were wholly alien. Part of the role of Christian preaching is surely to discriminate between the partial but real promise of the light, which may be discerned in responsible human conduct and belief, and the ultimate darkness of the hesitancy and refusal of the will in the face of the acknowledged good.

Every form of communication between persons, after all, has to be related to what is there already. Some kinds of sermon shock one by their assumption that the hearers' state of mind is one of unqualified half-heartedness. They shock because of their unreality. Whatever part convention and pious habit may have played in bringing this particular congregation into church, the preacher has no right to deny that there is some real desire to serve God in the minds of at least a good many of those who hear him. The analogy with the Church's role in a non-Christian culture in Africa or Asia is perhaps very limited. Nevertheless, it holds at least to this extent. The Church does not confront a total ignorance of God and of the good, so as to snatch as it were brands from the burning. She is there to preach Christ as Lord: which means, to 'unveil' the truth of every human situation so that the truth may be acknowledged and lived out. She is there to preach a relationship with Christ which is the way of salvation: which means, to make possible the integration of lives only imperfectly human into the life of the 'proper man'.

And correspondingly, conversion does not mean a simple turning of the back upon the past of the individual and upon the past history of the community within which he stands. It involves also a discernment of divine prevenience in both.

The attitude to non-Christians advocated by the Second Vatican Council, and shared by many outside the Roman Communion, does not, then, imply any lack of confidence on the part of the Church in the uniqueness of the gospel committed to her. For that gospel *identifies* the Christ whose work outside his Church may be as visible as his work within her. Perhaps, indeed, Kraemer is right in rejecting the idea that the New Testament gospel 'completes' a revelation outside Christianity, if this suggests the filling out of an already recognisable torso needing only a few specific additions. To acknowledge the presence of many adumbrations of the gospel in the non-Christian religions is not to deny their fragmentariness. There must be discrimination between one element and another, there must be criticism and correction. But this does not mean any kind of rejection out of hand of what has preceded Christianity in men's consciences and affections.

It follows from all this that the purpose of the Church's mission is more far-reaching than simply recruitment. Certainly she hopes and prays that, as a result of what she is seen to be doing as well as saying, God will move individuals and families to ask for baptism. But she is not there simply to enrol new members. The energies of those who serve her must rightly be often directed into work not immediately likely to bring about conversions.

There is something disquieting, then, about the claims recently made by Donald Macgavran (the Director of the Institute of Church Growth at the North-western Christian College, Eugene, Oregon) that 'the objective, measurable growth of the Church' is the only proper aim of mission, the only aim governing the attitude of the Christian to the non-Christian. Rejecting the interpretations of missionary strategy which are based on the 'open' approach to other faiths already indicated, he regards 'Church-planting' and recruitment as the only objectives of mission. To this end, moreover, he urges the adoption of techniques which look remarkably like the application of market analysis. The Church is urged to study those situations in which the most marked and rapid multiplication of conversions has taken place, in order to prepare a strategy in which comparable situations may be given priority in the deployment of resources. There is much that is disturbing here. There is an obvious danger of making 'rice Christians' by directing the efforts of corporations which, at any rate by local standards, will appear very wealthy, towards the evangelisation of the least advanced groups in the population (for these are sometimes the most responsive groups). Moreover, a mass approach of this kind gives the impression of treating human beings in a less than personal way by regarding them principally as potential increments to statistics of Church growth.

But more alarming than these considerations is the tacit withdrawal from any mission to the national culture as a whole. Once again, it is a matter of 'this oughtest thou to have done, and not left the other undone'. No-one denies that the local Church congregation is the place where Christ is active through his sacraments and in the lives they nourish; that this is the place where salvation is met in a form that is not 'anonymous'; that here the new life is preached, sacramentally imparted, and to some extent lived, in a way approximating to the will of Christ. Of course, therefore, the growth of the local congregation means the possibility of more human persons reaching the fulfilment of their humanity in the 'life that is life indeed' through communion with Christ. But 'growth' is a word which in this context needs more examination. 'Numbers and growth are important in God's arithmetic', writes Weber; 'not necessarily large and increasing numbers, but representative numbers, and growth in grace'. And where the last is not taking place, the preaching of the gospel ought, as he points out, to lead to a diminishing, not an increase, of numerical strength. To regard numerical, quantitative expansion as the only criterion for the effectiveness of mission is to give all too much justification to the comment of a group of Muslims passing an open-air meeting in a town in Eastern India: 'Oh, these are just Christians trying to get us to join them.'

Christian mission means far more than the expansion of essentially alien and unrelated communities within a non-Christian culture; it involves attention to, and relationship with, that culture itself. And this goes further than an external indigenisation of the style of worship. So in various ways contemporary missionary practice aims to establish 'Christian presence' within the non-Christian setting, hoping in the first place to understand, to interpret, and to serve, and in some cases deliberately refraining from active evangelism. A striking though unusual example is the work of the Dutch missionary, J. Van Pinxteren, who for five years shared the life of the Masai in East Africa without attempting any regular explicit or formal evangelism, 'which was bound to be considered a negation of their own heritage.' He has described how, on a basis of mutual respect, a growing interest emerged in the faith which impelled him to go to such lengths; and how, too, a curious relationship of trust was built up. 'God has given you great power', Fr Van Pinxteren was told by the tribe's priest, 'to bring blessing and to do good for our people'; and he speaks of the reverence with which the Africans, pagans as they were, heard his Mass. This may sound like an invitation to syncretism. But this would be very far from the truth. Here was a real attempt to come near to the non-Christian, not on any basis of superiority or religious 'imperialism', of which Christian mission may be so easily suspected, but through a genuine appreciation of the existing faith of the tribe in question and through gaining their confidence and respect.

On a wider scale, the Little Brothers and Little Sisters of Jesus – the communities originating from the vision of Charles de Foucauld – exemplify the same principle. The present Prior General of the Little Brothers, René Voillaume, has thus described the missionary aspect of their ideal of sharing the lives of those furthest from the gospel, while abstaining from any explicit attempt to draw them into the Church:

> 'Pursuing the apostolate through friendship can perhaps best be described as making oneself a brother . . . to every man, and trying to help men to discover, through this means, something of the love God has for them, very likely without their knowing anything about it.'

The Little Brothers' vocation has few if any parallels outside the Roman Catholic Church. It is a very costly way of expressing, among the poorest groups of all, the approach of humility and respect to the non-Christian. And Fr Voillaume's words just quoted enable us to see how, in this context also, the results of the Christian presence may be an 'unveiling' to the consciousness of the unbeliever of that love in which he is already sustained by God.

There are other ways, less detached from the Church's organised mission, in which a comparable principle may be seen. Thus Bishop Rutt's book already referred to shows the English priest working in Korea as an accepted member of the rural community, whose way of life he describes so delightfully and so accurately. The book shows, in particular, a familiarity with the poetry of old Korea which was the result of years of study. It shows a sensitivity to the values of an ancient culture in which there is little sense of pressures directed towards the short-term goal of individual conversions.

One could multiply examples of ways in which the contemporary Church is trying to effect a presence within non-Christian cultures whose aim is simply to be at the disposal of all comers and to serve their needs without obligation. The author of the book just mentioned was principally responsible, for instance, for the establishment of a study and enquiry centre in Seoul University. Here is a centre from which personal contacts of every sort can be developed on a pastoral and educational basis, as well as in the case of those under instruction for baptism. Very different in many ways was the Port Harcourt Industrial Mission project in Nigeria.[1] Yet here too was the attempt to be at the disposal of and to serve a newly industrialised society; to establish a ministry to people where they are, without an immediate and limited concern to recruit them into the Church.

Finally, it may be asked what attitudes towards the non-Christian ought to govern the missionary presence of the Church in the parishes of this country. For the situation *is* one of mission. However extensive may have been the 'staining' of habits of thought and conduct by Christian moral principles, and however justly surveys of mass opinion may reveal widespread adherence to religious practices such as personal prayer, it remains a truism that most of the population is at some distance from the life of the Church. If Christian discipleship is believed, as it must be, to entail participation in the prayer, and above all in the eucharist, of a particular congregation, then the Church has a responsibility for those outside its life. Again, the simple desire to recruit is unrealistic. The Christian's approach to the members of his own society who have lapsed from, or with varying degrees of decision 'contracted out of', organised religion, demands quite as much understanding as in the case of the non-Chrsitian: understanding, that is, not merely in the broader sense of sympathy and pastoral tact, but as taking seriously the religious position of the person concerned, however negative. A member of the Anglican Franciscan Community who combines professional social work with parish responsibilities in East London, has described how slow a process it is, in conversations with non-Christian colleagues, to overcome their deep-seated resentment and distrust of organised religion, springing from a variety of causes. In the English situation, and no doubt the same is true in many other post-Christian communities, the Christian's approach to his unchurched neighbour must often involve an awareness of the

[1] It is hoped to continue this Industrial Mission work as soon as circumstances permit.

failures of the Church as well as the faith that God has not ceased to be active in the minds and wills of the lapsed, however bitter their antagonism.

It is all the more important, then, that the local congregation should become fully aware of its relationship to neighbours and friends who are out of touch with the Church. There are no doubt many parishes in which – as in the one served by the priest just mentioned – the friendship and example of individual members have attracted strangers who have ultimately asked for confirmation. More particularly, small study and discussion groups have proved, here as so often, a point of growth. For here, to a far greater extent than in more formal meetings, there can take place what is of such great importance, not only for the spiritual growth of the individual, but also for the more personal 'realising' and apprehension of Christian truth on the part of those present who may be only partly convinced: the articulation, in terms of the individual's own experience, of a faith long accepted in a rather passive way. Thus, part of the preparation for a Franciscan mission to a parish in the Black Country took the form – as is often the case – of house-meetings; and in these the purpose was not to 'sell' the Christian faith so much as to 'unveil' and to articulate the reality of God and of grace as the truth about concerns and relationships of which the participants were already aware. In such a context, the Christian preaching – in the widest sense – means bringing a latent or dormant Christianity, often at the level of 'feelings', to an explicit acknowledgment of Christian truth.[1]

Christian mission, then, in any setting, is only partly a disclosure of what is new. The gospel proclaimed is the gospel of God who has already been present in the situation; it articulates, and answers, much that is already present in the consciousness of those to whom it is offered. The Christian approaches the non-Christian as one with whom he already

[1] I am grateful to have been been able, in these paragraphs, to draw on the experience of Brother Bernard s.s.f. of the Franciscan house in Plaistow.

has much in common: and the discovery and exploration of this common ground is a great part of his task. Above all, his approach must be made on a basis of respect and of love. For, if the Gospel is not to remain in the end something unrelated to what is most real in people's experience, it is only by means of intelligent respect and love that the truth of Catholic and Christian faith as relationship with God in Christ can be conveyed.

FURTHER READING

G. H. ANDERSON (ed), *The Theology of the Christian Mission*, S.C.M. Press

KENNETH CRAGG, *The Call of the Minaret*, Oxford, Galaxy Books

ROGER GARAUDY, *From Anathema to Dialogue*, (with introduction by Karl Rahner), Collins

H. D. LEWIS and R. L. SLATER, World Religions: *Meeting Points and Major Issues*, Watts

GEOFFREY PARRINDER, *Comparative Religion*, George Allen and Unwin

R. C. ZAEHNER, *At Sundry Times: an essay in the comparison of religions*, Faber and Faber
The Convergent Spirit. Towards a Dialectics of Religion, Routledge and Kegan Paul

M. A. C. WARREN (ed), *The Christian Presence Series*, S.C.M. Press

GEORGE APPLETON, *On the Eightfold Path. (Buddhism)*

KENNETH CRAGG, *Sandals at the Mosque. (Islam)*

RAYMOND HAMMER, *Japan's Religious Ferment. (Faiths Old and New)*

J. V. TAYLOR, *The Primal Vision. (African Religion)*